BETWEEN HUME'S PHILOSOPHY AND HISTORY

Historical Theory and Practice

Spencer K. Wertz

University Press of America,® Inc.
Lanham • New York • Oxford

Copyright © 2000 by
Spencer K. Wertz

University Press of America,® Inc.
4720 Boston Way
Lanham, Maryland 20706

12 Hid's Copse Rd.
Cumnor Hill, Oxford OX2 9JJ

British Library Cataloging in Publication Information Available

Library of Congress Cataloging-in-Publication Data

Wertz, Spencer K.
Between Hume's philosophy and history : historical theory and practice / Spencer
K. Wertz.
p.   cm.
Includes bibliographical references and index.
l. History—Philosophy. 2. Hume, David, 1711-1776—Contributions in philosophy of
history.   I. Title.
D16.7W47 1999   901—dc21   99—050369 CIP

ISBN 0-7618-1543-0 (cloth: alk. ppr.)
ISBN 0-7618-1544-9 (pbk: alk. ppr.)

⊗™ The paper used in this publication meets the minimum
requirements of American National Standard for Information
Sciences—Permanence of Paper for Printed Library Materials,
ANSI Z39.48—1984

For Susan Lee

CONTENTS

ABBREVIATIONS OF HUME'S WRITINGS

D = *Dialogues Concerning Natural Religion*, edited by Norman Kemp Smith. New York: Macmillan Company, 1947. References made to page numbers parenthetically after citation unless otherwise noted; sometimes general references to parts.

DP = "A Dissertation on the Passions," in *Essays and Treatises on Various Subjects*. Stereotype Edition. Boston: J. P. Mendum, n.d. References to sections and page numbers.

E = *Essays, Moral, Political, and Literary*, edited by Eugene F. Miller. Revised Edition. Indianapolis: Liberty Press, 1986. References to page numbers.

H = *The History of England from the Invasion of Julius Caesar to the Abdication of James the Second, 1688*, edited by William B. Todd. 6 volumes. Indianapolis: Liberty Press, 1983-85. References made to page numbers and volume; sometimes general references to chapters.

IU = *An Inquiry Concerning Human Understanding*, With a Supplement: "An Abstract of *A Treatise of Human Nature*," edited by Charles W. Hendel. New York: Macmillan Company, 1955. References to sections and page numbers.

IM = *An Inquiry Concerning the Principles of Morals*, With a Supplement: "A Dialogue," edited by Charles W. Hendel. New York: Macmillan Company, 1957. References to sections and page numbers.

L = *The Letters of David Hume*, edited by J. Y. T. Greig, 2 vols. Oxford: Clarendon Press, 1932. References to page numbers and volume.

LC = *Life and Correspondence of David Hume*, by John Hill Burton, 2 vols. Edinburgh: William Tait, 1846. References to page numbers and volume.

LS = *Letters of David Hume to William Strahan*, edited by G. Birkbeck Hill. Oxford: Clarendon Press, 1888. References to page numbers.

NH = *The Natural History of Religion*, edited by H. E. Root. Stanford, California: Stanford University Press, 1956. References to page numbers.

NL = *New Letters of David Hume*, edited by Raymond Klibansky and Ernest C.

Mossner. Oxford: Clarendon Press, 1954. References to page numbers.
PH = *David Hume: Philosophical Historian,* edited by D. F. Norton and R. H.
Popkin. Indianapolis: Bobbs-Merrill, 1965. References to page numbers.
T = *A Treatise of Human Nature,* analytical index by L. A. Selby-Bigge, with
text revised and notes by P. H. Nidditch. Second Edition. Oxford: Clarendon
Press, 1978. Contains the Abstract of the *Treatise.* References to Book, Part, and
Section (e.g., I,II,VI) or to page numbers.

ACKNOWLEDGMENTS

The work before you grew out of thirty years of study of the Scottish Enlightenment thinker David Hume (1711-1776), and much of it has appeared in scholarly journals and has been read at various meetings of philosophical societies, although all of this has been rewritten with an eye on the overall form of this book. Chapter 1 is a contribution to *Southwest Philosophy Review* (1994); chapter 3 appeared in the *Journal of the History of Ideas* (1975); chapter 4 in part was published in a supplement volume of *Philosophical Topics* (1981); and chapter 6 was included in *Southwest Philosophy Review* (1991); chapter 7 appeared in *Hume Studies* (1996); chapter 8 was selected for the *Journal of the History of Ideas* (1993). I wish to thank the editors of these publications for their permission to reprint these articles in a newly revised form in this humanistic study of one of the greatest philosophers of the Western world.

A word about a couple of editions I have selected of Hume's *Inquiries*. The Hendel editions were chosen because they contain all the variations—the inclusions and omissions—of the numerous editions that Hume made during his lifetime. Some of these are extremely important; for example, in the first *Inquiry*, section three, "Of the Association of Ideas," Hendel has included a discussion of historical and literary narration as an expression of the association of ideas. This is central to my arguments in chapters 5 and 6. The other editions of Hume's *Inquires* do not have these additional discussions, and with their exceptions, these editions can be easily used instead of Hendel's to follow my main argument and interpretation. I have usually given reference to section and its title to facilitate scholarship. The other editions of Hume's writings I have used are generally accepted by Hume scholars as the best available and readily accessible.

Many people have assisted me over the years, and I want to thank them for their generous criticism of my work; especially, Nicholas Capaldi, Roger

Emerson, Anthony Flew, Ted Klein, Donald Livingston, Kenneth Merrill, E. C. Mossner, J. H. Plumb, and numerous members of The Hume Society. These distinguished individuals, and many more, have dramatically contributed to the finished product. My most persistent critics, though, have been by wife, Linda Loflin Wertz, plus a masterful copy editor of my other books, Matthew Abbate, and the department's secretaries, Maura Carmody Cuny, Elizabeth Woodfin, and Sandy Jacoby, the latter of whom typed and edited the final stages of the manuscript—without them, there probably would not have been a book.

S. K. Wertz
Weatherford, Texas
January 10, 1999

INTRODUCTION

Let me start with the book's title. My inquiry occupies a space between Hume's philosophy and history; it is not philosophy of history or history of philosophy as we understand those areas today, but a precursor to both. Let us begin with the philosophical and then we will move to the historical dimension. The work Hume did on the *Treatise of Human Nature* while at La Fleche, France (1735-1737), was solely philosophy in its preoccupation and execution.[1] The origin or the way of ideas[2] and its systematic inquiry are topics he inherited from René Descartes's *Meditations* (1641), so it is only fitting that young David did his meditations in a place where Descartes had received his formal education—a course of study that lasted nine years at the Jesuit School. Descartes set out to demonstrate that the self (soul), God, and the world could be discovered through reason alone. Hume set out to demonstrate the contrary, i.e., that the understanding unassisted by experience could know none of these things. (This is the project of Book One of the *Treatise*.) What we know of ourselves and the world and how we know them are the agenda of the remaining Books (Two and Three) of the *Treatise*, "Of the Passions" and "Of Morals," and his subsequent writings—the *Inquiries*, the *Essays*, and the *History*. The latter two works provide important development of ideas which are found as suggestions in the *Treatise* and *Inquiries*, and this is the historical dimension I spoke of above.

Besides a *reductio ad absurdum* of Cartesianism, what else did Hume accomplish in the *Treatise*? R. G. Collingwood, in *The Idea of History*,[3] still provides the best answer:

I would not go so far as to call his entire philosophy a reasoned defence of historical thought, but that was undoubtedly one of the things which it implicitly undertook; and it seems to me that when he had finished his philosophical work and asked himself what he had accomplished in it, he could have said with justice that one thing at any rate was the demonstration that history was a legitimate and valid type of knowledge, more legitimate in fact than most others because not promising more than it could perform and not depending on any questionable metaphysical hypotheses.

Chapters 3 through 8 demonstrate Collingwood's main thesis, but contrary to his central argument, they attempt to show an alliance between history and philosophy in Hume's thought. Donald Livingston[4] and myself (1970/1975) were among the first to explore the historical dimension of Hume's philosophy. Lately, John Danford has contributed an important study of this aspect of Hume's thought,[5] so Collingwood's thesis is not as uncommon in the literature on Hume as it used to be. However the story is far from complete and not as much to the forefront as it should be. Hopefully this book will contribute toward these ends and be a part of the philosophical conversation.

The main argument contained in this book is in three distinct stages. First is the nature of the *Treatise* (chapter 1) and its difficulties with the copy theory of ideas (chapter 2). Second is a discussion of four main ideas in Hume's thought: history and human nature (chapter 3) and experience and evidence (chapter 4). Third are chapters 5-8, which find these ideas manifested in writing and various levels of composition: historical narration (chapter 5), literature and the standard of taste (chapter 6), moral judgments in history (chapter 7), and the historiography of science (chapter 8).

The general plan of the book is as follows. Chapter 1 deals with the nature of Hume's "system" as it is especially manifested in the *Treatise*. Like Annette Baier,[6] I find that work a unified, developing progression of ideas, arguments, and analyses which exhibits a narrative structure. Since many of the preoccupations of Hume in the later writings either appear or are suggested in the *Treatise*, one needs to begin here. With this book I try to continue Baier's project: "In principle the sort of interpretation I advance here should be continued beyond the *Treatise* to the later works, and so I hope it will be, if not by me then by some sympathetic Hume interpreter, or group of us. For the moral of the story, as I am telling it, is that *all* our interpretations will 'loosen and fall of themselves' until they become cooperative and mutually corrective" (viii-ix). Her life-long work on Hume serves as an inspiration to all of us in Hume studies. Chapters 1 and 2 set up Hume's philosophy or theory of history by showing that the copy theory of ideas, i.e., ideas are copies of corresponding impressions, is by itself epistemologically bankrupt and that Hume subsequently modified the theory of ideas to include their history or histories. One of the main arguments that leads to this modification is Hume's famous thought experiment—the missing shade of blue—and it is the subject of chapter 2. Consequently the move from the *Treatise* to the *Inquiries*, the *Essays*, and the *History*, is more than stylistic—it reflects changes in Hume's methodology and his understanding of the way of ideas. So in providing an alternative to Cartesian rationalism, Hume modifies one of the main principles of empiricism—the copy theory of ideas—by enlarging "experience" from sensory individual experiences to non-sensory social experiences.

If Hume thought that history is a legitimate and valid type of knowledge, as Collingwood claims, then what is history? Many historians and philosophers have argued that Hume's idea of history is associated with erroneous assumptions—that human nature is static, that by "experience" Hume meant personal individual experience, that evidence is understood as authoritative. In chapters 3 and 4, I argue that these assumptions were imposed on Hume by his readers and that what he in fact meant by human nature, experience, and evidence is dynamic, social, and interpretational, respectively. Besides Giambattista Vico (1664-1744), Hume was the first philosopher in the Western intellectual tradition who took history seriously. This was at a time before cultural relativism and historicism, so it is particularly noteworthy. Hume shares some affinities with these nineteenth-century movements as we shall see below, especially in chapters 3, 7, and 8.

A key part of Hume's historical methodology consists of the concepts of narration, taste, and moral judgments. Chapters 5, 6, and 7 address these issues, and they are really the ones that show history as a valid, legitimate type of knowledge. In Hume's mind, history and philosophy are species of literature,[7] so it is quite natural to expect his discussion of taste and literary subjects to be pertinent here. Also in chapter 7, we find that rhetoric plays as crucial role in moral judgments in history. I conclude with a look at the historiography of science (chapter 8) for which I examine Hume's conception of science throughout his writings, but especially in the *History of England*. These chapters taken together demonstrate that philosophy and history are methodologically and epistemologically tied together in Hume's thought; this is a feature that makes his thought so interesting from a contemporary perspective. The subtitle of the book before you, *Historical Theory and Practice*, perhaps best describes it in that where Hume does not explicitly address an issue, his practice of the craft of history supplies us with hints of where his theory would go.

Interpretations demand a focus: Baier's is in the "Conclusion of this book" (Book One, Part IV, section VII), mine appears earlier in Part IV, section I, "Of scepticism with regard to reason." It is here where Hume has the central insight that history is the key to understanding the way of ideas. He announces that:

In all demonstrative sciences the rules are certain and infallible; but when we apply them, our fallible and uncertain faculties are very apt to depart from them, and fall into error. We must, therefore, in every reasoning form a new judgment, as a check or controul on our first judgment or belief; and must enlarge our view to comprehend a kind of history of all the instances, wherein our understanding has deceiv'd us, compar'd with those, wherein its testimony was just and true. Our reason must be consider'd as a kind of cause, of which truth is the natural effect; but such-a-one as by the irruption of other causes, and by the inconstancy of our mental powers, may frequently be prevented. By this means all knowledge degenerates into probability; and this probability is greater or less, according to our experience of the veracity or deceitfulness of our understanding, and according to the simplicity or intricacy of the question. (180)

Embedded in this extraordinary passage is the idea that *we must enlarge our view [of knowledge] to comprehend a kind of history*. (What kinds of history there are for Hume is discussed in chapter 8.) Coupled with this idea is the conception that "history *extends* our experience" ("Of the Study of History," E, 566; emphasis added). Descartes's solution is *complete enumeration* modeled on mathematics and yields absolute truth or certainty.[8] Hume's solution is *historical enumeration* where the order and sequence of their appearance (the enumerata) are important and yield probabilities. (This thesis is suggested by the missing shade of blue discussion; see chapter 2.) So in a span of not quite a century the way of ideas moves from a mathematical paradigm (with Descartes) to a historical paradigm (with Hume). Charting out of that historical paradigm in Hume's thought is the theme of this book. Both Descartes and Hume conceived of the origin or way of ideas as psychological and logical, but Hume went a step further and added the historical. Hume took Locke's "Historical, plain Method" (44) seriously and it became Hume's "Account of the Ways, whereby our Understandings come to attain those Notions [Ideas] of Things," as Locke described it (44). This addition opened up a whole new dimension in accounting for the nature of our ideas and paves the way for historicism, although I do not think that Hume was a historicist, much less a relativist.

Hume's program was enlarged after the *Treatise* (1740); it was no longer essentially philosophical, although his outlook was always philosophical. His pen became that of an essayist and a historian. And as time passed he became more and more humanistic—drawing upon several areas and disciplines to address his concerns. A good example of this is the opening section of the first *Inquiry* on the different species of philosophy. "Moral philosophy or the science of human nature," Hume begins, "may be treated after two different manners: ... one considers man chiefly as born for action and as influenced in his measures by taste and sentiment.... The other species of philosophers consider man in the light of a reasonable rather than an active being, and endeavor to form his understanding more than cultivate his manners" (IU,15). Taste (chapter 6) and sentiment (chapter 7) now sit alongside reason which had previously (in Descartes's thought) presided single-handedly over our ideas. Hume thinks that a mean between the two species of philosophy is the best course to take:

The most perfect character is supposed to lie between those extremes: retaining an equal ability and taste for books, company, and business; preserving in conversation that discernment and delicacy which arise from polite letters; and, in business, that probity and accuracy which are the natural result of a just philosophy. In order to diffuse and cultivate so accomplished a character, nothing can be more useful than compositions of the easy style and manner which draw not too much from life, require no deep application or retreat to be comprehended [as is the case with the *Treatise* Hume thought], and send back the student among mankind full of noble sentiments and wise precepts applicable to every exigency of human life. By means of such compositions virtue becomes amiable, science agreeable, company instructive, and retirement entertaining. (IU,17-18)

So Hume moves away from the traditional conception of philosophy which he associates with Descartes and his *Meditations*. Hume's way of ideas becomes civil and liberal. The former proved to be "abstruse thought and profound researches" inducing "pensive melancholy"—something Hume suffered from (1734) while laying out or preparing the contents of the *Treatise* (L,I,12-18). (This becomes the central focus of Baier's interpretation of Hume's "Philosophy in This Careless Manner" [ch. 1].[9]) Hume's advice by the time of the first *Inquiry* (1748) is: "Be a philosopher, but, amidst all your philosophy, be still a man" (IU,18). Such compositions are tempered by living and by history; the *Inquiries* are good examples. (This is probably the reason why Hume considered the second *Inquiry* (IM) his masterpiece.)

Hume thought there were good and bad ways of doing philosophy. In the latter, philosophy had become restrictive and out of touch with mankind; it no longer attempted to address its needs. In the former, philosophy corrects these deficiencies by staying within the bounds of human experience. And by "experience," Hume means more than personal, individual experience; collective, social experience or history is the paradigm for that term. Throughout his writings he distinguished between different kinds of philosophy so that his would not be confused with his predecessors' and contemporaries'. In the *Treatise*, he thought that true philosophers were closer to the vulgar or common man in their opinions than what he called false philosophers (I, IV, III). They are closer because of their moderate skepticism and because the relationships among ideas are not indicative of the connections among objects. As he says early in Book One:

Nothing is more requisite for a true philosopher, than to restrain the intemperate desire of searching into causes, and having establish'd any doctrine upon a sufficient number of experiments, rest contented with that, when he sees a farther examination would lead

him into obscure and uncertain speculations. In that case his enquiry wou'd be much better employ'd in examining the effects than the causes of his principle. (I, I, IV)

In the first *Inquiry* Hume talks about philosophy less in terms of "true" and
"false," and more in terms of rhetorical notions: the easy and obvious philosophy on one hand, and the abstruse and profound philosophy on the other hand
(16). But these distinctions are not equivalent to one another. Hume thought
some abstruse and profound philosophy was necessary for true philosophy. The
first *Inquiry* had to have some abstruse or deep thought in order to be true philosophy. By this time (1748), Hume had tempered his conception of philosophy
not only with living but also with history. The locus of Hume's thought became
this area between philosophy proper and history. The contour of this space, then
is three-fold. First there is a suggestion that there is a difference between the
Treatise and the later writings which is that in the earlier work Hume accepted
a view of the nature of ideas (the "copy theory") which he later modified, and
that this modification consisted of including in the account of ideas "their history or histories." Second, there is the suggestion that Hume has been wrongly
accused of understanding history in terms of "erroneous assumptions" about
human nature, experience and evidence. Third there is the suggestion that
Hume's philosophical methodology was itself historical, with an emphasis on
narrative and temporality. In the following chapters there are arguments and
analyses developed to assist substantiating these three suggestions. Also the
subsequent chapters sample what this area has to offer. If they stimulate further
interest among Hume scholars, they will be successful from my perspective.

    Let us now turn to the *Treatise* itself and ask, what sort of systematic unity
does it possess? Chapter 1 is an attempt to answer that question, for it is here
where everything begins in Hume's thought.

ONE

THE STATUS OF THE SYSTEM

In the classic, early twentieth-century expositions of David Hume's thought, there is an interesting chapter that belongs to Charles Hendel and William Parry,[1] and it deserves to be reopened. The first edition (1925) of Hendel's *Studies* included a chapter (5), which was omitted from the new edition, where he admits that he "had gone too far in treating both space and time as impressions in which some 'operation' of the mind is reflected analogous to the case of casual inference." His mistakes regarding space and time were made, Hendel reports, because *he had made Hume's thought more systematic than it really was*. There is no doubt that Hendel had misinterpreted Hume on this score, but it was not for the reason Hendel suggests, as I shall try to establish here. In a word, I think Hendel has conceded too much to Parry on the "system" business in Hume's *Treatise*. Little research has been done on Hume's conception of system,[2] so I intend to amend that here.

Hendel gives some details on assimilating a system referred to in one Part of the *Treatise* with that in another:

The "system" mentioned in Part Two where he treats of *perception* need not be considered perfectly homogeneous with the general system that pertains to *"reasoning"* and to "knowledge and probability" in Part Three. There could be a system in regard to the perceptions of space and time without invoking the imagination. [Hendel's emphases]

Granted that the two systems need not be *perfectly* homogeneous, nonetheless they need to be "homogeneous" in the sense that they form one solitary system that is complete and consistent. A system, after all, is a pattern of thinking. It does not make sense to talk about independent systems in different Parts of the *Treatise*: this would violate its Newtonian spirit. Hume does, indeed, speak of a "system" throughout the *Treatise*, so we should expect it to be singular rather than plural. In fact, I cannot recall a use of "systems" except when he is speaking of philosophies; for example, in the opening paragraph of the Introduction (xiii).

If we posit different, multiple systems in Hume's *Treatise*, then its unity is seriously questioned along with any sort of logical rigor we would expect of it. Generally, Hume was careful with language, especially in his use of terms with technical connotations which "system" obviously had, i.e., it is Newtonian in nature, consisting of deductions from principles either established by experiments or accepted on intuition (see note 4). Perhaps the better thing Hendel should have done in the passage above was to talk about different *stages* in Hume's system, noting that discussions of perception and reasoning have different roles assigned to the imagination in these mental processes. The imagination becomes increasingly important in his theory of ideas as we progress through the *Treatise*.

We should expect some systematic rigor from Hume's *Treatise* and demand consistency among the various employments of "system" when he refers to his scheme. Otherwise, remarks like E. C. Mossner's "Hume was but more rigid and systematic than Hutcheson"[3] do not make much sense. We either have one system or none at all. As Hume announces in the Introduction to the *Treatise*: "In pretending, therefore, to explain the principles of human nature, we in effect propose *a compleat system* of the sciences, built on a foundation almost entirely new, and the only one upon which they can stand with any security" (xvi; emphasis added). Completeness is one of the characteristics of a system, especially of a formal system, but as Hendel asserts, we do not want to take this analogy too far. Hume's system is not a mathematical or logical system. Still, completeness suggests one system—not two or more. A system S is *complete* if all the statements one desires to be accounted for are in fact derived from S. What then did Hume envision by "system"? Has he derived everything he wanted to or should have? So when the term "system" is applied to intellectual productions (patterns of thinking), the system can be characterized either in terms of its methodology or in terms of the end it hopes to achieve. When Hume's system is characterized in this way, it can be said that it is a system that aims to explain the principles of human nature.

As I mentioned earlier, Newton's system of natural philosophy[4] is one Hume has in mind when he writes of his own system. However, there is some linguistic evidence that Hume had a less formal conception of a system than Newton's work itself exemplifies. In the Abstract, Hume says of the author of the *Treatise*: "He asserts, that the soul, as far as we can conceive it, is nothing but a *system or train* of different perceptions, those of heat and cold, love and anger, thoughts and sensations; *all united together, but without any perfect simplicity or identity*" (657; emphases added). But "train" for Hume is close to "chain," a metaphor (and it is only a metaphor) he uses when he speaks of argument or casual connection: every link in the chain must hang upon the other if they are to be capable of sustaining the whole (83). This conception clearly depicts a deductive understanding of a system, but with the main implications running only from beginning to end (as a string of conditionals) and not interchangeable as they are in an axiomatic system. The Parts of the *Treatise* imply each other in their order and are not logically equivalent or freely substitutive without constraints. Hence, this is the major difference between the Humean system and a formal system.

Another source of Hume's conception of system is A. A. Cooper, Third Earl of Shaftesbury. In Book I, Part II, of *An Inquiry Concerning Virtue, or Merit*, Shaftesbury employs the notion of a system; e.g., "For shou'd there be any where in Nature a *System*, of which this living Creature [Man] was to be consider'd as *a Part*; then cou'd he no-wise be allow'd *good*; whilst he plainly appear'd to be such *a Part*, as made rather to the harm than good of that System or *Whole* in which he was included."[5] And, "Male and Female," Shaftesbury adds Platonistically, "have a joint-relation to another Existence and Order of things beyond themselves. So that the Creatures are both of 'em to be consider'd as Parts of *another System*: which is that of a particular Race or Species of living Creatures, who have some one *common Nature*, or are provided for, by some one *Order or Constitution* of things subsisting together, and co-operating towards their Conservatism and Support" (9-10). Shaftesbury continues to talk about "a System of Animals" (10) and "one planetary System or *Vortex*" (11). Such remarks, no doubt, had considerable impact on the young Hume. They can be appreciated in his uses of the term "system" in the sense in which organisms are systems and in which the nervous system, digestive system, respiratory system and so on are subsystems of the system, the organism itself being a system of systems. Hume uses "system" in that sense when he talks about the identity that can be ascribed to a ship, or a building, over a period of time, even though all of its parts have been replaced, and he says that this is the kind of identity that can be ascribed to plants and animals. And I believe that he supposes that the "soul" is this kind of system. So Shaftesbury and the Physiological Library of Edinburgh are clearly present in this kind of analysis as influences.

Hendel came to appreciate the order of the *Treatise*, which is easily ignored because Hume claims throughout the book to have a "system." Hendel adds:

When he speaks of "my system" in Part Two treating of space and time it is quite natural for the reader to assimilate "system" in that Part to the system elsewhere and to suppose that somehow the imagination operating in accordance with principles of association has a role in the production of the ideas of space and time. On reflection, and in the light of such criticism as I here report, I realize that this was a mistake.

It is one thing to carry out this assimilation within the *Treatise* and another to apply it to all of Hume's writings, as R. F. Anderson has done.[6] Such an abstraction, which obliterates the differences great and small in Hume's works, should perhaps be called the Anderson fallacy. It is no wonder that he found fundamental contradictions among Hume's principles. Anderson treated Hume's system as if it were an axiomatic formal system:

Inasmuch as Hume is presenting a system, then, I suggest that sound evidence may be found in influences which that alleged contradiction may have upon the remainder of his doctrine. If these principles be truly fundamental, and be truly contradictory to one another, then lesser contradictions are to be expected as consequences in that philosophy, insofar as it is a system; and a discoverable lesser inconsistency might be traceable to that more fundamental contradiction which I pretend to find. (170)

Hendel's lesson is that such a procedure is not applicable to Hume; or, if it is applied, it is not surprising that contradictions are discovered. There is an application of the ideas in the *Treatise* to later works (chapters 3-8 intend to show this), but it is not a *deductive* application that Anderson's study suggests. Hume, I contend, makes an *interpretive* application of the ideas developed in the *Treatise*.[7] Spinoza's *Ethics* is probably the only philosophy which can be treated deductively or as a formal axiomatic system that disregards its narrative order. Spinoza himself does this because he always looks back to previous Definitions, Propositions, Proofs, and Notes in order to establish the next element in his system. His system consists of backward or past references, once the Definitions, Axioms, and initial Propositions are put forth. These backward references appear in the *Ethics* with the opening Propositions and remain in the Proofs throughout.

In contrast, Hume's system consists of both forward or future references and backward references. There are 16 forward references in the *Treatise*: 12 in Book One, 4 in Book Two, and 0 in Book Three. More of these references occur *earlier* in the *Treatise*, which is to be expected, so the system does anticipate its elements and their order. These references indicate that their order is important for Hume's arguments and the development of his system. There are 36 backward references in the *Treatise*: 21 in Book One, 5 in Book Two (4 to Book One and 1 to the Eight Experiments, 347), and 10 in Book Three (and these are to the previous two Books, in spite of Hume's Advertisement where he claims that the third volume is "in some measure independent of the other two," opposite 454). More of these references occur *later* in the *Treatise*, which is as expected. Both types of reference imply that narrative order is important in understanding Hume's system, especially in appreciating its development. Hume made some introspective discoveries along the way.

Let us look more carefully at how this narrative order displays itself in Hume's text. One of the clearest indications of this is from the opening of Book Three where he states: "I am not, however, without hopes, that *the present system of philosophy will acquire new force as it advances* [emphasis added]; and that our reasonings concerning *morals* will corroborate whatever has been said concerning the *understanding* and the *passions*" (455). Elsewhere, Hume selects the phrases "the precedent system" (see, e.g., 120 and 154) and "the present system" (see, e.g., 120, 145, 455), which implies that Parry may be right that we have two different "systems," in some sense. We can distinguish between a micro sense, as in "the preceding system of the passions" (in Book Three, 473), and a macro sense, as we have seen from previous uses (xvi, 455) and "the whole scheme or system" (580). The micro uses are obviously subordinate to the macro. (This is analogous to the system organism sense.) So, it seems to me that the best way to treat Hume here is to attribute *one* system to him and to witness the development of it from Book One to Book Two to Book Three and their respective Parts and Sections. After all, Hume does talk about the "progress of this treatise" (120). And Hume in the Abstract informs us that: "This treatise therefore of human nature seems intended for a system of the sciences. The author has finished what regards logic, and has laid the foundation of the other parts in his account of the passions" (646). (Mossner discusses this passage among others from the Abstract in his biography, 125ff.)

Hume's use of "system" falls in between our axiomatic conception of a formal system and a popular eighteenth-century use of the term, as when he speaks of "the vulgar system" of the double existence of perceptions and objects (211), "the vulgar systems of ethics" (297), and "a system or set of opinions" (272). This last use will perhaps capture Hume's, if we think of the set as an *ordered set* where the arrangement of the elements is crucial for their understanding. But Hume's system is far more than *opinions*; it is experiments, arguments, descriptions, and analyses—all rolled up into one work. His use of the "train," "channel" (157), and "chain" metaphors suggest this interpretation. Hume's system is *synthetic*: it grows, changes, and undergoes development and expansion. Hume's is a system in much more than that weak sense in which every philosopher—including Nietzsche—has a "system."

In a perceptive review Humphrey Palmer claims, I think quite correctly, that Hume's system is not "a single-source system of philosophy" in the sense that axiomatic geometrical systems are.[8] Rather, "it was meant to hang together, and not to contain inconsistencies, some parts of it were seen as following from other parts, some parts needed to be expounded first." However, I take issue with Palmer that the system was not thought out or presented as a *deductive* one. It is "deductive" in a limited sense—again Newtonian in nature and spirit. Moreover, we should think of Hume's Lockean background for what we mean by "deduction." Locke and Hume both used "demonstration" to mean that one idea led to another with intuitive certainty.[9] Also Hume speaks of an argument as a demonstration if its denial results in a contradiction (T, e.g., 161). Or, in more contemporary terms, if the premises (propositions or ideas) are true, then the conclusion (subsequent proposition or idea) necessarily follows from them. However, we must be careful not to give an anachronistic reading of "demonstration" as a formal derivation or deduction, where a sequence of statements or ideas are true in virtue of their form or pattern.[10] With this in mind let us look at a string of sentences from the *Treatise* pertaining to the notion of a system. Hume confidently remarks: "What principally gives authority to this system is, beside the undoubted arguments, upon which each part is founded, the agreement of these parts, and the necessity of one to explain another" (154). He then follows with this definitive statement: "All these phenomena lead directly to the precedent system; nor will it ever be possible upon other principles to give a satisfactory and consistent explication of them."[11] And in Book Three Hume says in passing: "Nor need any one wonder, that tho' *I have all along endeavour'd to establish my system on pure reason,* and have scarce ever cited the judgment even of philosophers or historians on any article, I shou'd now appeal to popular authority, and oppose the sentiments of the rabble to any philosophical reasoning" (546; emphasis added).

The foregoing enumerations sound deductive to me and distinctly Cartesian in their bold outlook. Nor does it end here. As with any system there are givens, and Hume's are his *impressions,* which he takes to be clear, distinct, self-evident, incorruptible—all those characteristics that Descartes attributed to *ideas.* In fact, Thomas Reid in the *Inquiry* (1764) was one of the first philosophers to see that Hume's system was a Cartesian one: "The system which is now generally received, with regard to the mind and its operations, derives not only its spirit from Des Cartes, but its fundamental principles; and, after all the improvements made by Malebranche, Locke, Berkeley, and Hume, may still be called *the Cartesian system.*"[12] And Reid observes: "That the modern skepticism is the natural issue of the new system; and that, although it did not bring forth this monster until the year 1739 [the year Hume's *Treatise* appeared], it may be said to have carried it in its womb from the beginning" (112). So Kreimendahl is not completely off base on the system question.[13] An intermediate position between Anderson-Kreimendahl and Palmer is probably the best characterization of Hume's conception of system. How do we obtain that position? As Palmer reminds us: "As to the actual structure of Hume's system, that can only be elicited by reading what he wrote" (177). And I might add, that is more than what he wrote in Book One of the *Treatise.*[14] When one characterizes his system in terms of his methodology (xvi), one looks back to the machinery that is provided in Book One of the *Treatise*, although it gets modified in its details in Books Two and Three. The skeptical consequences of the use of this methodology is summed up in Part IV of Book One. He claims that he has shown that the understanding when it acts "according to its most general principles . . . leaves not the lowest degree of evidence in any proposition, either in philosophy or common life" (267). Of course, he will be saved by nature, but then goes on to say that "in this blind submission, I shew most perfectly my skeptical disposition and principles" (269). It is in tracing Hume's applications of the methodology described in Book One that we see the full development of Cartesian principles. Consequently Reid's interpretation stands. The point to be made here is that *method leads to a system* and that *a system is a result of inquiry*.

Characterizing Hume's philosophy in these two ways—system as organism and as intellectual production—does not imply that there are two systems. It is possible that the characterizations would pick out exactly the same system. Nevertheless, as a matter of fact, I believe that there is much that Hume wants to say that cannot be incorporated within his Cartesian framework. These are beliefs, typically labeled "fictions" by Hume, that nature forces upon us.[15] What cannot be adapted into his system are certain very important mental dispositions, so Hume did not derive everything he wanted from his system. Dispositions are excluded because the way of ideas does not provide a way of having an adequate concept of what a disposition is. The villain of the piece is the copy theory of ideas. Every simple idea is a copy of an impression, and, what may not be generally realized, every complex idea is also a copy if the idea is an idea of anything (and everything) that is real. But a disposition is not anything that we can have an impression of, at least not in a straightforward sense. Hume turns to human nature and history for an account of dispositions and more lasting traits or qualities of persons or their character.

Did Hume have one and only one system? I am certain that Hume would have said that he had only one system. He had as much interest in formulating a philosophical system as Kant did. But many beliefs that Hume wants to license do not receive their license from that system. The Cartesian verdict on these beliefs is that they are beliefs in fictions. Perhaps it would be wrong to say that these fictions comprise a system; nevertheless, they are all linked by the fact that Hume regarded each of them as a general, and original, principle of human nature. The following passage, though it is from the first *Inquiry*, is true to the spirit of the *Treatise*:

They [the other species of philosophers] regard human nature as a subject of speculation; and with a narrow scrutiny examine it, in order to find those principles, which regulate our understanding, excite our sentiments, and make us approve or blame any particular object, action, or behavior ... they attempt this arduous task, they are deterred by no difficulties; but, proceeding from particular instances to general principles, they will push on their inquiries to principles more general, and rest not satisfied till they arrive at those original principles by which, in every science, all human curiosity must be bounded. (15-16)

"What most people think of as a philosophical system," R. G. Collingwood laments, "is a collection of doctrines deliberately invented by an individual philosopher in the attempt to reduce the whole of his experiences to private formulae. I do not believe that such things exist. What I find in the writings of any one philosopher is nothing like that; it is more like *a series of attempts to think, more clearly and consistently than his contemporaries, in ways more or less common to them all.*"[16] This is especially true of Hume in the *Treatise*: some of the early critics of Hume made his system out to be a collection of doctrines, but Collingwood's characterization of a system is more faithful to Hume's intentions. That philosophical system, as Collingwood characterizes it, finds its way into the explanations of the *Essays* and the *History of England*. This is one reason why the latter work was described as philosophical history by those who followed in Hume's footsteps.[17]

To conclude then, Hume's system is a set of principles. One important member of that set is the "maxim" (a principle for Hume) that all the perceptions of the mind are divided into impressions and ideas and that the latter are derived from the former.[18] I shall discuss this maxim next in relation to a thought experiment called the missing shade of blue.

TWO

THE MISSING SHADE AND ITS IMPLICATIONS

This chapter is divided into two unequal sections. The first section discusses Hume's thought experiment known as the missing shade of blue and the critical literature it generated especially as of late with the first principle of his system—the priority of impressions over ideas. The second section speculates on the implications the thought experiment has for his philosophy and history. In some instances it provides us with an explanation where none seem to be readily apparent. I find this especially true of historical conjectures. Be that as it may, let us first examine the missing shade of blue and its literature.

I

In the opening section of the *Treatise*,[1] David Hume puts forth a thought experiment which has been a constant source of puzzlement in recent Hume scholarship.[2] He invites us to entertain the following situation:

Suppose ... a person to have enjoyed his sight for thirty years, and to have become perfectly well acquainted with colours of all kinds, excepting one particular shade of blue, for instance, which it never has been his fortune to meet with. Let all the different shades of that colour, except that single one, be plac'd before him, descending gradually from the deepest to the lightest; 'tis plain, that he will perceive a blank, where that shade is wanting, and will be sensible, that there is a greater distance in that place betwixt the contiguous colours, than in any other. Now I ask, whether 'tis possible for him, from his own imagination, to supply this deficiency, and raise up to himself the idea of that particular shade, tho' it had never been conveyed to him by his senses? (6)

Hume believes that this individual can imaginatively supply the deficiency. (The person is a woman in my account.) This case proves "that ... simple ideas are not always derived from the correspondent impressions." Some commentators think that this admission is devastating to Hume's system and he cannot possibly hold that "the instance is so particular and singular,...and does not merit that for it alone we should alter our general maxim." Hume thinks the phenomenon proves "that 'tis not absolutely impossible for ideas to go before their correspondent impressions" (5). Apparently Hume did not find the instance counter to his previous reasoning, so what is it that commentators have missed? Why did Hume write this?

Hume's text is a bit misleading here because of the talk of the person perceiving a blank. This is nonsense. One does not perceive the *absence* of something which has not been there in a person's experience. Objects are perceived but not their omission. How would one perceive a blank? Consequently this portion of Hume's text leads us into directions we need not traverse. The route we need to take is to examine the relationship between ideas and impressions that Hume gives us a few pages earlier. He describes ideas as "exact representations" of the impressions he felt in his chamber (3). "In running over my *other* perceptions," Hume adds, "I find still the same resemblance and representation" (emphasis added). So he concludes that "ideas and impressions *appear always* to correspond to each other" (emphasis added). So far, so good; but it is at this point at which the commentators quit reading and move on to the thought experiment. Seemingly Hume was dissatisfied with the above description of the relation between ideas and impressions. He starts the next paragraph with "[u]pon a more accurate survey I find I have been carried away too far by the first appearance, and that I must make use of the distinction of perceptions into *simple and complex*, to limit this general decision, *that all our ideas and impressions are resembling*" (Hume's italics). Now ideas are not copies or exact representations (8), but only resemble one another *as they do in complex situations*. (See note 3.)

Hence, if all the different shades of blue, except the one particular shade of the color the person has not experienced, are placed before her in descending shades from darkest to lightest, then she will be able to supply the missing shade because of the *other* impressions which lie on either side of the missing shade: "there is a greater distance in that place betwixt the contiguous colours." He is mistaken to have labeled the missing shade a simple idea, but having done so we are obliged to explain this. (The thought experiment, Hume writes, "may serve as a proof, that *simple* ideas are not always derived from the correspondent impressions" (6; emphasis added).) From this remark it is inferred that Hume takes the missing shade of blue and the spectrum as a discussion of simple impressions and simple ideas. *Blue* is a simple idea if it is derived from a simple (singular) impression. *A shade of blue* is a complex idea derived from a simple impression and other ideas, i.e., the color spectrum.[3] In other words, if we imagine *merely blue* then we possess a simple idea, but if we are asked to think of its shade or saturation, we have a complex idea made up of idealized components. We have parceled out the idea and in the process made it complex. As long as we think blue we have a simple idea, but when we are asked *about the blue* then we move from simple to complex: we begin to apply other ideas and/or impressions to it. That application changes the idea of blue from a simple to a complex idea. Karann Durland offers an interesting account of this on Hume's terms by employing his "distinctions of reason" (T,25). "Since such partial resemblances [of colors, see T,637] are possible only if the perceptions themselves have distinguishable aspects," Durland argues, "Hume is committed to the view that simple impressions have disguishable features" (115). Consequently, "when Hume tells us simple perceptions 'admit of no distinction or separation,' he is not denying that they possess components distinguishable by reason; he is saying that their features are not distinguishable and separable in reality" (116). Even though Hume speaks about the "perfect simplicity" (T,637), C. L. Hardin counters, "it is precisely the lack of such simplicity in [phenomenal] colors which makes it possible to interpolate Hume's 'missing shade of blue'" (128). Durland sees the interpolation by distinctions of reason, i.e. our agent seeing "a greater distance in that place betwixt the contiguous colours" (T,6), the lightness (or darkness) of the color, or hue of the color, are done by "reason," or really in Hume's case, the imagination. The distinctions of reason plus the other impressions are sufficient for the imagination to supply the simple idea of the missing shade of blue.

The presentation of all the different shades of blue to a person is a complex impression and idea. So Hume's accounts of complex impressions and ideas need to be applied to the color shading presentation. He asks, "I have seen *Paris*; but shall I affirm I can form such an idea of that city, as will perfectly represent all its streets and houses in their real and just proportions?" The answer is obviously No. A complete enumeration of such ideas is not possible nor desirable. (Descartes is in the background here, for he thought that most ideas—complex ideas, like mathematical, physical, and metaphysical ones—needed complete enumeration for there to be an adequate explanation.[4]) Hume claims that "many of our complex impressions never are exactly copied in ideas" and this is consistent with the thought experiment where one of the impressions (the missing shade of blue) of the complex impression (the color shading presentation) is supplied by distinctions of reason, just as in someone's idea of Paris. Someone sees some particular streets and some particular houses, and on the basis of these, fills in the conception with resembling (supplied) streets and houses. After all, this is what we mean by someone possessing *a concept of a city*. Likewise if one possesses a concept of a color/shading spectrum, we expect a similar imaginative enumeration based on the sample given. In the case of a city, like Paris, the imaginative enumeration is large, but in the color/shade presentation, the imaginative enumeration is decidedly easy, and this is the reason why Hume sees no threat to his maxim and system by the thought experiment. Hume's fallacy or mistake is in thinking that "the different shades of the same colour, that each of them produces a distinct idea, [are] *independent of the rest*" (6; emphasis added). These shades are not *independent* of one another, because they *resemble* one another *if* they occur next to each other in their gradual arrangement from darker to lighter. (Again see the theory of color outlined in note 3.) Contrary to some of the commentators, the thought experiment adds a sophisticated clarity to the nature of complex impressions, complex ideas, and their relationships which is absent to that point in Hume's *Treatise*.

At this stage I need to tidy up my analysis by discussing briefly what Hume understands the relation of resemblance to be. He says it can produce a new impression in the mind (T,165), but admits that resemblance is the most fertile source of error (T,61), so it is not a sure thing that she can produce the new idea of the shade of blue. However, he does hold that resemblance is a demonstrable relation which is discovered by intuition (T,69,70). Thus, if she has good intuitions, our agent will be able to supply the missing shade.

Another question raised by my analysis thus far is, how does the distinction between simple and complex "*limit* this general decision" (T,3; emphasis added), i.e., "ideas and impressions appear always to correspond to each other?" To require that two things or activities resemble one another is not to ask much of them in terms of relation. A football game and a fight resemble each other but they share no important features in common, like belonging to the class of games, and games like football and solitaire belong to the same class but do not resemble one another.[5] So far from limiting his maxim, it seems to make it almost unlimited! Representation appears to become possible in ideas with exact (appropriate) impressions, but given by those in the same class (the other shades of blue or the particular streets and houses of Paris). So the representation of the missing shade is not the actual *shade* but what represents it, the greater distance between the two shades she uses as a clue to the new idea. Her reason or imagination is one of space and not of color. Does this matter to Hume's theory of ideas? Probably not, because she can still imaginatively produce the new idea of the color—it is just done by space rather than by the missing shade itself. This is a major reason why the thought experiment is so interesting philosophically, because of its controversial nature: in one sense she cannot supply the missing shade and in another sense she can. Commentators disagree on the possible resolutions of the case. However, these resolutions seem compatible to me and do not forge any contradictions to Hume's theory. If anything, they open it up to the point where it may not even be capable of contradiction, especially the primary maxim. Not only are all impressions covered or copied, but all ideas are "copies" by some member of their sensible class which may not be their appropriate sub-class, i.e., a spatial impression rather than the shade impressions. Contrary to David Pears, such a "lateral" move in Hume's theory is there, i.e., to be formed in the text and not something foreign to it which we attribute to it.[6] So Hume's point seems to be that *other* (i.e., similar or ordered) impressions can serve as the basis for simple ideas. This significantly changes the meaning of "copy" in the copy theory of ideas. Hume's empiricism is less restricted than the first principle of his system suggests. His other point is: no impressions, no ideas. If there are ideas, then they are derived from corresponding impressions (this is the strongest reading) or from resembling impressions from a series (this is the weaker reading).

Another problem with using "a greater distance" between two shades for her to detect the missing shade of blue is that we have no impression of space in Hume. "But my senses convey to me only the impressions of colour'd points, dispos'd in a certain manner .... [T]he idea of extension is nothing but a copy of these colour'd points, and of the manner of their appearance" (T,34). As Alexander Rosenberg has observed: "Hume's analysis has proved circular.... [C]onsider the 'manner of appearance' that relates the sensible minima: the manner of appearance of these coloured points has them either to the left or, to the right of, above, or below one another. But where do these ideas come from? They presuppose space."[7] So Hume's subsequent analysis of space is of no help to him here. If anything, it makes matters worse.

Descartes's answer to Hume's thought experiment would be that she would be able to supply the missing shade of blue by reason and not by imagination. He asks of Pierre Gassendi, "How do you know that there is no idea of colour in a man born blind.?"[8] He argues (fallaciously I think): "From time to time we find in our own case that even though we close our eyes, sensations of light and colour are nevertheless aroused." (Descartes means by "sensations" what Hume means by "ideas.") Apparently Descartes entertains the possibility that the idea of color is an innate idea, so consequently he has an easy solution to Hume's experiment: she can produce it by reason; there is no need for her to have an impression. Or that "sensations" of color can be aroused by way of reason. But Berkeley counters this line of reasoning by arguing in *A New Theory of Vision* (1709), sec. 10,[9] that "no idea which is not itself perceived can be the means of perceiving any other idea." This implies that ideas which are themselves perceived (the other shades of blue) can be the means of perceiving another (the missing shade of blue). So the plausibility of the thought experiment might stem from the argument in Berkeley's *Essay*. As with other secondary qualities, color is equated with "a particular sensation in the mind,"[10] which leads Berkeley to conclude that "[f]rom all which, should it not seem to follow, that *all colors are equally apparent*, and that none of those which we perceive are really inherent in any outward object?" (21; emphasis added). So following Berkeley, Hume thinks that the mind can perceive the missing shade of blue, since the other shades are "particular sensation(s) in the mind."

The reader can tell that Hume is comfortable with the analogy he draws between ideas and colors in the *Treatise*: "If you make any other change [besides the increase or diminish of its force and vivacity] on it [an idea], it represents a different object or impression. The case is the same as in colours. A particular shade of any colour may acquire a new degree of liveliness or brightness without any other variation. But when you produce any other variation, 'tis no longer the same shade or colour" (96). Our agent in the thought experiment produces another variation, i.e., the greater distance between the two shades on either side of the missing one, and she produces the missing shade. So there seems to be the mental causal mechanism in Hume's thought for it to appear plausible for her to produce it. A shade, for Hume, is a variation of a color and an idea which he takes to be simple. Both Berkeley and Hume conceived of the defining properties of color as subjective (mental) and hence the plausibility of the thought experiment; whereas today we conceive of the defining properties of color as relational (see note 3), and consequently its plausibility diminishes.

I have already discussed Hume's assumption of the independence of the ideas (of shade) in the thought experiment. But its implausibility is perhaps brought out more clearly if we bring in some of the considerations of the nature of sensible qualities in the debate between Michael Dummett and A. J. Ayer.[11] The thoughts that lead up to the thought experiment are mistaken, but instructive. Hume argues:

Now if this be true of different colours [tho' at the same time resembling], it must be no less so of the different shades of the same colour, that each of them produces a distinct idea, independent of the rest. For if this shou'd be deny'd, 'tis possible, by the continual gradation of shades, to run a colour insensibly into what is most remote from it; and if you will not allow any of the means to be different, you cannot without absurdity deny the extremes to be the same. (T,6)

Hume's reasoning here is incoherent because of two factual considerations. The first is that sensory qualities, like shades of the same color, constitute a continuum, and as Dummett and Ayer point out, "with the result that the relation of indiscernibility between qualities of the same kind is not transitive" (8). Consequently, for instance, in the case of color, if we have three shades of the same color in a series, x is indiscernible in color from y and y from z but x is discernible from z. (Dummett's indiscernibility condition for simple observational qualities is "that, if one object possesses the quality, and no relevant difference between it and another object can be perceived, then the second object possesses it" (9).) The condition is satisfiable as long as we stay within the series, but if there is any gap (as there is in Hume's thought experiment, the blank), then the two objects compared can be distinguished or discerned. They remain indiscernible only if the two objects or shades of the same color are *continuous* throughout the spectrum. The upshot of this discussion from the Dummett/Ayer debate is that Hume is right about them producing a distinct idea only if taken out of sequence, like x and z, but that each shade is not independent of the rest because they are continuous on the spectrum and form a series. It is here where "ideas...go before their correspondent impressions" (5). So along with the assumption of independence goes Hume's conjecture that what applies to the means applies to the extremes. This is the second factual consideration and it overlooks the properties of the spectrum, i.e., it is continuous and serial by nature. One will not "run a colour insensibly into what is most remote from it." They become "sensible" or discernible, if the series is interrupted or a gap is detected as in the missing shade of blue. If the shades ran insensibly together, there would be no possibility of her detecting the missing shade. Hence Hume sets up the thought experiment in such a way as to satisfy Dummett's challenge in spite of what theoretical remarks he prefaces the thought experiment with. Hume gets the color relationships correct in the description of the thought experiment, but errs in their explanation.

II

What are the implications of the thought experiment? In Hume's system a distinction is drawn between imagination and memory——the former is "free" and the latter is "orderly." This distinction seems to collapse, since the missing shade of blue demonstrates that the imagination (in supplying the missing shade) can be as "orderly" as memory.

Hume claims "the instance [the missing shade of blue] is so particular and singular" that it does not merit our altering the general maxim. Commentators, like D. M. Johnson, show that if Hume permits this instance in visual perception that we need to permit it in other experiences, i.e., auditory, gastronomical, and so on. Any experiences which are "orderly," i.e., in a series which forms some kind of continuum. Johnson plays the trombone and has had analogous experiences when sight-reading music (109-110). So these experiences are not as "particular and singular" as Hume had thought. Even though he does not mention the thought experiment again, he does not forget about it and that it looms large in his arguments and analyses especially in regard to history. Hume came to recog-

nize that history, as R. G. Collingwood expresses it, "is an integral part of experience itself" (IH,158). Hume's empircism was considerably broadened by his
historical endeavors.

The historian is like our agent in the missing shade of blue experiment. He
knowns certain things and facts and on the basis of them he reasons or conjectures about others. The best statement of the function of conjectures in history
comes from the first *Inquiry*:

the most usual species of connection among the different events which enter into any narrative composition is that of cause and effect; while the historian traces the series of
actions according to their natural order, remount to their secret springs and principles, and
delineates their most remote consequences. He chooses for his subject a certain portion of
that great chain of events which compose the history of mankind: each link in this chain
he endeavors to touch in his narration; sometimes unavoidable ignorance renders all his
attempts fruitless; sometimes he supplies by conjecture what is wanting in knowledge;
and always he is sensible that the more unbroken the chain is which he presents to his
readers, the more perfect is his production. (IU,34)

I will save the discussion of the nature of historical composition or narration for
later chapters, but I do want to briefly look at the idea of historical conjecture
since it has a certain similarity with the missing shade of blue experiment. An
illustration can be taken from Hume's history of King Edward II:

Before I conclude this reign, I cannot forbear making another remark, drawn from the
detail of losses given in by the elder Spenser; particularly the great quantity of salted meat
which he had in his larder, six hundred bacons, eighty carcasses of beef, six hundred muttons. We may observe, that the outrage of which he complained began after the third of
May, or the eleventh new style, as we learn from the same paper. It is easy, therefore, to
conjecture, what a vast store of the same kind he must have laid up at the beginning of
winter. . . . From this circumstance, however trivial in appearance, may be drawn important inferences with regard to the domestic economy and manner of life in those ages.
(H,II,180)

Here we have an excellent example of conjectures functioning in historical
narration——obeying the succession of time or temporal order by Hume's observation of the quantity of salted meat Spenser had in the *spring* and then conjec-
turing how much more there should have been during the *winter* months. After
all, it stands to reason and in conformity with experience of the times that there
would be a greater quantity of salted meat in the winter than in the spring, for
food was scarce during those harsh months and salted meat was the principal

food source and also because of storage practices among the ancient Britons. Nowhere in the documents does it mention these general conditions of the period which Hume writes about. All that is mentioned is the quantity of salted meat in the spring. (This document is really just an inventory.) Using only that information for the circumstances in the winter months is insufficient evidence; thus conjectures rather than probabilities are supplied to fill in and make complete the succession of time. This is a reasonable practice for historians to engage in if they are to give a complete picture of what happened. We know what the food supplies were like in the spring and we do not know for the winter. We (reasonably) assume the same general conditions hold through the period. So given the same impressions we form new ideas in a way analogous to the agent in the missing shade of blue experiment. Hence, this instance or situation gives us a basis for understanding historical conjectures within Hume's system.

An important consequence of the nature of historical conjectures is that they were Hume's way of overcoming the view that historical facts and chronology are based on authorities—a view of history Collingwood labels the "common sense view" (IH, 234ff.). Hume with this practice was moving toward what Collingwood calls *historical construction*. In other words, Hume's conjectures parallel Collingwood's concept of interpolation, where the critical historian constructs his or her own idea of the past, using himself or herself as the sole authority, or using his or her own picture of the past as the criterion, for deciding the true and the false in memorabilia. One does not discover the past; one invents it. (For more details of this view, see chapter 4.)

Hume's way out of the problem of the missing shade of blue is to look beyond simple sensible qualities and the ideas annexed to them. This gaze took him to history and human nature as more plausible ways to explain the way of ideas. What Hume had found true of the missing shade of blue, he later discovered was true of history. This is especially true of historical narration since it too is in a series (via chronology) much like the color spectrum (see chapter 5).

THREE

HISTORY AND HUMAN NATURE

I

David Hume has been frequently accused by his critics of having grossly misunderstood the nature of historical judgment, and consequently, of failing to grasp the elements constituting the historical enterprise. General consensus has it that his idea of history is inadequate for a reason not unique to Hume but shared by all eighteenth-century historians and perhaps the most predominant (if not the most remembered) characteristic of eighteenth-century historiography. The major flaw in Hume's understanding, as the critics see it, is in his conception of human nature. The statement from Hume most frequently quoted in this regard comes from the first *Inquiry*: "Mankind are so much the same, in all times and places, that history informs us of nothing new or strange in this particular. Its chief use is only to discover the constant and universal principles of human nature" (IU,93). In the course of this chapter, I shall examine the interpretation and argument that critics have based on these two sentences, and then reexamine Hume's writings in the light of the accusations. I shall show that the critics' view is simply mistaken or unfounded, and that Hume's idea of history is far more sophisticated and individual than the critics' view of it.

David H. Fischer is one of the historians to single Hume out in this regard, and has gone so far as to say that this type of reasoning employed in history constitutes a fallacy. Fischer dubs this "the fallacy of the universal man."[1] This fallacy is allegedly committed when a historian makes inferences on the assumption that a people or individuals are intellectually and psychologically the same in all times, places, and circumstances. But such an assumption does not rest on historical premises; a historical judgment or conclusion should be based on historical statements—not on nonhistorical assumptions like the above. Fischer cites an American Civil War historian, Kenneth Stampp, as an example: "I have assumed that the slaves were merely ordinary human beings, that innately Negroes *are*, after all, only white men with black skins, nothing more, nothing less."[2] The fallacy that occurs here is the assumption as self-evident that Stampp himself would have responded in much the same way an African Negro slave would have in his predicament, and hence, that an African Negro slave *did* respond in the same way as a white liberal professor of history who worked in twentieth-century Berkeley, California, would have if he were shackled, put on a block, and then sold to a nineteenth-century plantation owner in Bibb County, Alabama. Such armchair reasoning is no substitute for empirical investigation when the latter is called for. Needless to say, African Negros—much less nineteenth-century ones—do not fit into this white liberal stereotype. This sort of reasoning ignores important cultural differences and certain institutional changes at that time which did affect the Black consciousness and behavior, and these changes and differences need to be listed as among the characteristics of the African Negro—they should be reflected in the historian's judgment or reasoning. The conclusion does not follow from the premise supplied; hence the argument is a *non sequitur*, and more precisely, a fallacy of *a priori* motivation.

A passage from Hume's *History of England* which is suggestive of this sort of fallacious reasoning occurs in his discussion of the scandals in the political parties of late seventeenth-century England, where Hume adds that:

Charles I was a tyrant, a Papist, and a contriver of the Irish massacre: the church of England was relapsing fast into idolatry: puritanism was the only true religion, and the covenant the favourite object of heavenly regard. Through these delusions the party proceeded, and what may seem wonderful, still to the increase of law and liberty, till they reached the imposture of the popish plot, a fiction which exceeds the ordinary bounds of vulgar credulity. *But however singular these events may appear, there is really nothing altogether new in any period of modern history*: and it is remarkable, that tribunitian arts, though sometimes useful in a free constitution, have usually been such as men of probity and honour could not bring themselves either to practise or approve. (H,VI,533; emphasis added)

"Man-in-general" or mankind does not change from one time, place, or circumstance to another; this is the reason behind Hume's (italicized) remark. So when we find Hume opening his narrative as follows, what we shall expect to find in the *History of England* when he makes historical comparisons is similarities and continuities: "The only certain means by which nations can indulge their curiosity in researches concerning their remote origin, is to consider the language, manners, and customs of their ancestors, and to compare them with those of the neighbouring nations" (H,I,4). Another historiographer, J. B. Black, would also support Fischer's interpretation. Black argues that "Hume sees only similarity."[3] These conceptions form a commonplace view of Hume that may be seen most clearly in Black's account, and, for convenience, may be labeled as "the standard interpretation."[4]

Black, on behalf of the standard interpretation, maintains that: "Hume did not grasp the elements of the problem [of historical explanation], because he was dominated, as indeed were all the eighteenth-century *philosophes*, by the belief that human nature was uniformly the same at all times and places" (86). Nor is Black alone on this point. Alfred Stern also holds that "Hume maintained the thesis of an invariable human nature."[5] And R. G. Collingwood likewise held that Hume, like other men of the Enlightenment, was barred "from scientific history by a substantialistic view of human nature which was really inconsistent with his philosophical principles [his skepticism]," and that "[h]uman nature was conceived substantially as something static and permanent, an unvarying substratum underlying the course of historical changes and all human activities. History never repeated itself but human nature remained eternally unaltered."[6]

So critics agree that the concept of human nature is central to Hume's idea of history, and in this connection he is often grouped with his contemporaries, Montesquieu and Voltaire. However, this interpretation has been pushed so far that when one carefully looks at Hume and then at the standard interpretation, one becomes suspicious, for there exists a marked difference between his words and their interpretation. Indeed, one begins to understand why a historian like Laurence L. Bongie makes the methodological remark: "He [the historian] should consult Hume and Montesquieu, not the reason of the Age of Reason."[7] Much of Hume's argument and reasons are missed by the standard interpretation. In fact, much of this view, I shall argue, is not representative of Hume's idea of history at all. Collingwood goes so far as to suggest that the historical outlook (the Enlightenment's and Hume's) was not genuinely historical (77). Thus we are lacking a portrait of Hume as a philosophical historian struggling with problems and attempting to find historical solutions.

In the remainder of this chapter, I shall construct a competing interpretation that is truer to the spirit of Hume's letter than the standard interpretation. I shall also attempt to show that the statements singled out in the standard interpretation that lead Fischer and others to conclude that Hume was a victim of the fallacy of universal human nature in his historical procedure suggest a different meaning and implications than what has been attributed to them.

II

Let us first make some concessions. As a historian Hume was very much concerned with continuities and similarities in making historical comparisons. A glance at any of the six volumes of the *History* testifies to that; for example, his comparison between the government of England in the reign of Elizabeth and that of Turkey (H,IV,376). A preoccupation with similarities and continuities is part of the historian's disease. But as Fischer says, "Significant elements of continuity cannot be understood without a sense of the discontinuities, too" (204). This is obviously a large part of what constitutes historical understanding; the location of some happening or phenomenon into its period (or some equivalent concept) with the sort of observations and judgments that reflect a delicate balance between periodization and individualization— between continuity and discontinuity—is one of the marks of the historian's activity. Now the question is, Does Hume possess any such balance? Does he have a sense for discontinuities, too? To answer these questions, let us look at Hume's narrative.

In his discussion of Charles I, Hume makes the following judgment:

But as these [strict legal] limitations were not regularly fixed during the age of Charles, nor at any time before; so was this liberty totally unknown, and was generally deemed, as well as religious toleration, incompatible with all good government. No age or nation, among the moderns, had ever set an example of such an indulgence: and it seems unreasonable to judge of the measures embraced during one period, by the maxims which prevail in another. (H,V,240)

This passage suggests that Hume was aware that the historian must be careful not to fall into the error of reading one's own concepts and values back into those of other periods. In a passage from the *Treatise*, which offers some explanation as to why one is tempted to reason this way, Hume states:

To this principle [sympathy] we ought to ascribe the great uniformity we may observe in the humours and turn of thinking of those of the same nation; and 'tis much more probable, that this resemblance arises from sympathy, than from any influence of the soil and climate, which, tho' they continue invariable the same, are not able to preserve the character of a nation the same for a century together. (II,I,XI)

So what similarity the historian observes within a given period or nation is to be sought for in (and attributed to) *sympathy*. And furthermore, similarities observed between periods and nations in historical comparisons have the same origin, on Hume's account.[8] So the historian's observed similarities are based on the principle of the uniformity of human nature. But it is here that the critics of Hume have done less than justice to his historical epistemology.

Hume identifies the uniformity of "the humours and turn of thinking" with "the character of a nation." This is given content by Hume's argument concerning liberty and necessity in the first *Inquiry*:

The mutual dependence of men is so great in all societies that scarce any human action is entirely complete in itself or is performed without some reference to the actions of others, which are requisite to make it answer fully the intention of the agent.... In proportion as men extend their dealings and render their intercourse with others more complicated, they always comprehend in their schemes of life a greater variety of voluntary actions which they expect, from the proper motives, to co-operate with their own. In all these conclusions they take their measures from past experiences. (IU,98)

When Hume adds that "men ... are to continue in their operations the same that they have ever found them," he has in mind something like the following example from the first *Inquiry*: "He [an artisan] also expects that when he carries his goods to market and offers them at a reasonable price, he shall find purchasers and shall be able, by the money he acquires, to engage others to supply him with those commodities which are requisite for his subsistence" (IU,99). Hume does not have in mind, as many have suggested, the specific actions of the artisan in this economic-socio-political framework as part of the uniformity, such as what the artisan was thinking about along the way, why he must sell on this particular day, that he chose this market rather than another because his relatives were there, and so on. Hume makes this perfectly clear in the following statement on method from the *Inquiry*: "The philosopher, if he be consistent, must apply the same reasonings to the actions and volitions of intelligent agents. The most irregular and unexpected resolutions of men may frequently be accounted for by those [that is, a historian or biographer] who know every particular circumstance of their character and situation" (IU,97). In the contemporary idiom of philosophy of history, the latter type of explanation seems to be accomplished for Hume by detailed description, an idea similar to one argued for by Collingwood and William Dray.[9] And, of course, explanation through narrative description is quite a different concept from the idea of explanation according to the principle of uniformity or regularity, which is the one generally attributed to Hume.

The appearance of scientific rigor must not be overlooked when evaluating Hume's contribution to philosophical historiography and the philosophy of history. The Newtonian influence and Hume's success in employing the conceptual achievements of the "new science" in a study of man separates him from previous British historians. The uniformity Hume sought was one that would make a study of man, including history, a discipline comparable to the new science. His early work, the *Treatise*, marks a step toward laying a theoretical foundation that would make history a respectable, scientific pursuit for modern man, a "moral science." This foundation was needed in part because the science of man has to utilize concepts and techniques that are essentially historical in character. Uniformity was one such concept; it can perhaps be better understood in the context of the Introduction to the *Treatise*, in which Hume argues that a science of man is not only superior to the other sciences but is also the basis for the others. There is a dependence of the other sciences on the science of man because in the latter the connection with human nature is "more close and intimate"; and this connection is, of course, sympathy. As he states in Book Two: "Every human creature resembles ourselves, and by that means has an advantage above any other object, in operating on the imagination" (II,II,V). Because of this "fact," inquiries that have as their objects human action and human nature are the only ones in which we can expect assurance and conviction. (This assurance and conviction is reflected in Hume's manner of exposition in the *History*; see chapter 7.)

Hume's expectations would be viewed today as an over-simplification of human psychology, if not actually premised on a number of falsehoods. Nonetheless, his expectations are also premised on the discovery he thought he had made in finding sympathy and sensitivity as the keys to understanding man's behavior in the past as well as in the present.[10] Before we leave the *Treatise*, the claims of the standard interpretation need special attention, especially to the extent that Hume held to the uniformity of human nature. I have already given some indication as to what kind of uniformity was sought and what was presupposed by his view. However, to exhibit the variety of meanings of the word *uniformity*, one may observe the reasoning in the following theory from the *Treatise*. It is also an excellent statement of the philosophy of history that is reflected in Hume's other writings:

The skin, pores, muscles, and nerves of a day-labourer are different from those of a man of quality: So are his sentiments, actions, and manners. The different stations of life influence the whole fabric, external and internal; and these different stations arise necessarily, because uniformly, from the necessary and uniform principles of human nature. Men cannot live without society, and cannot be associated without government. Government makes a distinction of property, and establishes the different ranks of men. This produces industry, traffic, manufactures, lawsuits, war, leagues, alliances, voyages, travels, cities, fleets, ports, and all those other actions and objects, which cause such a diversity, and at the same time maintain such an uniformity in human life. (II,III,I)

A careful reading of the above passages indicates that Hume makes allowance for diversity, and hence has a probabilistic account of uniformity on this level.[11] From a contemporary point of view, this is what is minimally required of explanations in history. As Karl Lambert and Gordon Brittan have pointed out: "The laws that the 'Humean' account requires can be either deterministic or statistical."[12] And both kinds of laws are found in Hume. Moreover, it is the statistical or probabilistic account that we find in his historical explanations of specific actions. (Evidence for this claim will be presented below.) The stronger sense of *uniformity* (which Black mistakenly regarded as the only sense for Hume) is *Hume's belief in the uniformity of "the whole fabric" of human life.* This belief is in terms of the very conditions of likelihood, the limits of explanation; it is the limits that are deterministic. The distinction between these two levels, the deterministic and the statistical, in Hume's theory of explanation has not been fully appreciated. On the basis of such a distinction, we are able to answer the question: How does Hume think it is possible for "actions and objects ... [to] cause such a diversity, and at the same time maintain such a uniformity in human life?" Hume's best reasoning in support of this assertion is in the following argument taken from the first *Inquiry*:

I grant it possible to find some actions which seem to have no regular connection with any known motives and are exceptions to all the measures of conduct which have ever been established for the government of men. But if we could willingly know what judgment should be formed of such irregular and extraordinary actions, we may consider the sentiments commonly entertained with regard to those irregular events which appear in the course of nature and the operations of external objects. *All causes are not conjoined to their usual effects with like uniformity.* An artificer who handles only dead matter may be disappointed of his aim, as well as the politician who directs the conduct of sensible and intelligent agents. (IU,96; emphasis added)

This is the context of the question that Hume raises in the first *Inquiry*: "What would become of *history* had we not a dependence on the veracity of the historian according to the experience which we have had of mankind?" (IU,99). To this potent rhetorical question, Hume succinctly adds: "It seems almost impossible, therefore, to engage either in science or action of any kind without acknowledging the doctrine of necessity, and this [includes] *inference* from motives to voluntary action, from characters to conduct" (IU,99).

This statement leads Hume to affirm uniformity, and his concept is markedly different from that of previous thinkers on this point, in that the inferences he speaks of in the above passage are based upon an appeal to analogical reasoning from probabilities. Here the inference is from human action. The statement, of course, never has the certainty of an *a priori* statement or a limiting principle, so that sort of uniformity is ruled out. Words in Hume's writings like "necessity," "contradiction," and "certainty" are highly misleading (if they are read in a literal, formal way) and probably have increased misunderstanding. An example of this is: "This possibility is converted into certainty by further observation ..." (IU,96). Probabilities are confirmed by observations, but possibilities are obviously not, since these are modal considerations of logic. Furthermore, Hume almost always adds qualifications to his statements in the *Inquiry*. These qualifications, like the following one, are left out in the standard interpretation: "This [the manners of men different in different ages and countries] *affords room for many general observations concerning the gradual change of our sentiments and inclinations*, and the different maxims which prevail in the different ages of human creatures" (IU,95; emphasis added). And the preceding paragraph is another, important qualification which Hume readily admitted:

We must not, however, expect that this uniformity of human actions should be carried to such a length as that all men, in the same circumstances, will always act precisely in the same manner, without making any allowance for the diversity of characters, prejudices, and opinions. Such a uniformity, in every particular, is found in no part of nature. On the contrary, from observing the variety of conduct in different men we are enabled to form a greater variety of maxims which still suppose a degree of uniformity and regularity. (IU,95)

This single passage is sufficient to dispel the myth of the standard interpretation. It makes you wonder how a first rate philosopher like Collingwood would not appreciate this significant qualification by Hume on the uniformity of human nature.

So from the *Inquiry* passages above we can expect significant change in the details of nations or national characters. Hume's reasoning seems to confirm, as historians today would agree, that it would be a fallacy for a historian to attribute a characteristic of one national character to another without proper observance of the above maxim.

III

Let us now turn to the *History* to see if our reconstruction of Hume's idea of history and its foundations adequately portrays his account of human nature and action in the narrative. The question concerning the uniformity of human nature in the *History* is a complex one, and cannot be answered straightforwardly as in the *Inquiry*. There are passages that suggest that what Hume meant by "uniformity" does not exclude contingency in human affairs. A possible counterexample of this from Hume is "We may change the names of things; but their nature and their operation on the understanding never change" (T,II,III,II;IU,100). But the kind of uniformity to which Hume is referring here is physical (rather than moral) necessity; for instance, a chain of events which are necessary but not sufficient conditions for the existence or the occurrence of an event. Hume's example makes this clear: "...if he throw himself out of the window and meet with no obstruction, he will not remain a moment suspended in the air." However, in the first *Inquiry*, Hume thinks an analogous type of necessity is present in moral subjects too: "Were a man whom I know to be honest and opulent, and ... with whom I lived in intimate friendship, to come in my house, where I am surrounded with my servants, I rest assured that he is not to stab me before he leaves it in order to rob me of my silver standing." Hume adds, unless he be seized with a frenzy, but this is to "change the suppositions" (IU,100). The presumption here is in the idea that morals change gradually (IU,95).

Hume attributes "moral necessity" to much of human behavior. It is here that he allows for contingency. For example, when a historian reads in a document about the execution of a prisoner who resists it, the historian, through an imaginative effort of what Hume referred to as "physical necessity" (deterministic laws), can consider what that event was like for that particular individual. Thus, the uniformity Hume speaks of is inferred from the principles of sympathy and resemblance. No understanding of the past would be possible without these presuppositions. Hume's example clarifies this:

The same prisoner, when conducted to the scaffold, foresees his death as certainly from the constancy and fidelity of his guards as from the operation of the ax or wheel. His mind runs along a certain train of ideas: The refusal of the soldiers to consent to his escape, the action of the executioner: the separation of the head and body; bleeding, convulsive motions, and death. (T,II,III,II;IU,100)

According to Hume, the historian can imagine this train of ideas and use them in his narrative as "fact" (soft data). The events are molded together by their physical (and moral) necessity. On this basis, Hume allows the notion of fact to include imagination, but only insofar as it follows a chain such as is evidenced by nature. It is from this basis and its implications that we find Hume writing the *History* as he does, with its many passages that suggest the interpretive approach. A historical example is the execution of Queen Anne Boleyn, in which Hume uses only one secondary source (Burnet), and in which the narrative follows the above pattern of reasoning and interpretation of the event:

The queen now prepared for suffering the death to which she was sentenced. She sent her last message to the king, and acknowledged the obligations which she owed him in thus uniformly continuing his endeavour for her advancement. From a private gentlewoman, she said, he had first made her a marchioness, then queen, and now, since he could raise her no higher in this world, he was sending her to be a saint in heaven. She then renewed the protestations of her innocence, and recommended her daughter to his care. Before the lieutenant of the Tower, and all who approached her, she made the like declarations; and continued to behave herself with her usual serenity, and even with cheerfulness. "The executioner," she said to the lieutenant, "is, I hear, very expert, and my neck is very slender:" upon which she softened her tone a little with regard to her protestations of innocence. She probably reflected that the obstinacy of Queen Catherine, and her opposition to the King's will, had much alienated him from the Lady Mary. Her own maternal concern, therefore, for Elizabeth, prevailed, in these last remarks, over that indignation which the unjust sentence, by which she suffered, naturally excited in her. She said that she had come to die, as she was sentenced by the law: She would accuse none, nor say anything of the ground upon which she was judged. She prayed heartily for the king, called him a most merciful and gentle prince, and acknowledged that he had always been to her a good and gracious sovereign; and if any one should think proper to canvass for cause, she desired him to judge the best. She was beheaded by the executioner of Calais, who was sent for as more expert than any in England. Her body was negligently thrown into a common chest of elm-tree, made to hold arrows, and was buried in the Tower. (H,III,238)

In this passage, statements like "When brought, however, to the scaffold, she softened her tone..." and "She probably reflected that the obstinacy of Queen Catherine..." and "Her own maternal concern..." are difficult to explain in terms of hard data (documents and monuments). However, according to what Hume means by physical necessity and moral evidence (and necessity) in the *Treatise*, there is a basis or justification for the above psychological assertions about Queen Anne. Also, there is a pragmatic element in statements like these; they make the narrative interesting and supply connections among the hard data. Character analysis of historical figures is indicative of the historian's understanding of human nature; and in Hume, the above statements and one like "...the unjust sentence, by which she suffered, *naturally* excited in her" utilize his notions of sympathy and resemblance in historical understanding. The statement "She *probably reflected* that the obstinacy of Queen Catherine ...," ending with the "conclusion" that "Her own maternal concern, therefore, for Elizabeth, prevailed, in these last moments ...," is based upon two interrelated principles. One is the analogy Hume draws between Queen Anne and Queen Catherine in their behavior. The second is the principle of resemblance: there is the "similar station in life" between the two women. Hume utilizes this principle to such an extent that he will premise character analyses on statements like "The method in which we find they [the nobility] treated the king's favourites and ministers is proof of their usual way of dealing with each other" (H,II,179).

From the context one may say that this statement is a general law or methodological principle and that the particulars are subsumed under it or "covered" by it. But these passages and others do not show that Hume believed, implicitly or explicitly, in a constancy of human nature which entails that "history is simply a repeating decimal."[13] *Constancy of human nature, for Hume, is a methodological principle that makes history possible; that is, possible for there to be any consistency and credibility in what the historian says.* Apparently Black incorrectly identifies constancy of human nature with historical events, but this identification is not suggested by Hume. This error is probably due to Black's failure to draw the distinction between methodological and substantial uniformity. For instance, "No people could undergo a change more sudden and entire in their manners, then did the English nation during this period" (H,VI,141). Hume makes other statements in the *History* that answer Black's "repeating decimal" charge:

It is needless to be particular in enumerating all the cruelties practised in England during the course of three years that these persecutions lasted: the savage barbarity on the one hand, and the patient constancy on the other, are so similar in all those martyrdoms, that the narrative, little agreeable in itself, would never be relieved by any variety. Human nature appears not, on any occasion, so detestable, and at the same time so absurd, as in these religious persecutions, which sink men below infernal spirits in wickedness, and below the beasts in folly. (H,III,437)

This passage illustrates a significant idea. The emphasis Hume puts on the narrative being relieved by variety shows that dissimilarity was considered important to Hume not only in the structure of a historical narrative, but also in the presentation of an adequate, well-rounded picture of the past.[14] Also, Hume's historical thoughts on individuals and periods are reflected by his use of the notion of human nature in his narrative. His discussion of Queen Elizabeth, which illustrates how little Hume subscribed to the myth of absolute constancy of human nature in history, perhaps better exhibits this point: "She knew the inconstant nature of the people ..." (H,IV,46). Novelty in history, Hume recognized, arises from individual human actions.

With regard to passion and reason in human nature, Hume remarks about Mary, Queen of Scots:

In order to form a just idea of her character, we must set aside one part of her conduct, while she abandoned herself to the guidance of a profligate man; and must consider these faults, whether we admit them to be imprudences or crimes, as the result of the inexplicable, though not uncommon, inconstancy in the human mind, of the frailty of our nature, of the violence of passion, and of the influence which situations, and sometimes momentary incidents, have on persons whose principles are not thoroughly confirmed by experience and reflection. (H,IV,251-52)

Noteworthy here is the reference to persons and their principles, which is a methodological technique for evaluating the historical figures within Hume's narrative. It appears from this passage that Hume would assert that what seems to be an inconstancy in human nature for one person or group may not be so for another. This is because the question of the constancy or inconstancy of human nature is couched in the light of principles that are premised on the historian's understanding, or in this case, on Hume's understanding. Also, Hume's idea of historical explanation includes the inconstancy of human nature (in the relative sense) and the exceptional. The individual events are not sacrificed; rather, as the *History* testifies:

We must here, as in many other instances, lament the inconstancy of human nature, that a person endowed with so many noble virtues, generosity, sincerity, friendship, valor, eloquence, and industry, should, in the latter period of his life, have given reins to his ungovernable passions, and involved not only himself but many of his friends in utter ruin. (H,IV,338)

This reflective remark by Hume plays a central role in his concept of history. If there are many instances, or memorable events and characters, that demonstrate the lamentable inconstancy of human nature, and if man is subject to ungovernable passions that affect his life and others, then there are instances that fall outside the uniformity which Newtonian science and philosophy demand. So Collingwood is right in claiming that Hume is not scientific in the Newtonian sense. For example: "[Charles's] attachment to France, after all the pains which we have taken, by inquiry and conjecture, to fathom it, contains still something, it must be confessed, mysterious and inexplicable" (H,VI,448). Because there are instances like these (ones where not all or enough of the particulars are known), and because they are memorable to man, history is of the utmost importance to Hume. Accordingly, historians should be challenged to provide an explanation of such instances. According to Humean thought, the significant contribution of history is that it discloses the consequences of irregular changes that affect the course of human history. This can be seen in the following passage from the *History*: "This event [the rise and eventual political power of Sir John Savile] is memorable, as being the first instance, perhaps, in the history of England, of any king's advancing a man on account of Parliamentary interest, and of opposition to his measures. However irregular this practice, it will be regarded by political reasoners as one of the most early and most infallible symptoms of a regular established liberty" (H,V,93). This typifies a common explanatory model: the irregular shown to be regular.

If all these passages exemplify the subject matter of history, then the principle of sympathy may be seen as the cornerstone of Hume's *History*. For sympathy, and what Hume refers to as "conjecture" (the supplying the missing particulars), are the only means to an understanding of the data of history. The consulting of common experience creates the standard or criterion. Hume's slogan in the *Treatise*, "Consult common experience" (III,II,II), operates as a disciplinary guide for the historian's imaginative or conjectural use of his or her data. In detail:

By means of this *guide* [the principles of human nature] we mount up to the knowledge of men's inclinations and motives from their actions, expressions, and even gestures, and again descend to the interpretation of their actions from our knowledge of their motives and inclinations. The general observations, treasured up by a course of experience, give us the *clue* of human nature and teach us to unravel all its intricacies. (IU,94: emphasis added)

This important passage cannot be overemphasized. It gives us a reasonable account of the activity of a critical historian who is in the process of assessing evidence.

IV

Since we have reconstructed the general lines of Hume's idea of history, we are now in a better position to conclude our earlier discussion on inconstancy or diversity in human action by observing some important ideas that may be seen in several interesting passages from the *History* within their philosophical framework. At times Hume uses the phrase "human nature" to refer both to man's nature and to the actions that proceed from his nature, but he applies it as well to actions that are atypical. Constancy and inconstancy of human behavior on a socio-political level form a tacit criterion for Hume's historical judgments concerning importance and merit for narration. This can be seen in detail by the following passages from the *History*:

[Elizabeth] had established her credit on such a footing, that no sovereign in Europe could more readily command any sum, which the public exigencies might at any time require. During this peaceable and uniform government, England furnishes few materials for history; and except the small part which Elizabeth took in foreign transactions, there scarcely passed any occurrence which requires a particular detail. (IV,178)

The great popularity which she [Elizabeth] enjoyed proves that she did not infringe any established liberties of the people; there remains evidence sufficient to ascertain the most noted acts of her administration; and though that evidence must be drawn from a source wide of the ordinary historians, it becomes only the more authentic on that account, and serves as stronger proof that her particular exertions of power were conceived to be nothing but the ordinary course of administration, since they were not thought remarkable enough to be recorded even by contemporary writers. If there was any difference in this particular, the people in former reigns seem rather to have been more submissive than even during the age of Elizabeth. (IV,355)

Such passages indicate that what is most central to Hume's concept of history is not the similarity among events or persons in different periods; rather, the novel, the extraordinary, and the remarkable are characteristics of change and are the data of history. Obviously there are rhetorical reasons for stressing extraordinary events; it makes the narrative more interesting and represents a more complete picture of that period of the past that is under investigation, for it approximates how we experience and comprehend the present. Once the novelty of some event has been recorded and interpreted, historical interest diminishes. In other words, it is the appearance (origin) of some new turn in the drama of mankind that is of central concern to history and the historian.

But the reason for novelty in history goes far beyond this. In the essay "Of Tragedy," Hume gives first a psychological basis and then a rhetorical one:

Novelty naturally rouses the mind, and attracts our attention; and the movements which it causes are always converted into any passion belonging to the object, and join their force to it. Whether an event excite[s] joy or sorrow, pride or shame, anger or good-will, it is sure to produce a stronger affection, when new or unusual. And though novelty of itself be agreeable, it fortifies the painful, as well as agreeable passions. /Had you any intention to move a person extremely by the narration of any event, the best method of increasing its effect would be artfully to delay informing him of it, and first to excite his curiosity and impatience before you let him into the secret. (E,221)

The last of the above quotations concerning Elizabeth illustrates a technique Hume uses throughout the *History*. Whenever Hume feels that documentation is necessary to substantiate a particular fact in his narrative, he will cite as many primary or secondary sources as agree on that point. Hume decides on the authenticity of the evidence from this consensus.[15] Hume's slogan, "consult common experience," means in the *History* "consult the consensus in reports." Hume's procedure here concerning the actions of men, which is derived from a consideration of their motives, temper, and situation, depends on the assumption or notion that people involved in documenting events do not purposefully try to falsify their material. The most obvious counterexample to this (one to which Hume himself fell victim) comes from the Elizabethan period, in which personalities and records were distorted and falsified to please the ruling family.

A declaration that the historian employs other means, such as reasoning in the absence of consensus, is suggested in the following synoptic remark:

At this era, it may be proper to stop a moment and take a general survey of the age, so far as regards manners, finances, arms, commerce, arts, and sciences. The chief use of history is, that it affords materials for disquisitions of this nature; and it seems the duty of an historian to point out the proper inferences and conclusions.[16]

So besides the use of history for discovering the principles of human nature, which Black and other historians of history are fond of quoting, there is this other use—one Hume labels also as a chief use.

The foregoing analysis of Hume on history and human nature has suggested conclusions that are contrary to Black's. The result is that Hume's view of human nature and its use in historical inquiry is more diversified and complex than the standard interpretation has made it out to be. Any failure on Hume's part to provide an adequate conception of history and theory of historical explanation will not be found in an inadequate static conception of human nature. That concept in Hume's philosophical thought and historical practice is not as impoverished as some critics have led us to believe.[17] The debate on whether Hume's conception of human nature is static or dynamic continues in the Hume literature. For example, in their discussion of Hume's theory of morality, David Norton[18] and Terence Penelhum[19] handle the natural virtues in different ways. For Norton, they "are embedded as fundamental propensities of human nature itself. The evidence suggests that every human being, from the most primitive times to the present, has been motivated by these inherent virtues" (164). For Penelhum, they *evolve* and he speaks of our nature as "creative," by which he means that "[h]is [Hume's] view of our beliefs is essentially a Darwinian view" (124). The *History* sides more with Penelhum on this issue because Hume thought the remote past is not worth studying because the actions of primitive people lacked moral causes. (Civilized people's actions could be explained by their moral causes.)

We shall now turn to an antithetical problem in dealing with Hume's thought. Other critics and philosophers have construed his notion of experience as personal or individual, and consequently have held that his historical enterprise falls for other reasons; the next chapter examines these concerns.

FOUR

EXPERIENCE AND EVIDENCE

I

David Fate Norton has put forth an important and challenging interpretation of David Hume that is centered around some of the points in the latter's methodology.[1] Norton's thesis is worthy of specific attention because (1) it is one of the best attempts to undermine the method Hume used in both his philosophy and his history, and (2) there are some noted Hume scholars who accept it, namely, James Noxon,[2] Donald Livingston,[3] and David Wootton.[4]

Almost all of Norton's thesis rests upon an interpretation of a crucial passage in Hume's famous discussion of miracles which appears in the *Inquiry Concerning Human Understanding* (section X). Consequently, I shall direct most of my comments and arguments to the interpretation and to the passage in question. The passage is as follows:

When any one tells me, that he saw [for example] a dead man restored to life, I immediately consider with myself, whether it be more probable, that this person should either deceive or be deceived, or that the fact, which he relates, should really have happened. I weigh the one miracle against the other; and according to the superiority, which I discover, I pronounce my decision, and always reject the greater miracle. If the falsehood of his testimony would be more miraculous, than the event which he relates; then, and not till then, can he pretend to command my belief or opinion. (IU,123-24)

That is the text. Now let us look at Norton's handling of it. First, when Norton uses it in his discussion, he italicizes all the personal locutions which Hume used, for instance, all the pronouns "I," "my," and "myself." There are eight occurrences of self-referential, personal locutions. Their use suggests to Norton an interpretation of the passage on which he bases his entire thesis, which is: "By 'experience' Hume here means *personal* or *individual* experience" (PH,xlvi). Nor is Norton alone in this regard: Antony Flew has argued that experience for Hume is *essentially* private and has denied any public dimension.[5]

The interpretation leads Norton to say that "individual experience is our final standard" (PH,xlvi) and that "the subject of miracles seems to have been chosen because it represents a clear instance of the necessity of deciding on the basis of one's own experience alone, and even before hearing it, what evidence to count and what to discount" (PH,xlvii). This line of thought takes Norton to the next point: "The process [of reasoning] is almost, but not quite circular—it is insular; that is, it results in insularity and a failure to establish the common ground that we regularly take to be a necessary condition of a genuine science" (PH,xlix).

The argument at this point leads Norton to make the following evaluations of Hume's thought. First, "Hume's critical method, and with it, the science of man, failed, failed as he surely suggests all enterprises conceived after his model must fail" (PH,xlviii). Second, "from what has been said here, it appears that Hume 'failed' as a philosopher because he failed as a historian"; or, "In other words, it may very well be that the most vexing problem Hume ever faced was that of finding out what the historical data were; because he failed to solve it, his philosophy collapsed into mere opinion" (PH,l). And, "We have found at last where Hume's historical work becomes a *non sequitur* of his philosophical work" (PH,xlix). One final statement is needed to complete Norton's thesis. It is as follows:

All too often, however, words creep in whose use belies a prior commitment to a more or less fixed point of view—words such as "natural" or "credible," "reasonable" or "consistent"—words whose use reveals that even with his critical apparatus, Hume's evaluations of evidence were in the last analysis not scientific, but to put it somewhat naively, subjective. They were not scientific because they rested solely, as Hume himself tells us they must, on his own personal experience, because his own unique background and biases, no more and no less, determined which direction these evaluations would take. (PH,lviii)

So here we have Norton's thesis, and in this last passage we find his use of the interpretation again. Hence let us go back and carefully look at it—what it means, whether it is true—and try to imagine an alternative or two to Norton's thesis.

The first claim of the Norton thesis that needs to be sorted out pertains to Hume's use of "experience." As I see it and as Norton openly suggests, the claim is the fundamental premise in his argument for the interpretation. However, as is the case with a large number of key terms in Hume's writings, the word "experience" is not used unequivocally and has been a source of much controversy among critics. In support of his interpretation of "experience" as personal or individual experience, Norton cites a passage from a letter Hume wrote to Hugh Blair: "No man can have any other experience but his own. The experience of others becomes his only by the credit which he gives to their testimony: which proceeds from his own experience of human nature" (PH,xlvi,403). Yet in the same letter Hume added the following forceful remark:

I find no difficulty to explain my meaning, and yet shall not probably do it in any future edition ["Of Miracles"]. The proof against a miracle, as it is founded on invariable experience, is of that *species* or *kind* of proof, which is full and certain when taken alone, because it implies no doubt, as is the case with all probabilities; but there are degrees of this species, and when a weaker proof is opposed to a stronger, it is overcome. (PH,403)

The statement "No man can have any other experience but his own" is analytic, and this, I think, is the gist of the former passage. One person's experience is obviously logically independent of someone else's experience (though they may be causally related); this is just an acknowledgment of the egocentric predicament. Whether or not Hume means more than this, as Norton implies, we shall see in a moment. As for the remark concerning testimony, its acceptability is measured by its credibility, and the credibility is allotted by one's experience of human nature. If a fellow is foolish or inexperienced, the credibility standards are low; if he is wise or is experienced in such activities, they are high. This "experience of human nature" is experience in a broad sense, meaning the background with which one faces a question or issue. It encompasses what he or she has read, heard, and lived through in learning about individuals and society. The latter quotation bears out this interpretation. Hume states his meaning in "Of Miracles" in the context of "proof," and not solely in terms of personal experience or opinion. But listen to Hume on the study of history: "A man acquainted with history may, in some respect, be said to have lived from the beginning of the world, and to have been making continual additions to his stock of knowledge in every century" (E,567). Hume himself was one of these men. A little later he adds, "There is also an advantage in that experience which is acquired by history, above what is learned by the practice of the world, that it brings us acquainted with human affairs, without diminishing in the least from the most delicate sentiments of virtue" (E,567). Does this sound as though "experience" were individual or personal in the sense of subjective bias or prejudice and independent of "testimony"? Surely not. Earlier Hume contends that: "history ... *extends our experience* to all past ages, and to the most distant nations; making them contribute as much to our improvement in wisdom, *as if they had actually lain under our observation*" (E,566-67; italics added). To this statement about the study of history, he adds: "There is also an advantage in that *experience* which *is acquired by history*, above what is learned by the practice of the world, that it brings us *acquainted* with human affairs, without diminishing in the least from the most delicate sentiments of virtue" (E,567; italics added). How Hume thought this was accomplished is another story—one I began in the previous chapter and will continue in ones to follow; so keep these in mind in this discussion; however, let's return to the argument at hand.

In fact, the passage in question has elements in it that cast doubt on Norton's thesis. Hume tells us that he *considers* "whether it [the event in question, for example, a dead man restored to life] be more probable" and "always rejects *the greater* miracle"; "if the *falsehood* of his *testimony* would be *more* miraculous than the event which he *relates*," then such testimony *commands* Hume's belief or opinion. All this considering and weighing in order to discover what is more probable is an expression of more than personal, subjective bias. Method, as little as there is, is present here. In the "Of Liberty and Necessity" section (VIII) of the first *Inquiry* Hume tells us "the benefit of that experience acquired by long life and a variety of business and company, in order to instruct us in the principles of human nature and regulate our future conduct as well as speculation" (IU,94). He elaborates: "The general observations, treasured up by a course of experience, gives us the clue of human nature and teach[es] us to unravel all its intricacies" (IU,94). These two uses of "experience" clearly mean social experience—not personal, individual experience.

In regard to Cardinal Wolsey's fall, Hume narrates:

But constant experience evinces how rarely a high confidence and affection receives the least diminution, without sinking into absolute indifference, or even running into the opposite extreme. The king [Henry VIII] now determined to bring on the ruin of the cardinal with a motion almost as precipitate as he had formerly employed in his elevation. (H,III,183-4)

Hume frequently uses "constant" with "experience" when speaking of social experience. The first sentence above is a psychological law of human nature that Hume applies to the situation—this is commonplace in his narrative of individuals' actions. Besides "constant," "regular" appears with "experience" when Hume means more than personal individual experience. For example, "[w]here such reports, therefore, fly about, the solution of the phenomenon is obvious, and we judge in conformity to regular experience and observation when we account for it by the known and natural principles of credulity and delusion"

(IU,136). For some parallels between Hume and Herbert Butterfield, see chapter 7, section II.

II

All of this reasoning in the text is an "experiment" Hume is performing. Hume himself is the experimenter in the passage in question; he is in the role of an arbiter of evidence. He is that learned man of history mentioned above. The probability of an event weighed against the record of time and human nature is the factor that decides whether a given testimony commands one's belief. Norton makes out personal opinion or "experience" in Hume to be something independent of all these methodological considerations. He suggests that things are either "objective" or "subjective" but not both, that there is no middle ground or mixture of these two. Here we have a dichotomy at work in Norton's reasoning; he employs it as simply an instance of the disjunctive syllogism rule. But this is too neat.

The personal locutions in the passage refer to Hume not just as an individual but as one who is "enlightened," a historian. This is most important in understanding Hume's historical methodology. The historian's point of view that Hume adopts in "Of Miracles" and in the *History of England* is either missed or undervalued by such an emphasis on personal locutions.[6] Moreover, the point of view is not as fixed or static as Norton suggests (PH,xlviii), nor does it reflect a prior commitment. Noxon has given us examples from the *History* where we would expect to find bias, but rather we find an absence of bias and of prior commitments (see note 6).

I now want to move to a point concerning the rhetoric of the passage. In the eighteenth century, English prose writers made use of pronouns as rhetorical devices, much as we today use "one," "individual," and the personal pronouns. This passage, however, clearly suggests that their meaning is also indicative of computational parameters. *Someone* has to compute probabilities. They do not arise by themselves. Starting with oneself in probabilities is roughly like starting with the number 1 in a mathematical induction proof. One starts or begins a sequence or succession just as the order of the integers is started by the number 1. Analogously, Hume's use of himself in the passage is for the purpose of performing the computations necessary for the probabilities, the lesser or greater proofs, beginning with himself. *Anyone* can make the necessary computations because anyone can use "I." "I" refers not only to Hume but to any reader (first-person pronouns function as variables do in arguments). Whoever reads the relevant passages is the individual making the inferences in the argument. This is one way Hume makes the argument rhetorically convincing.

Another possible rhetorical use of the pronouns is as a representation of "an ideal observer" or historian. Before the passage Norton quotes, Hume uses first-person-plural pronouns and third-person-singular pronouns. Observe the latter uses in the passage below, which are strikingly similar in the pattern of reasoning or "the critical apparatus" (as Norton calls it):

A wise man, therefore, proportions his belief to the evidence. In such conclusions as are founded on an infallible experience, he expects the event with the last degree of assurance, and regards his past experience as a full proof of the future existence of that event. In other cases, he proceeds with more caution: He weighs the opposite experiments: He considers which side is supported by the greater number of experiments: To that side he inclines, with doubt and hesitation; and when at last he fixes his judgment, the evidence exceeds not what we properly call probability. All *probability*, then, supposes an opposition of experiments and observations, where the one side is found to overbalance the other, and to produce a degree of evidence, proportioned to the superiority. A hundred instances or experiments on one side, and fifty on another, afford a doubtful expectation of any event; though a hundred uniform experiments, with only one that is contradictory, reasonably beget a pretty strong degree of assurance. In all cases, we must balance the opposite experiments, where they are opposite, and deduct the smaller number from the greater, in order to know the exact force of the superior evidence. (IU,118-19)

Shall we play the "numbers game" with Norton to see how many occurrences there are of personal locutions—this time, though, of third-person singular? There are nine this time, with a couple of first-person plural "we's" thrown in and an instance of "a wise man" at the opening. So Hume's use of first-person pronouns in this passage has fewer uses than the above, more-detached rendering of the method (perhaps to draw less attention to his own instance or use of the method?).

It is not too difficult to imagine that Hume intentionally employed this method in the passage in question. Also, it may be that Hume is doing no more than simply varying his use of pronouns, as good writers are expected to do. Or, even better, perhaps he considered himself (in all his modesty) as an instance of the wise man mentioned in the opening of the above paragraph. How else can an individual "know the exact *force* of the superior evidence" unless he or she computes it? (I have in the back of my mind here Wittgenstein's discussions of calculation and the force of a conclusion in the *Remarks on the Foundations of Mathematics*.[7])

If the above account is accurate, then it seems that Norton has mistaken a premise for a conclusion. According to Hume's method, the argument form would be something like this:

1.A premise which states something about the common experience of mankind, or a uniform experience of X, whatever X might be.

2.Hume's personal experience is tabulated as an instance of (1).

3.Thus, if probabilities greater, then admissible; if probabilities less, then inadmissible, given the calculations in (1) and (2).

Premise (1) is to be interpreted as dynamic rather than static; as Hume remarked in a note in the essay "Of the Liberty of the Press," "the experience of mankind *increases*" (E,604; my emphasis) over time and with the study of history. (These are interpretive points established in the previous chapter.) Norton has taken (2) to mean and function as (3), as a conclusion, when in fact it is not. Norton sees only prejudice and mere opinion. Can we see this as anything else? Surely. Below is an example.

III

Norton argues that Hume "failed" as a philosopher and as a historian because of his unsatisfactory solution to the problem of data. It is not surprising that Norton comes to the conclusions he does, given the erroneous assumptions he makes. For example, his argument oversimplifies the question over the nature of the given. How do we ascertain truth from given facts or data? This is perhaps a mistaken or misguided question for Hume since he clearly anticipated Collingwood and others in arguing that there are no givens. There are no given ready-made facts or data—there is only evidence. And historians must judge for themselves whether or not something is "fact." There are no authorities who are in possession of ready-made truths and facts that have historians at their mercy. Norton's fundamental assumption is that Hume had this common sense view of history rather than a critical reconstructive concept of history (historians and philosophers alike who have written on Hume and history have made this crucial interpretive assumption). There are elements of both in Hume; however, the critical reconstructionist view is more predominant in Hume's thinking than scholars have recognized.

Hume's use of personal pronouns is similar to that of Collingwood, and I think that Hume has attempted to weave a web close to the one Collingwood did. In detail:

The web of imaginative construction [of the historian] is something far more solid and powerful than we have hitherto realized. So far from relying for its validity upon the support of given facts, it actually serves as the touchstone by which we decide whether alleged facts are genuine. Suetonius tells me that Nero at one time intended to evacuate Britain. I reject his statement, not because any better authority flatly contradicts it, for of course none does; but because my reconstruction of Nero's policy based on Tacitus will not allow me to think that Suetonius is right. And if I am told that this is merely to say I prefer Tacitus to Suetonius, I confess that I do: but I do so just because I find myself able to incorporate what Tacitus tells me into a coherent and continuous picture of my own, and cannot do this for Suetonius.[8]

Hume's comment about his idea of experience in his letter to Blair has affinity with Collingwood's imaginative reconstruction idea, and a strong one at that, when coupled with examples from the *History*. This analogy is made more convincing when we examine the nature of historical narration (chapter 5).

Norton's labeling of Hume's constant interjection of himself into the account or narrative as mere subjectivism is simply wrong. It is, rather, that the historian is equipped by training and experience with a measure of insight whereby to judge or assess theories or the status of facts. Such a measure is reflected in his reconstruction. I think that Hume was aware of this to some extent, and it was for this reason that his personal remarks *as critical historian* show up in the *History* as well as in his discussion of miracles in the first *Inquiry*. If the "wise man" who performs the balancing procedures Hume recommends in assessing testimony is the enlightened historian, how does the enlightened historian know where to find enlightenment in the first place? Human nature—both collectively and individually (i.e., socially and psychologically)—provides the answer for Hume. He is a naturalist so he does not think there is much of a problem about what "history" refers to and he finds the circularity innocent enough in having putative history sorted from possible myth by someone who is enlightened by a knowledge of human nature as displayed by history. This may be troubling for those who do not accept Hume's answer, but it is the one he gave and he felt it was better than the alternatives he had.

Finally in the last two chapters (3 and 4), we examined Hume's ideas of history, human nature, experience, and evidence, and we see connections among them. In the next four chapters (5-8), we shall see how they are reflected in writing and in different levels of composition. The first chapter of this group (5) addresses the nature of historical narration because it appears in one form or another in the remaining topics treated.

FIVE

THE NATURE OF HISTORICAL NARRATION

I

David Hume wrote a great deal that would qualify as narration and specifically as historical narration. So it is not too surprising to find various remarks on the nature of historical narration in his writings, although given how much has been written on other aspects of Hume's thought it is astonishing that historical narration has not been discussed at any length. The most well-known analysis of the philosophical significance of the concept of narrative in Hume's thought is Donald Livingston's *Hume's Philosophy of Common Life*. However, Livingston does not address directly the concept of historical narration. This chapter is an attempt to describe and analyze Hume's statements on the subject and to relate them to his and other historians' practice of the craft. A portion of Hume's characterization of narration has a contemporary ring to it, and to make this more obvious I will from time to time bring in recent contributions to the topic. All of this is interesting historically, because Hume wrote on narration at a time when modern historiography was just beginning, and some of his insights apply remarkably well to it as well as to his own writing. However, his view is not without its troubles. Let us first examine some of the essential features of the idea of historical narration.

The first revealing statement on historical narration appears in the *Treatise*. It reads:

We always follow the succession of time in placing ideas, and from the consideration of any object pass more easily to that, which follows immediately after it, than to that which went before it. We may learn this, among other instances, from the order, which is always obser'd in historical narrations. Nothing but an absolute necessity can oblige an historian to break the order of time, and in his *narration* give the precedence to an event, which was in *reality* posterior to another. (II,III,VII)

So the order of time seems to be requisite for an adequate description of historical narration. Hume himself observes this mark in his *History of England* (1754); for example, "We come now to mention some English Affairs which we left behind us, that we might not interrupt our narrative of the events in Scotland, which form so material a part of the present reign" [Elizabeth I] (IV,117). And looking back over that reign, we find that temporal order is thought of as chronological sequence. The intellectual historian H. Stuart Hughes would most certainly agree with Hume on this point when he says: "the telling of a story will continue to be an indispensable feature of our endeavour. After all, it is chronological sequence that most sharply distinguishes the writing of history from all other pursuits."[1]

Apparently Hume did not find reversing the succession of time in narration too difficult, since he did this in writing the *History*. Hume started with the reigns of Charles II and James II and moved to earlier reigns, finally ending with the commencing of the nation of Great Britain with the invasion of Julius Caesar. Hume began with the period closest to his own, developed a narrative understanding of it, then proceeded to the next earlier period, and so on.

Consequently narrative structure is first of all to be analyzed in terms of temporal predicates. Why can't we (as historians) break the temporal order? The answer to this question (and subsidiary ones) from Hume's perspective is the subject of the rest of this chapter. In short, though—to give a glimpse of things to come—it is because of the requirement of a narrative to be smooth and uninterrupted, and to exhibit the components of Hume's principle of causation. Let us first notice Hume's causal requirement of a historical narrative, since its analysis leads to the other distinguishing marks just mentioned.

Hume's best discussion of historical narration appears in the first *Inquiry*, section 3, "Of the Association of Ideas," which was included in some editions (K, L, N) and omitted in others. Apparently Hume was ambivalent about its inclusion, although he did see its great importance: "These loose hints I have thrown together in order to excite the curiosity of philosophers, and beget a suspicion at least if not a full persuasion that this subject [narration] is very copious, and that many operations of the human mind depend on the connection or association of ideas which is here explained" (IU,39). (I was excited and convinced.) He later concludes the section with the following remark: "The full explication of the principle [the association of ideas] and all its consequences would lead us into reasonings too profound and too copious for these Essays. It is sufficient for us, at present, to have established this conclusion, that the three connecting principles of all ideas are the relations of *resemblance, contiguity,* and *causation*" (IU,39). These last two remarks need to be kept in mind as evaluational parameters in reviewing what Hume says about narration, for there is much lacking in terms of a complete analysis or even an adequate description of historical narration. However, we can piece together a cursory view from what remarks he had made and from the narrative itself, *The History of England from the Invasion of Julius Caesar to the Revolution in 1688*.

II

The key passage from the *Inquiry*, which has embedded in it most of Hume's ideas and assumptions, is the following:

The most usual species of connection among the different events which enter into any narrative composition is that of cause and effect; while the historian traces the series of actions according to their natural order, remounts to their secret springs and principles, and delineates their most remote consequences. He chooses for his subject a certain portion of that great chain of events which compose the history of mankind: each link in this chain he endeavors to touch in his narration; sometimes unavoidable ignorance renders all his attempts fruitless; sometimes he supplies by conjecture what is wanting in knowledge; and always he is sensible that the more unbroken the chain is which he presents to his readers, the more perfect is his production. He sees that the knowledge of causes is not only the most satisfactory, this relation or connection being the strongest of all others, but also the most instructive; since it is by this knowledge alone we are able to control events and govern futurity. (IU,34)

The view that Hume espouses (which claims that the most usual, instructive, important, and the strongest connection among events in a narrative is causal) is a commonplace one, especially among positivists. For example, Morton White's conception of a historical narrative is defined in causal terms: "A history is predominantly, though it need not be completely, integrated from a causal point of view."[2] He further elaborates on this idea by introducing the notion of a chronicle: "A chronicle of a subject ... is a conjunction of noncausal singular statements which expressly mention that subject and which report things that have been true of it at different times" (222). So, "A history will in the familiar way be distinguished from a chronicle by the fact that a history contains causal statements" (223). The familiar way, as White calls it, is the Humean way or model.

The sort of actual histories we expect to find fitting this model are the ones that are explanatory narratives or ones that attempt to answer questions like, "What brought about *X*?" where *X* may be instantiated with terms like revolution, rebellion, reformation, renaissance, and so on. Generally, it is where a historian traces the development of some given entity, and that development is por-

trayed by way of causal connections among its events. For example, Hume's
burning question toward the end of the *History* is: What were the events that led
to the English Revolution? He concludes: "Thus have we seen, through the
whole course of four reigns, a continual struggle maintained between the crown
and the people ..." (VI,530). Afterward, he wrote, "the revolution forms a new
epoch in the constitution ..." (VI,531), namely an epoch in which a state of tran-
quility and peace was achieved or resulted. Hume's causal interpretation and
narrative here could be construed as an instance of "abnormalism." According
to this view, the cause of an event is what interferes with normal conditions; historians seek to explain facts that are abnormal or unusual. The cause of an
abnormal event is also thought to be abnormal itself. For example, Hume
explains the Revolution because it is unusual for the English to have revolutions—their normal state is peace and stability—by accounting for the struggle
(itself abnormal) leading up to the Glorious Revolution.[3]

So it would seem that Hume would be in initial agreement with White's
model; as he says again later in the *Inquiry*, "in history the connection among
the several events which unites them into one body is the relation of cause and
effect" (IU,38). Nor does their agreement end here. When we examine the
nature of this relation, we find further agreement. For instance, in answering the
question of whether this relation is semantic or pragmatic, both Hume and
White respond that it is definitely pragmatic.

The appearance of contrary-to-fact conditionals in historical discourse (for
instance, "If Napoleon had not invaded Russia, he could have maintained the
Empire") is used by White to illustrate that focusing on semantics or on the syn-
tax of explanatory laws is not particularly helpful in understanding the notion of
explanation (70-77, *inter alia*). Attention must be paid to psychological and
pragmatic features that exhibit our ordinary linguistic habits. And White adds:

In a sense I have adopted a quasi-Humean approach to the problem, arguing that reference to more than law is required when we come to analyze an explanatory statement,
and that extra something may well be *custom*.... Moreover, if it is custom that decides,
custom may decide differently in different cultures. (77)

For Hume, the inference from cause to effect is the only legitimate one concerning matters of fact that allows the historian to go beyond the evidence supplied by the senses and memory. Causation carries the historian's attention to
the usual cause from the effect (or *vice versa*, depending on whether he or she
is narrating or inquiring), which is acquired by habit or the constant conjunction
of events. As Hume says in the Abstract: "it is custom alone, not reason, which
determines us to make it the standard of our future judgments. When the cause

is presented, the mind, from habit, immediately passes to the conception and belief of the usual effect."[4] We can infer from this that a historical narrative is to enhance this smooth, immediate passage in the reader's mind. Although Hume says in the *Inquiry* that: "All events seem entirely loose and separate. One event follows another, but we never can observe any tie between them. They seem *conjoined* but never *connected*" (IU,85), the events in a historical narrative are nonetheless connected, not merely conjoined. We are here talking not just about events, but about narrated events—about what the historian does with these events when he writes a narrative.

There are two items in Hume that confirm the above interpretation. One is his extensive use of the link-chain metaphor in talking about both historical narration (see the first quote from the *Inquiry*) and the principles of association. Concerning the latter, Hume says in the Abstract: "these are the only links that bind the parts of the universe together or connect us with any person or object exterior to ourselves" (IU,198). By the time Hume writes about the principles in the *Inquiry*, he has toned the subject down from the universe to the mind's organization of phenomena. The Abstract comment, then, would surely hold for such "objects" or entities as the French Revolution, the Great Plains, the Restoration, etc. The second point is that Hume in the *History* conceives of the historian's job as making connections among events and including these statements in his narrative. He remarks:

At this era [The Restoration], it may be proper to stop a moment, and take a general survey of the age, so far as regards manners, finances, arms, commerce, arts, and sciences. The chief use of history is, that it affords materials for disquisitions of this nature; and it seems the duty of an historian to point out the proper inferences and conclusions. (VI,140)

An excellent example of this idea of the historian's duty comes from Hume's discussion of the reign of Edward II. It reads:

Before I conclude this reign, I cannot forebear making another remark, drawn from the detail of losses given in by the elder Spenser; particularly the great quantity of salted meat which he had in his larder, six hundred bacons, eighty carcasses of beef, six hundred muttons. We may observe, that the outrage of which he complained began after the third of May, or the eleventh new style, as we learn from the same paper. It is easy, therefore, to conjecture, what a vast store of the same kind he must have laid up at the beginning of winter; and we may draw a new conclusion with regard to the wretched state of ancient husbandry, which could not provide subsistence for the cattle during winter, even in such a temperate climate as the south of England; for Spenser had but one manor so far north as Yorkshire. There being few or no enclosures, except, perhaps, for deer, no sown grass, little hay, and no other resource for feeding cattle, the barons, as well as the people, were obliged to kill and salt their oxen and sheep in the beginning of winter, before they became lean upon the common pasture; a precaution still practised with regard to oxen in the least cultivated parts of this island. The salting of mutton is a miserable expedient, which has every where been long disused. From this circumstance, however trivial in appearance, may be drawn important inferences with regard to the domestic economy and manner of life in those ages. (II,180)

So the unity of a historical narrative is achieved by causal statements, just as links compose a chain. However, Hume recognized that a total unity in the subject (which the metaphor misleadingly suggests) is rarely accomplished in a narrative. One reason for this, which I mentioned earlier, is the existence of gaps or of ignorance in the historian's understanding of the subject. The historian conjectures about what is wanting in his knowledge. (This I briefly discussed in chapter 2, section II.) The above passage from the reign of Edward II illustrates this idea in Hume's account of historical narration. The other reason, according to Hume, is in the nature of human action itself, or in the very nature of the historian's subject itself. Let us briefly examine each one of these reasons in turn.

It is easily seen that Hume's idea of conjecture is a symptom of his dependence on the link-chain metaphor. Positivists, like White, follow Hume in emphasizing causation as the most important relation to be found in a historical narrative, and they (including Hume) fall victim to the complaint that in articulating their conception of a historical narrative, they are "excessively under the sway of the causal chain."[5] Consequently, their model is one that does not fit actual histories. However there are important rhetorical considerations that Hume took account of, especially dealing with morality in history; see chapter 7.

Perhaps even more troubling than this criticism is one voiced by John Passmore.[6] The gist of his argument is something like this. Historians write books under preposterous titles like *The History of England* where omissions from the subject are inescapable. The omissions are in turn cited as proof of the historian's prejudice. However, the fact of the matter is that there is no such subject as *The History of England*. Such "general histories" are frauds—basing their appeals on a metaphysical notion that there is something called "Mankind" or "the whole community" that behaves like a single man. There is not the history of mankind as Hume had thought—just histories of men and nations. When a historian is purporting to write about "the history of England," he mars his book by including perfunctory and irrelevant chapters on every aspect of history he can think of. This is done in order to escape the charge of arbitrariness, since his selection is not determined by his subject matter. At best, these histories become no more than a collection of fragments.

Professor Hughes, I think, would generally agree with Passmore's judgment, especially when it applies to such historical entities as "England." Hughes's following comment is particularly relevant to our discussion:

One generalization immediately springs to mind—narrative history is far less simple a matter than it appears to be. On this, both its defenders and its detractors will agree. As the primary vehicle for historical literature through two and a half millennia of writing, the narrative has been refined and polished to a highly professional finish. Historians have developed a myriad of literary devices for gliding over what they do not adequately know or understand. With more schematic history, the gaps yawn embarrassingly wide: in narrative prose, they can be artfully concealed. Moreover, if the analytic historian makes a judgment, he is usually explicit about it: the storyteller can slip such a judgment into a highly colored adjective or a subordinate clause without alerting the reader to what he is doing. Thus more narrative history does not quite live up to its advance billing: it is neither as comprehensive nor as "objective" as it is popularly supposed to be (70-71).

Passmore and Hughes obviously reflect a bias toward analytical and topical histories.[7] And I do think that Atkinson has the more sensible attitude toward this debate of narrative vs. analytical histories when he reminds us that "explanatory history must include *both* truths of succession *and* truths of coexistence."[8]

Not only does most of Passmore's argument apply to Hume in particular, it applies to the view of historical narration that White has labeled "encyclopedism."[9] Hume's *History* is an excellent example of this view: "He [the historian] chooses for his subject a certain portion of that great chain of events which compose the history of mankind: each link in this chain he endeavors to touch in his narrative" (IU,34). The more comprehensive a historian's treatment of a given entity, the more truthful or superior it is. As Hume continues, "the more unbroken the chain is which he [the historian] presents to his readers, the more perfect is his production" (IU,34). Hence Hume is aiming, or he thinks the historian aims, at the whole truth rather than the essential truth.[10] (The passage from the *History* [VI,140] which I cited earlier illustrates this point, too.) Quantity of information rather than selection seems to be the standard for judging competing historical narratives. Passmore's criticism is particularly relevant here: "greater selectivity would be a step towards objectivity, not away from it." Hume cannot be accused of all of Passmore's criticisms. As we have seen from the previous chapter, "mankind" or "human nature" is not a single, collective entity, but a distributive one. The history of England was generally divided up in terms of reigns, and the activities of the isles placed within the context of the kings and queens. In other words, it is a political history. Next, in the essay "Of the Populousness of Ancient Nations," Hume foresees that: "It is a usual fallacy to consider all the ages of antiquity as one period, and to compute the numbers contained in the great cities mentioned by ancient authors as if these cities had been all contemporary" (E,426). So Hume cannot and should not be accused of treating "England" in a like manner. As David Wootton remarks: "Hume never claimed to identify a single *esprit* running through all aspects of the life of an epoch" (295), or, I might add, a nation.

White formulates a "modified" view of encyclopedism that is not quite as ambitious as the above-stated version. Here, "the notion of approximating the whole truth as a standard for basic statements may be replaced by the notion of organizing all of the evidence *available*" (251: my italics). So the idea of the whole truth is diminished to the point that "all" is thought of as the known data about the historian's subject at a given time (252). From Hume's correspondence about his *History* and its frequent editions,[11] it seems that his underlying conception of his narrative was that of "full" encyclopedism, the main evidence being that he thought he needed to incorporate the least bit of information he had discovered since the last edition.

How could Hume hold this view of historical narration and be able to overlook such serious defects in it? Probably because he was writing history at a time when the main concern of historians was to achieve an overall view that was orderly and unified. His most praiseworthy remarks on Robert Henry's *History of Great Britain* (1773) reflect that this is what Hume found important about his narrative. For instance:

By this delicate and well fancied method [of periodization], the thread of the narration is preserved unbroken, and some degree of unity and order introduced into a portion of the history of Great Britain, which has perplexed the acuteness of our most philosophical and accomplished historians.[12]

Hume himself attempted to achieve these same things for which he praised Robert Henry.

Trygve R. Tholfsen, a historian of historiography, suggests that the period concept was developed in Hume's time. Indeed, what Tholfsen says was first formed in Robertson's narrative is what I have found in Hume's: "Soon this new insight [treating political phenomena in the context of a larger social whole] came to be applied in the writing of history.... In his *History of England* (1754), David Hume interrupts his narrative at several points to include systematic descriptions of the constitution, laws, and customs. Williams Robertson's famous account of medieval Europe, in the introduction to his *History of*

Charles V (1769), assumes the existence of all-embracing civilization in the period, characterized by an identifiable unity, common to all its components. Thus, out of the fusion between the new sense of diversity and the concept of civilization came the period concept, so fundamental to historical thinking."[13] It is obvious that what Hume meant by *mankind*—those things he deemed worthy of narration (see, for example, H,VI,140) was civilization. So on my account of the *History*, coupled with the *Inquiry* discussion, Hume precedes Robertson on this matter. Tholfsen calls Hume's systematic descriptions "interruptions," but they were not that at all. They were aligned to notes and appendices so as not to interrupt the political narrative; see the fourth volume on Elizabeth (H,IV, chs. XXXVIII-XLIV and Appendix III). Again, Wootton has a pertinent comment here: "To make sense of Hume's *History*, we must take more seriously than commentators usually do the fact that his is a narrative history describing changing social and political circumstances. Hume's emphasis on change was, indeed, one of the most original aspects of his history" (298). This emphasis on change in Hume's history is one I made earlier in chapter 3 in regard to his view of human nature; in other words, the *History* reflects change because it gives an account of change in human nature and its manifestation in numerous important figures in English history. Again, I shall return to this discussion in chapter 7.

Hume's selection or choice of the history of England to narrate over other histories, it could be argued, was essentialistic, because not all histories are worth narrating, only those that show the rise of manners and civilization (see H, ch. I and note A). Once his choice of subject was made and he began his narrative, however, he was definitely an encyclopedist in how he conceived of its construction. Hume here serves as an excellent example of the following point White makes about encyclopedism: "that even those who speak of approximating the whole truth think of approximating that part of the whole truth which is *significant*" (251). Needless to say, Hume's criterion of significance is the prescription that the historian ought to account for the rise of manners and civilization; that's why the history of England is worth six volumes. But just as important, Hume narrates the threats to liberty and security from factions of extremism—whether political or religious.[14] Manners and civil practices are ones that we have paid a price for and must constantly do so. Checking extremism is one reason why Hume was in favor of a mixed constitution (see H, VI, 531).

Another way Hume obtains the unity of his narrative is by conjectures. Although such practice would be frowned upon by today's analytical historians, this approach was a common one among Scottish writers in the eighteenth century and was called theoretical or conjectural history.[15] Conjectures would be very much needed for Hume because the gaps were so frequent and large in his subject. Hence, they were a symptom of this study—"England"—and the link-chain image that dominated his model of historical narration. This is not only a problem for Hume, but for any encyclopedist whose conception of narration is dominated by a link-chain idea or by a notion of causal unity. Conjectures become a necessity under such a model as encyclopedism, if the truths are viewed under the link-chain image. But at least Hume said that the causal chain is always wanting, and hence his view is not as narrow as it could have been.

He made further allowances in his model away from a strict causal view, and these shall be examined in the next two sections.

III

At this juncture a distinction should be drawn over whether unconnectedness of events is within or outside the design of the historian. An illustration will make this clear. Given what we have seen of his view thus far, Hume would have had to allow for examples like that from G. E. Aylmer's narrative. In discussing the causes of the English Civil War and Revolution, Aylmer says:

There are many possible explanations as to why the Civil War began when and how it did. The unbridgeable gulf on political principles (the King's powers in relation to those of Parliament), the equally unbridgeable gulf on religious matters (between Root-and-Branch Puritans and Anglicans) provide two obvious ones. But these constitutional and ecclesiastical beliefs were probably only held strongly enough to have caused a resort to armed force by relatively small numbers on each side. Indeed it is most unlikely that more than a very small fraction of those involved had accepted that war was necessary, still less wanted war even as late as the summer of 1642. These differences alone could scarcely have produced a civil war dividing the country against itself. More important perhaps are the role of personality and the unfolding logic of the crisis: Charles' temperament and outlook, the fears and chronic mistrust which he generated in others, and on the opposite side the apparently aggressive intentions of Pym and his party. *The war would hardly have come about when it did but for a whole sequence of events partly unrelated in themselves, including the Irish rebellion.*[16]

The passage illustrates among other things what Hume was getting at in the following remarks from the first *Inquiry*:

An annalist or historian who should undertake to write the history of Europe during any century would be influenced by the connection of contiguity in time or place. All events which happen in that portion of space and period of time are comprehended in his design, though in other respects different and unconnected. They have still a species of unity amidst all their diversity. (IU,34)

Contrary to previous impressions formed on this subject, Hume does permit some unconnectedness among the narrated events of historical narration, although his view remains one of the encyclopedic variety. Still, Hume's view does not go far enough to cover Aylmer's account in all respects. Aylmer's account has explicit unconnected events *within* the historian's design. This is a particularly noteworthy feature because many narratives are written in such a way that the event is portrayed as if it were inevitable and followed some sort of "laws" of historical necessity. (This is the picture left by many historians even if it is unintentional; their selection of words—the very language—suggests such a view.[17]) Both Hume and Aylmer are fairly careful, in theory and practice, not to suggest such a deterministic view.

There is further agreement between example and model in (1) exemplifying the view of encyclopedism and (2) adhering to the idea that narrative unity sometimes is achieved solely from the contiguity among events. The view of (1) and the idea in (2) are probably interrelated; what unity a narrative constructed on encyclopedic lines has is just from the contiguity among events—their immediate surroundings. The italicized statement in Aylmer's account would only be admitted on the grounds of encyclopedism, for essentialism demands that all the salient truths of an event be connected by an essence—whether they were inside the historian's design or not. Such looseness in narrative unity, like Aylmer's and Hume's views, can be permitted only by encyclopedism. And it goes almost without saying that such looseness, as Aylmer's example illustrates, is an important feature of narrative unity. Sometimes the historian simply has to narrate what happened around an event (in both time and place), for he has nothing other than this to go on. This circumstance is probably the simplest and most primitive form of narration. Also, the contiguity feature is something that has been overlooked by many philosophers whose thoughts are dominated by causal explanation when discussing the nature of narration.

But the unity of a narrative is still to be accounted for. If this unity is not simply the relation of causation, then what else is it? *Smoothness* and *uninterruptedness*, primitive notions that are utilized and stressed by Hume, are likely answers. But these notions are not to be violated by allowing unconnectedness: "They [the events] have still a species of unity amidst all their diversity" (IU,34). Or elsewhere, as we have already mentioned, Hume speaks of the thread of the narrative being unbroken and of the idea that the more unbroken the chain the more perfect the historian's production. This unbroken quality of smoothness is partially explained by Hume's other two ideas of association: contiguity and resemblance. Concerning these, Hume has the following things to say.

IV

From the example Hume gives of "contiguity"—when St. Dennis is mentioned, the idea of Paris naturally occurs (IU,198)—I suppose what he has in mind in attributing this to the connectedness of historical narratives is that the natural surroundings of a given event are its context within a given narrative. This line of thought is also suggested by the passage I quoted earlier from the first *Inquiry*: "An annalist or historian who should undertake to write the history of Europe during any century would be influenced by the connection of contiguity in time and place" (IU,34). Another example Hume gives of contiguity is: "The mention of one apartment in a building naturally introduces an inquiry or discourse concerning the others" (IU,32).

Hume's discussion of contiguity anticipates Collingwood's "the *a priori* historical imagination"[18] and Danto's "conceptual evidence."[19] Let me try to illustrate the parallel: If a historian is reading a document that is, say, a social commentary on a town, and there are sentences dealing with urban housing from the given era, Hume's statement above (IU,32) would be a procedural remark that guides or "influences" the historian. For it follows from the very meaning of *apartment* that there are other dwellings. If there are not any other dwellings, then the writer has chosen the wrong term and he or she has misled us. This would also cast doubt on the documentary evidence, i.e., it would mean that the statement is false or it would cast doubt on the reporter's reliability. Narrated events are to be connected by the relation of contiguity in the mind of the historian and his or her readers. Contiguity is then one of the clues the human mind makes use of in determining concept and instance, and in determining how concepts cluster together. Perhaps this is what Hume had in mind when he says that "the historian traces the series of actions according to their natural order, remounts to their secret springs and principles, and delineates their most remote consequences" (IU,34).

Contiguity is also intimately connected with Hume's idea of causation. For instance, in the *Treatise* Hume says that the relation is one that is necessary to the idea of causation:

...whatever objects are consider'd as causes or effects, [they] are *contiguous*; and that nothing can operate in a time or place, which is ever so little remov'd from those of its existence. Tho' distant objects may sometimes seem productive of each other, they are commonly found upon examination to be linked by a chain of causes, which are contiguous among themselves, and to the distant objects; and when in any particular instance we cannot discover this connexion, we still presume it to exist. We may therefore consider the relation of CONTIGUITY as essential to that of causation. (I,III,II)

So here, too, we find the link-chain metaphor guiding Hume's thoughts on the relationship between the two ideas of association: causation and contiguity.

The most curious and puzzling of the three relations attributed to the idea of historical narration is *resemblance*. Here Hume has little to say specifically in the context of narration, so I will have to interpolate considerably. The only direct remark I have found on this matter comes from *The Natural History of Religion*, where he says: "An historical fact, while it passes by oral tradition from eyewitness and contemporaries, is disguised in every successive narration, and may at last bear very small, if any resemblance of the original truth, on which it was founded" (NH,25). The other comments below on this subject seem to be right in line with this one.

In the first *Inquiry*, Hume gives the following example: "A picture naturally leads our thoughts to the original" (IU,32). And later on in the same work, he extends his example from pictures to that of ceremonies in the Roman Catholic religion. His discussion of ceremonies in terms of resemblance is centered around the idea that when some actual object is present, the thinking associated with it is that much greater than in the case of the other two ideas of association (contiguity and causation). Hume offers this as a reason why the Roman Catholics made sensible types and images of the objects of their faith; these render the objects of faith "more present to them by the immediate presence of these types than it is possible for us to do merely by an intellectual view and contemplation" (IU,65). These sensible objects resemble and are related to those ideas they are supposed to convey. Hume adds: "I shall only infer from these practices and this reasoning that the effect of resemblance in enlivening the ideas is very common; and as in every case a resemblance and a present impression must concur" (IU,65). We have seen an exception to this principle in chapter 2 with the missing shade of blue thought experiment.

What about practices of the historian? If one substitutes the idea of narrative for picture or ceremony and actual event for original, we come up with the following line of reasoning. A narrative is supposed to resemble what actually happened. A narrative is the literary or linguistic counterpart of a person or an idea. The force of the idea of Great Britain is enlivened by a narrative of Great Britain because (1) it diminishes the distance of this expansive idea, which reaches far back into the past, and (2) the narrative at every stage must resemble some other stage (and hence, be the same idea) or every stage narrated must resemble some present impression or evidence of what did actually happen (that is, the event).

So at every stage of a given narrative, the historian records a resemblance to some present, corresponding impression. This is another way in which uninterruptedness and smoothness are achieved in a historical narrative; resemblance insures these narrative qualities.

How would Hume conceive of this process as being done? There is a passage in the *Treatise* that may provide some explanation of what he thinks historical construction and imagination consists. And we could equally well substitute "England" for "Rome" and get some idea of Hume's own theory of concept-formation in history, as in his *History of England*:

'Tis this latter principle [judgment] which peoples the world, and brings us acquainted with such existences, as by their removal in time and place, lie beyond the reach of the senses and memory. By means of it I paint the universe in my imagination, and fix my attention on any part of it I please. I form an idea of ROME, which I neither see nor remember; but which is connected with such impressions as I remember to have received from the conversation and books of travellers and historians. This idea of *Rome* I place in a certain situation on the idea of an object, which I call the globe. I join to it the conception of a particular government, and religion, and manners. I look backward and consider its first foundation; its several revolutions, successes, and misfortunes. All this, and everything else, which I believe, are nothing but ideas; tho' by their force and settled order, arising from custom and the relation of cause and effect, they distinguish themselves from the other ideas, which are merely the offspring of the imagination. (I,III,IX)

There is much wrong with Hume's seemingly naive theory of concept-formation in history, but I do not want to concentrate on its negative aspects. What I am interested in showing is that his passage illustrates the three ideas of association, and in addition gives us a better picture of how Hume conceived of historical narration. Where Hume speaks of the idea of Rome being connected with impressions he remembers having received from the conversation and books of travellers and historians, he probably has in mind the relation of resemblance, for he has little else to offer for justification of such a remark. (The other two ideas of association can be easily seen or illustrated in the passage.)

The ideas exemplified in this passage from the *Treatise,* however, are not as naive as they seem on the surface. History is predominantly practiced and taught in schools and universities, hence the discipline is academic: the study is learned from reading and hearing others who have mastered the craft. Those who aspire to be masters learn their conceptions from them, and these stay with them throughout their careers and are used as appraisal indicators. Collingwood in the conclusion of *The Idea of History* (Part V, the Epilegomena) has an admirable description of the sort of situation I am describing, so I need not dwell on this here, but Collingwood's conception of history unfolds in various chapters of this volume.

A contemporary counterpart to what Hume is saying (or at least a part of it) about resemblance and narration can be found in A. R. Louch's study of historical narration. In detail:

His [the historian's] object is to lay out a continuum of events related in such a way as to meet the condition of narrative smoothness. These connections are not causal or statistical. The condition is met instead when one sees a narrative constructed out of adjacent descriptions which closely resemble one another, and when one is entitled to assume that there is some persisting thing or process to which this sequence of closely resembling descriptions applies. It can also be seen why it has often been claimed that the historian must deal in the unique and the unrepeated. The historian is seeking to discover a chain of similarities that will exhibit the evolution of an historical feature or process; he is not presuming similarities (e.g., all revolution-type events) in order to discover other factors constantly associated with them.[20]

In Louch's description of the narrative process one finds language and concepts similar to those we found in Hume; references to resembling and adjacent (or contiguous) descriptions, narrative smoothness, the link-chain metaphor, and so on. Hence, Hume's model persists in contemporary philosophy of history, whether the participants are aware of Hume's contribution or not.

V

We are now in a position to return to the initial question of our study, that is, why cannot historians break the temporal order? The governing idea of historical narration, aside from the ideas of association, is *time*. Why the temporal order of historical narrations cannot be broken except by "an absolute necessity," as Hume says in the *Treatise* (II,III,VII), is shown in the *Inquiry* (IU,32) when he states that the historian selects a portion of the history of mankind to narrate. So there is this entire space of time—past, present, and future—of which his subject, for example England in the case of Hume, is a part, in addition to the historian and his or her time as well. For instance, Hume in his discussion of King Edward II makes reference to both the past and the present in the following discussion:

All the European Kingdoms, especially that of England, were at this time [1315] unacquainted with the office of a prime minister, so well understood at present in all regular monarchies; and the people could form no conception of a man, who, though still in the rank of a subject, possessed all the power of a sovereign, eased the prince of the burden of affairs, supplied his want of experience or capacity, and maintained all the rights of the crown, without degrading the greatest of nobles by their submission to his temporary authority. (II,160)

It is through complex temporal sentences like this one that Hume is able to exhibit the historical development or evolution of a given subject, like that of a political office. Hume's *History* abounds with sentences that illustrate this mark of narrative structure.

In concluding, there is one further comment I want to make about Hume's view of historical narration. His theory or view is best characterized as a pluralistic one. What I mean by this is that Hume does not have one single mode of explanation or a monistic theory of what happened in the past; rather he employs numerous and varied approaches to narrating the history of England.[21] In other words, it would take a pluralistic theory of historical narration to satisfy what Hume says about narration and for us to adequately characterize his narrative. From White's categories Hume's narrative can be viewed as examples of abnormalism and "full" encyclopedism, but in his selection of his topic he was an essentialist.

Toward the end of the section "The Association of Ideas" in the *Inquiry*, Hume makes the following assessment of what he thinks he has accomplished: "If we consider all these circumstances [Hume's experiments with the ideas of association], I say, we shall find that these parts of the action have a sufficient unity to make them be comprehended in one ... narration" (IU,39). Here we learn Hume's motive for employing the ideas of association: to explain how something (like a narrative) has unity when all of its elements seem to admit of such diversity. This is one way that Hume explains the unity of an object, like that of a narrated event or entity: in terms of the ideas of association. In addition to these associative ideas are the passions, which equally involve transition, continuities and discontinuities. They too have "associations" and these are seen in human nature and its dispositions. So it is not surprising to see Book Two, "Of the Passions," of the *Treatise* at work by Hume the historian as he narrates historical figures. They too have "long train[s] of passions, [such] as grief, hope, fear" (T,276) which Hume narrates in such a way as to involve those of the reader; see chapter 7 for examples. These same associative ideas and passions he discusses in relation to the standards of taste and to literary subjects which we shall take up in the next chapter. As we shall see, Hume's concern for history also plays a role in literary theory and the theory of taste.

SIX

THE PARADOX OF TASTE

Mary Mothersill has written an interesting and philosophically challenging essay on David Hume and the paradox of taste that I wish to revisit here.[1] While I am in agreement with her about a paradox of taste in Hume's thought, I have a different account of it that involves less speculation and less anachronistic readings of him. Therefore let us carefully look at Professor Mothersill's interpretation of Hume's essay "Of the Standard of Taste" (1757). The first part is conventional and offers no surprises. Even a cursory reading of his famous essay shows that Hume is faced with a genuine problem in trying to resolve the premises that (1) aesthetic preference depends on feeling as distinct from reason and ultimately is dependent upon observation or factual evidence, and that (2) people differ dramatically on what they like or dislike about the arts. "How," Mothersill asks, "does it happen that there are some opinions—not many, perhaps, but some—that are instantly discussed as false (or agreed to as true) by anyone who has the right to be listened to at all?" (270). Why Hume thought that "taste" provided an answer to this problem has perplexed many a reader, and it has Mothersill up in arms: "Can Hume have failed to notice this? It seems implausible, and yet he does not concede failure or even any doubts." She then offers an intriguing hypothesis to explain this paradoxical situation.

What Hume did, Mothersill speculates, is to *ignore* the incoherence he had found in the neoclassical doctrine. She continues:

When he did, he discovered—could not have *failed* to discover—that it was embarrassingly incoherent. But to get to the heart of the problem would have meant going back to the kind of detailed analysis practiced in the *Treatise*, and he was unwilling to do that. Kant recognized as Hume did not (or did not quite) that beauty is a good that is distinct from moral good, and when faced with Hume's problem (which he presents as "The Antinomy of Taste"), Kant saw that any plausible solution would have to be pretty complicated and so devoted the first part of *The Critique of Judgment* to a new "transcendental deduction." (270)

Mothersill mentions Kant here because she thinks that "Hume entertained, at least in outline, a view that is much closer to Kant than has been supposed" (271). This view she derives from a subtext in "Of the Standard of Taste," and she argues that when it is "suitably amplified, [the subtext] provides the clue to a solution of the paradox that is both simpler and more intuitive than anything to be gleaned from the third *Critique*." This last part of her reading of Hume's essay is unconventional and breaks new interpretive ground, and hence it is worth a closer look.

Upon reflection, Mothersill's reading does not speak well of Hume. Are we to suppose that Hume compromised the truth about neoclassical doctrine in order to enhance the sale of *Four Dissertations*? (Hume sold out.) Did he really ignore the incoherence of neoclassicism? (Hume was less than a prudent scholar.) Would it really have taken the sort of detailed analysis that he gave of the question of external existence in the *Treatise* (190ff)? I do not think it would have; after all, Hume wrote the essay some twenty years after the *Treatise* and his abilities as writer and thinker had improved substantially, as the two *Inquiries* and the *Dialogues* demonstrate. He could have given an analysis similar to those found in the later works that would not have detracted from the style of the essay and *Four Dissertations*. So I do not think Mothersill has done justice to Hume on this biographical note concerning the nature of philosophical analysis. Be that as it may, let us examine her subtext idea and its interpretation of his essay.

Concerning the argument of the subtext, Mothersill claims:

... there are no laws of taste, hence no principles or rules of composition. There are particular works, such as the *Iliad*, which please universally "in all countries and in all ages." "The *Iliad* is beautiful" is not merely true; it is an eternal truth. A critic who failed to recognize this would be a "pretender" and not a "true judge." The critic with "delicacy of taste" is known by his ability to identify the particular features of, say, the *Iliad* that contribute to its beauty. The standard of taste is set for each of the arts by the works that are acknowledged masterpieces, as is the *Iliad* for epic poetry. The subtext is in part explicit (e.g., the bits about Homer) and in part derived by implication (e.g., the vacuity of principles as it emerges from the discussion of Ariosto). (285)

It is curious that in the age of deconstruction Mothersill not only offers us a definitive reading of the text, but also develops a subtext from it. I find evidence for her premises, but find little support for her initial conclusion. How can she assert that Hume held (either implicitly or explicitly) that there are no laws of taste and hence no principles or rules of composition when we find extensive discussion of such things throughout the essay? On my count, I found ten references to a "standard," twelve uses of "principle" or "principles," nine of "rules," and one to "laws" as in "laws of criticism" (E,231). Furthermore, Hume talks about "judging" and forming "judgements" eleven times, and in this context mentions formulating comparisons between artworks four times. Given that the essay is relatively short (thirty-three paragraphs), it is safe to say that Hume in no way questions the existence of such principles or rules governing composition and that these are derivable from a standard of taste. He even speaks of a standard of taste as a rule (E,229); not only does Hume presume such things, he also produces examples, e.g., "Every work of art has also a certain end or purpose, for which it is calculated; and is to be deemed more or less perfect, as it is more or less fitted to attain this end" (E,240). Where do such principles come from?

Hume does assert that "the general rules of avowed patterns of composition" are "drawn from established models" (E,235), like Homer, so Mothersill is right about this. The models come from history—in this case, the history of epic poetry. Hume classifies the rules gleaned from them as general observations (E,231) and states that they are fixed by experience and not by reasonings *a priori*. History affords us with this experience. To this he adds the following qualification: "But though poetry can never submit to exact truth, *it must be confined by rules of art, discovered to the author* either by genius or observation" (E,231; emphasis added). Consequently from this brief sketch of Hume's essay, we see that he is in general agreement with neoclassical doctrine and makes the same assumptions that Addison, Johnson, Hutcheson, and others do about the existence and validity of such principles. But such a discussion as this should not be restricted just to the essay. Mothersill is simply wrong in claiming that the essay alone is definitive of Hume's position on critical theory (270). He provides additional insightful statements in other works that assist us in placing the essay in historical perspective. In fact in these other places, Hume provides analysis akin to that provided in the *Treatise*. We shall now briefly examine four of these other writings.

Toward the end of his Abstract of the *Treatise*, Hume ties his discussion of ideas to composition. He does not rest content with analyzing the nature of ideas, but works out the implications his theory has for other phenomena (like writing). Hume concludes that:

if any thing can intitle the author to so glorious a name as that of an *inventor*, 'tis the use he makes of the principle of the association of ideas, which enters into most of his philosophy. Our imagination has a great authority over our ideas; and there are no ideas that are different from each other, which it cannot separate, and join, and compose into all the varieties of fiction. But notwithstanding the empire of the imagination, there is a secret tie or union among particular ideas, which causes the mind to conjoin them more frequently together, and makes the one, upon its appearance, introduce the other. Hence arises what we call the *apropos* of discourse: hence the connection of writing: and hence that thread, or chain of thought, which a man naturally supports even in the loosest *reverie*. (T,661-62)

Hume is not satisfied with suggesting the *apropos* of discourse with his use of the association of ideas (Resemblance, Contiguity, and Causation). We have seen this in connection with historical narration in the previous chapter. In the first *Inquiry* (in editions K, L, and N), he works out an application of the principles of the association of ideas to composition. In this pursuit, he consciously follows in the footsteps of Francis Hutcheson.[2] Apparently, though, Hume was never happy with his analysis because he omitted it from the final editions of the *Inquiry Concerning Human Understanding*, but fortunately Charles Hendel has preserved that exposition.[3] It helps us fill in some details of Hume's analysis that are lacking in the essay.

We must be careful, however, in using it to amplify the essay, since Hume had mixed feelings about it. Hume gives the same principle that I just cited from the essay in this section: "In all compositions of genius, therefore, it is requisite that the writer have some plan or object"(IU,33). He says that this rule admits of no exceptions and that actions or events narrated are united "under one plan or view ... which may be the object or end of the writer in his first undertaking." So the principle of unity is explained by Hume as expressions of his principles of the association of ideas: resemblance (examples are Ovid and Milton), contiguity (histories and Milton again are illustrations), and causation (an important quality of historical narrations). "These loose hints," Hume remarks, "I have thrown together in order to excite the curiosity of philosophers" (IU,39). He concludes that "The full explication of this principle [i.e., 'By introducing into any composition personages and actions foreign to each other, an injudicious author loses that communication of emotions by which alone he can interpret the heart and raise the passions to their proper height and period'] and all its consequences would lead us into reasonings too profound and too copious for these Essays" (IU,39). Again, Mothersill is correct about Hume not employing the kind of analysis of "abstruse philosophy" (this term is from the first *Inquiry*, IU,16) characteristic of portions of the *Treatise*. But the analysis he did provide in this section (III) of the first *Inquiry* "is sufficient for us," Hume adds, "at present, to have established this conclusion, that the three connecting principles of all ideas are the relations of *resemblance, contiguity,* and *causation*" (IU,39). And Hume has shown that literary principles that govern composition, like Aristotle's unity of action (IU,34f), are explicable in terms of the laws of association. Concerning Ovid, Hume claims that he "formed his plan upon the connecting principle of resemblance. Every fabulous transformation produced by the miraculous power of the gods falls within the compass of his work. There needs but this one circumstance, in any event, to bring it under his original plan or intention" (IU,33-34). This sounds plausible, but it is Hume's Milton description that probably led him to omit this portion of the section:

It may be objected to Milton that he has traced up his causes to too great a distance [hence violating the connecting principle of contiguity], and that the rebellion of the angels produces the fall of man by a train of events which is both very long and very casual [hence violating the principle of causation]. Not to mention that the creation of the world, which he has related at length, is no more the cause of that catastrophe than of the battle of Pharsalia, or any other event that has ever happened. But if we consider, on the other hand, that all these events, the rebellion of the angels, the creation of the world, and the fall of man, *resemble* each other in being miraculous, and out of the common course of nature; that they are supposed to be *contiguous* in time; and that, being detached from all other events, and being the only original facts which revelation discovers, they strike the eye at once, and naturally recall each other to the thought or imagination—if we consider all these circumstances, I say, we shall find that these parts of the action have a sufficient unity to make them be comprehended in one fable or narration. To which we may add that the rebellion of the angels and the fall of man have a peculiar resemblance, as being counterparts to each other, and presenting to the reader the same moral of obedience to our Creator. (IU,38-39)

Hume's analysis is grossly wanting. It treats *Paradise Lost* as a historical narrative, and leaves out the more important literary features—style, compositional order, and story. However, Hume reminds us in the *Treatise* that: "All the rules of this nature [general ones] are very easy in their invention, but extremely difficult in their application" (T,I,III,XV).

Then there are rules of composition which Hume establishes that appear to be blatantly false and that even neoclassical writers would have found exceptions and objections to: e.g., "every writer," Hume declares, is "to form some plan or design before he enter on any discourse or narration, and to comprehend his subject in some general aspect or united view which may be the constant object of his attention" (IU,37). In going over the later editions of the first *Inquiry*, Hume probably saw the naivete of his analysis and decided to abandon the literary discussion altogether in the third section on the association of ideas;

hence, he does concede failure by its final withdraw. Probably not a bad idea, but the discussion does substantiate the points I have wanted to make about Mothersill's treatment of Hume.

A third source outside of the essay on the standard of taste that bears on this general topic is an unpublished essay of Hume's titled "Of the Poems of Ossian" (PH,389-400), probably written in the spring of 1775. I mention this essay in passing, because it shows Hume at work as a literary critic arguing against the alleged authenticity of the poems as works from antiquity. Again, the criticism is in line with neoclassicism. And fourth, Hume has several discussions of rules or principles of composition in the second *Inquiry*; e.g., "it is a rule in criticism, that every combination of syllables or letters, which gives pain to the organs of speech in the recital, appears also from a species of sympathy harsh and disagreeable to the ear" (IM,51). He continues talking about "unharmonious compositions" (Section V, Part II). From what he says here, it is obvious that the harmonious ones are a product of principles, too. In fact, some of the narrative discussion that was omitted in the final editions of "Of the Association of Ideas" found its way into several sections of the second *Inquiry*. Evidently Hume thought the subject of narrative and composition was more suitable for the second *Inquiry*, since sentiment is addressed there rather than ideas, and he probably decided that the former is the *source* of the principles rather than the latter. He entertained a Kantian move, but settled on a Dubosian/Hutchesonian one. The validity of an epic, like the *Iliad*, is determined by sentiment, by its ability to move and engage its reader and the pleasure it affords.[4] This is why the epic has a history—it initiates these responses in individuals generation after generation and age after age. This is what its "eternal truth" consists in, i.e., its history.

It is now time that I give my account of the paradox of taste in Hume. He does think that there are rules or principles (contrary to Mothersill's subtext conclusion)—he just gives generally a negative account of them. In his analysis of knowledge and probability in the *Treatise* (I,III,XIII,), Hume catalogues unphilosophical (ordinary) species of probability; the fourth kind of probability is derived from general rules, "which we rashly form to ourselves, and which are the source of what we properly call *Prejudice*." So general rules, like rules of composition, are or can be the source for prejudice. Hume elaborates:

An *Irishman* cannot have wit, and a *Frenchman* cannot have solidity; for which reason, tho' the conversation of the former in any instance be visibly very agreeable, and of the latter very judicious, we have entertain'd such a prejudice against them, that they must be dunces or fops in spite of sense and reason. Human nature is very subject to errors of this kind; and perhaps this nation [England] as much as any other.

Rules of composition can produce similar negative generalizations, such as: A narrative cannot have a design that does not comprehend its subject matter in some general aspect or united view that is the constant object of the writer's attention. If a critic who entertains such a rule encounters a narrative without a design of this sort, the critic will find the composition lacking. The narrative will be judged against some standard or rule, which in turn becomes another rule. And these rules, Hume says, "are in a manner set in opposition to each other." Yet he thinks that only through such conflict can prejudice be corrected or minimized. In his words, "The following of general rules is a very unphilosophical species of probability; *and yet 'tis only by following them that we can correct this* [i.e., the procedure of following general rules], and all other unphilosophical probabilities" (emphasis added). And in the second *Inquiry* Hume says that: "*General rules* are often extended beyond the principle whence they first arise, and this in all matters of taste and sentiment" (IM,37).

This is Hume's statement of the human predicament: we are riddled with prejudice. His solution or way of overcoming prejudice is to correct or modify it with other general rules. Another way to correct prejudice is to employ rules admitting possible exceptions (T,III,II,VI). So things that fall short become exceptions rather than deficiencies. The exceptions become uniform and generalizations in turn. That rules and principles *change* is the moral of Hume's story. The paradox of taste lies in his notion of a rule and its uses on one hand to create prejudice and on the other hand to correct it. The Hume of the *Treatise* is very skeptical of what rules do and what we accomplish with them because of this paradox. Standards or rules of taste are not different from other generalizations in this respect. Adrian Oldfield distinguishes prejudice and judgment this way: "The prejudice we assert is the product of judgments we have made in the past, but this does not affect the nature of a judgment, nor the distinction between a judgment and a prejudice: the one is reflective, the other not."[5]

Perhaps the best interpretation we can give of Hume on principles of taste (and hence rules of composition) is to attribute the position of *skeptical realism*[6] to his critical theory. Hume does not deny that there are principles of taste and rules for composition—he believes that they exist and govern such things—we just don't know them in their detail. The fact that taste and composition exist is enough for Hume to accept that there are laws and rules that govern their operations. My conjecture is that he was so committed to the theory of the association of ideas that he thought the rules or laws must exist even though he was unable to glean adequately them from literary compositions, or at least not to his satisfaction. Nevertheless, they are there to be discovered, or so Hume believed. In more Kantian terms, if we possess a concept of taste and a concept of composition, then there are rules that govern them and ones we can derive by a transcendental deduction. This is where we find an affinity of Kant with Hume.

A colleague of mine[7] asked: "What is the difference between saying there are not any principles governing composition and claiming there are such principles but we don't know them or haven't discovered them yet?" Pragmatically there may not be a difference, but there is metaphysically and epistemologically. The skeptical realism claim matters because it suggests that principles of composition do populate the universe. Since human nature is governed by principles, so, too, is composition because it is a by-product of human nature if it is not too artificial. As Hume concludes in "A Dialogue" (IM,158):

When men depart from the maxims of common reason and affect these *artificial* lives, as you call them, no one can answer for what will please or displease them. They are in a different element from the rest of mankind, and the natural principles of their mind play not with the same regularity as if left to themselves, free from the illusions of religious superstition or philosophical enthusiasm.

Epistemologically, the admission of principles is important because it means that writers and critics should continue to search for the principles. Writers or critics must rid themselves of artificiality and think "naturally" in order for the principles of the mind and composition to become evident. Who knows, they may some day be discovered, whereas if the principles are outright denied then we will not attempt to look for them. Hence the position of skeptical realism is significant in respect to principles of composition.[8]

We now move from the literary to the rhetorical dimension of Hume's conception of history and how it fits into the way of ideas.

SEVEN

MORAL JUDGMENTS IN HISTORY

"History is but the shadow of ethics."
anonymous

Introduction

This chapter consists of four sections; the first part is a brief description of the problem of moral judgments in history from the standpoint of contemporary analytic philosophy of history. With this context, Hume is introduced into the debate and it is asked where he would stand on this issue. In this second section, his notion of history and conception of moral judgment are examined with an eye on illustrations (like Hume's account of the fate of Montrose) from the *History of England*. As Hume's position emerges, it is compared and contrasted with Butterfield's and Collingwood's. Common experience, sympathy, and pre-sensation appear to be the Humean basis of historical understanding. Hume anticipates the Butterfield-Collingwood theory of historical imaginative reconstruction. Section three continues this argument with a look at various accounts of Cardinal Wolsey—including Hume's and Lord Acton's. The last section (four) attempts to analyze Hume's crucial concepts of common experience, sympathy, and presensation in light of later theories (Smith, Burke, Dilthey, Freud, Livingston, and Capaldi).

I

One of the long-standing and important issues in the philosophy of history is the permissibility or desirability of moral judgments in written history. The contributions of R. F. Atkinson,[1] Herbert Butterfield,[2] and Adrian Oldfield[3] supply the context for a discussion of David Hume on this issue. What is at stake, of course, is whether or not historians should make such judgments in their narratives. Butterfield (127) thinks that if they do, the narratives lose objectivity and transform the historical enterprise into a new and different one. This sounds very much like a positivistic doctrine, and Butterfield goes on to amend this argument: "the historical realm emerges as a moral one in what we may regard as a higher sense of the word altogether" (103). Unfortunately he does not tell us what that sense is, so we have to try to determine what he means from the clues he provides. So the question is not whether or not moral judgments are made, but *how* they are made—are they either implicit or explicit in the historian's story? Either way their presence demands explanation and argument.

Butterfield's argument is primarily directed against Lord Acton's view that pronouncing moral verdicts is central to the task of history (see Atkinson, 198).[4] Butterfield denies that moral judgments make their appearance in narratives as pronouncements. Rather, he adds:

There is one way in which the historian may reinforce the initial moral judgment and thereby assist the cause of morality in general; and that way lies directly within his province, for it entails *merely describing*, say, the massacre or the persecution, laying it out in concrete detail, and giving the specification of what it means in actuality. It is possible to say that one of the causes of moral indifference is precisely the failure to realise in an objective manner and make vivid to oneself the terrible nature of crime and suffering; but those who are unmoved by the historical description will not be stirred by any pontifical commentary that may be superadded. (123; emphasis added)

So it is by description that the historian communicates or invites moral judgments on the part of the reader. Moral judgments are embedded in narrated actions that *move* the audience to interpret them. Sounding very much like R. G. Collingwood,[5] Butterfield says: "Working upon a given historical event, then, the historian knits around it a web of historical explanation" (120) by way of description.[6] Moral judgments are woven into the very fabric of human life, and if history is to adequately reflect that fabric, history will have to possess them. You and I as human beings recognize them in the historian's portrayal of human actions and deeds. Pronouncements or verdicts are unnecessary and indeed unwarranted. Moral judgments, according to Butterfield, can be conveyed in another way—by description.[7] Butterfield (who is a Christian historian) holds that moral judgments emerge upon reflecting on the whole narrative—a view (as we shall see) that is attributable to Hume.

How moral judgments are "conveyed" by description is not clear from Butterfield's account. However, Atkinson gives us an idea of how this might be carried out: "A somewhat sophisticated moral attitude is here required, involving stepping aside from one's own standards ['the historian's own substantive standards should be kept out of history,'], in recognising that the agent has and is guided by his own" (204). Moreover, "it is a central feature of historical activity that it should tend to [fill] ... in the sort of context that enables the people of the past to be seen as exercising moral agency" (205). Atkinson concludes that "moral merit is manifested in an agent's living up to his *own* standards" (205). And, "The historian, operating in a characteristic manner, may thus enable past people to be seen as moral agents; but not in a way which involves his passing moral judgements of his own on them" (205). It takes moral sensitivity on the part of the historian to be able to do this. "In morals," Atkinson reminds us, "we are all practitioners" (207), so the historian has firsthand experience to assist in his reconstruction of past people as moral agents. We all know what it is to live up to our moral expectations and to fall short of them. The understanding of our moral psychology is reflected in the historian's portrayal of individuals, events, institutions, and policies of the past.

Adrian Oldfield extends this line of argument by introducing the concept of the contemporary:

> If sympathetic understanding of the man of the past is required, then this can be conveyed with much more subtlety, and ultimately more effect, if the historian, instead of pronouncing his own moral judgments, speaks through the mouths of contemporaries, using their recorded thoughts and opinions as pieces of evidence much like any other. If he is skillful, the historian can still make us aware of his own moral reasoning. But, because he is using contemporary utterances, he can also make us aware of the views and opinions of those whose moral positions diverge from his own. Contemporary moral judgments enable us to enter the lives of the men of the past. We begin to see "heroes" and "villains" in their terms, and thus to appreciate more fully not just their circumstances, but the moral choices and judgments that they themselves made. (271)

It goes without saying that with any narrative technique, the use of contemporary voices can be abused just like any thing else in the historian's craft. Oldfield is talking about sensitive, skillful historians. He adds: "The advantage which the historian possesses over the contemporary is hindsight—he does know what followed the actions of his subjects" (275). This hindsight enables the historian to create a coherence that is not present in lived experience. The historian is able to look at an agent's experience and events and see them as a series. These series are normally assessments of meaning and significance that lie beyond mere temporal ordering within a narrative. Here Oldfield borrows Louis Mink's term, "synoptic judgments" (276), to describe the kind of considerations that are held together in those kind of judgments. Oldfield concludes that "the historian *cannot* avoid acting, from time to time, as moral educator" (277; emphasis added). The premises in the argument are:

When historians write about individual actions, they are likely to find that the language they use in describing and assessing such action has moral connotations. To describe and assess action is, in the broadest sense, to educate; and part of this is moral education. As much as any educative effort, this is an issue which requires handling with clarity and sensitivity. (276)

At this point we have sufficient context of the philosophical issue of moral judgments in history to introduce Hume. We shall now turn to his writings; however, the context above shall be brought into the discussion from time to time.

II

Let us first look at Hume's conceptions of history and of moral judgments before we examine what his position would be on this issue. Concerning the nature of history we need to peruse the withdrawn essay "Of the Study of History" (1741). Because it was withdrawn does not diminish the importance of the theoretical statements that follow. Hence I take these propositions to be central to Hume's theory of history. To start with, he says that: "the advantages found in history seem to be of three kinds, as it amuses the fancy, as it improves the understanding, and as it strengthens virtue" (E,565). How does history strengthen virtue? The answer is by the examples it affords. The examples do two things. First, "experience ... is acquired by history" (E,567), and that would include moral experience—the virtues and the vices. Second, "[t]he virtues ... contributed to their [the past empires'] greatness, and the vices ... drew on their ruin" (E,566). So the subject matter of history—the revolutions of past empires—necessarily has this moral dimension. Hume continues: "the historians have been ... the true friends of virtue, and have always represented it in its proper colours, however they may have erred in their judgments of particular persons" (E,567). Hume gives Machiavelli's *History of Florence* (1523) as an illustration of a history that represents virtue "in its proper colours"—not Machiavelli the politician, but Machiavelli the historian.[8] Virtue can be properly represented apart from a historian's judgments of particular people. The crucial query is, How is this representation accomplished in history? Notice that Hume separates the representation of virtue and judgments. This is no accident on his part.

Hume makes the following claim: "The writers of history, as well as the readers, are sufficiently interested in the characters and events, to have a lively sentiment of blame or praise; and, at the same time, have no particular interest or concern to pervert their judgments" (E,568). The key terms here in the argument are "sentiment" and "judgment." Let us briefly look at Hume's use of them. In "Concerning Moral Sentiment," Hume addresses the issue of "how far either *reason* [judgment as 'cool approbation' (IM,57)] or *sentiment* enters into all decisions of praise or censure" (IM,104). His argument runs like this:

Premise 1: "The approbation or blame which then ensues cannot be the work of judgment but of the heart; and it is not a speculative proposition or affirmation, but an active feeling or sentiment" (IM,108).

Premise 2: "In moral decisions, all the circumstances and relations must be previously known; and the mind, from the contemplation of the whole, feels some new impression of affection or disgust, esteem or contempt, approbation or blame" (IM,108-109).

After dealing with some historical illustrations to establish the plausibility of these premises, he concludes that: "Nothing remains but to feel, on our part, some sentiment of blame or approbation, whence we pronounce the action criminal or virtuous" (IM,109).

Given this line of reasoning, the task of the historian is to describe all the circumstances and relations known about some event, so that the reader may from the contemplation of the whole, i.e., the event and its context, feel some *new* impression of a passion. As Hume tells us earlier in the second *Inquiry*: "The perusal of a history seems a calm entertainment, but would be no entertainment at all did not our hearts beat with correspondent movements to those which are *described* by the historian" (IM,50; emphasis added). What I take Hume to be suggesting here is that it is just the presenting of the information in context and with significant relationships depicted, including temporal relationships such as patterns and evolutions or responses to earlier events, which presensation itself so informs the understanding of the readers that because of that understanding the readers are able to grasp those relationships and "map" them to what they know and feel of their being in the world, that then the moral sentiment arises as an impression within them, directly felt (because of the double relation). This sounds very similar to Butterfield's procedure: the one way for the historian to assist the cause of morality is merely by describing some event—not by giving any "pontifical commentary" or judgment. But at times Hume does pronounce judgments as well as describe. So Hume goes beyond Butterfield's positivistic description of historical practices.

Hume's argument above offers us some explanation as to why he thought that history strengthens virtue. Every reader has the capacity for moral feelings or sentiments. These sentiments may be awakened or strengthened by the historian's narrative. The narrative description excites or enlivens the reader to feel some new impression of a passion. The "mechanics" of this psychological process is unclear, but as well as I can make it out, it is as follows. Virtues and vices are moral sentiments. "What each man feels within himself," Hume proclaims, "is the standard of sentiment" (IM,5). Yet, "he must observe that others are susceptible of like impressions" (IM,3). In other words, you can not tell other persons how it feels or how it *should* feel (this would be a moral pronouncement). All you can do is to describe the situation in such a way that they may have the occasion to feel or experience it for themselves. This points to a difference between moral and aesthetic judgments. Some can merely describe a situation and he or she can make moral assessments of it, but not so with aesthetic judgments. You have to see it for yourself in order to pronounce it as beautiful or ugly. I can describe a car in great detail, but you cannot deduce its beauty—you have to see it, then and only then you might infer that. (Hume was aware of this difference in evaluations; see IM, 5). The observations or ideas that lie before the reader are converted by sympathy into internal impressions, and are "lived" again in those readers. The "conversion" is best explained in Book Two, "Of the Passions," of the *Treatise*. Hume announces that: "No quality of human nature is more remarkable, both in itself and in its consequences, than that propensity we have to sympathize with others, and to receive by communication their inclinations and sentiments, however different from, or even contrary to our own" (T, II, I, XI). His conception of sympathy is a species of communication: "When any affection is infus'd by sympathy, it is at first known only by its effects, and *by those external signs in the countenance and conversation*, which convey an idea of it. This idea is presently converted into an impression, and acquires such a degree of force and vivacity, as to become the very passion itself, and produce an equal emotion, as any original affection" (T, II, I, XI; emphasis added). So given the nature and situations of events in human history, they turn out to be emotionally charged by the very language the historian uses to describe them, and we in turn as readers interpret these through sympathy.

James Farr[9] has fortunately given an excellent analysis of Hume's use of the principle of sympathy in his theory of history, so I need not dwell on this point, except to amend Farr's account. I focus on it here because Hume anticipates the Butterfield-Collingwood theory of historical imaginative reconstruction. Butterfield gives this account of that process:

The historian can never quite know men from the inside—never quite learn the last secret of the workings of inspiration in a poet or of piety in a devout religious leader. For the same reason he can never quite carry his enquiries to that innermost region where the final play of motive and the point of responsibility can be decided. The historian fails to pierce the most inward recesses and the essential parts of a man; and all he can depend on is a general feeling for human nature, based ultimately on self-analysis, but further enlarged in a general experience of life. Much can be achieved by a constant practice of that kind of imaginative sympathy which works on all types and varieties of men and acquires a certain feeling for personality. But the only understanding we ever reach in history is but a refinement, more or less subtle and sensitive, of the difficult—and sometimes deceptive—process of imagining oneself in another person's place. (116-117)

Hume would probably be more forceful and less cautious about the historian knowing people from the inside because of the extraordinary powers he attributes to sympathy: "expect a correspondence in the sentiments of every other person, with those themselves have entertained" (T,II,II,I). He then goes on to make this remarkable statement: "we are not subject to many mistakes in this particular, but are sufficiently guided by common experience, as well as by a kind of *presensation*; which tell us what will operate on others, by what we feel immediately in ourselves" (T,II,II,I; Hume's emphasis).[10] So he would add to Butterfield's "general experience of life" (which Hume himself affirms) "a kind of presensation," by which he means an introspection that reveals universal principles of human nature and which serves as the basis for a feeling of something before it happens, i.e., an anticipation of what will occur, or what did occur if we are examining the past. In this respect, Hume is closer to Collingwood than Butterfield, for Collingwood, too, thinks that:

The gulf of time between the historian and his object must be bridged, as I have said, from both ends. The object must be of such a kind that it can revive itself in the historian's mind; the historian's mind must be such as to offer a home for that revival. This does not mean that his mind must be of a certain kind, possessed of an historical temperament; nor that he must be trained in special rules of historical technique. It means that he must be the right man to study that object. What he is studying is a certain thought: to study it involves re-enacting it in himself; and in order that it may take its place in the immediacy of his own thought, his thought must be, as it were, pre-adapted to become its host. (IH,304)

The process of preadaptation and reenactment of object and thought[11] is analogous to Hume's notion of presensation, although the latter is clearly not as sophisticated as Collingwood's description of human appropriation. Where Collingwood talks about the right kind of person and object, Hume says "the force of the passion depends as much on the temper of the person, as on the nature and situation of the object" (DP,108). Surely Hume would have thought that this holds for presensation in individuals. Presensation is another way for

Hume to depict the human agent as active rather than passive in his or her mental operations: it is *how* we know the sentiments of others, just as how we know external objects is by our sensations. A historian's presensation becomes the bridge for the gap between him or her and the historical personage. In other words, a historian's presensation is his or her reenactment of the agent's experience from whatever documents or evidence have been left for posterity. What more we can say of "presensation" is speculation, since he does not discuss it anywhere except in that one place in the *Treatise* (II,II,I). We can probably assume that "[i]t is a constitution of nature of which we can give no farther explication" (DP,103). Presensation is an odd item for Hume to include in his inventory of human nature, given his empirical leanings in the opening of Book One of the *Treatise*, but then his whole treatment of sympathy is most unusual. Since he denies reason any significant role in human conduct, he must have other faculties and abilities performing that role, and presensation and sympathy are among them.

"This is the nature and cause of sympathy," Hume declares, "and 'tis after this manner we enter so deep into the opinions and affections of others, whenever we discover them" (T,II,I,XI). James Farr supplies us with the following clarification: "In Hume's metaphor, therefore, we 'enter so deep into' all those various states of mind which Hume shows sympathy opens up to us: sentiments, feelings, opinions, principles, and the like. For example, when we sympathize with an agent we at first form an idea of, say, his repugnance or horror at some heinous deed, and then through the enlivening process of the association of ideas, *we then share that idea and eventually feel* ('enter so deep into') *that very repugnance and horror*" (294; emphasis added). A skillful historian will narrate a past event in ways such that he or she communicates the sympathetic elements which comprise that event to his or her audience. Historians are to recapture the states of mind of the agents they describe in their narratives. Notice that Farr illustrates the enlivening process with a moral judgment in history, i.e., "some heinous deed which moves the reader to feel that very repugnance and horror felt by a historical agent."

Numerous examples abound in the *History of England*, but one that particularly stands out in this context is Hume's account of the fate of Montrose—one of Charles I's loyal generals (H,VI,ch. LX). Hume begins his account of the marquis with the indictment: "When he was carried before the parliament, which was then sitting, Loudon, the chancellor, in a violent declamation, reproached him with the breach of the national covenant, which he had subscribed; his rebellion against God, the king, and the kingdom; and the many horrible murders, treasons, and impieties, for which he was now to be brought to condign punishment" (H,VI,22). Hume then gives an evaluation of Montrose in terms of his own standards—something Atkinson (205) suggests as a way to assess an agent's moral worth: "Montrose in his answer maintained the same superiority above his enemies, to which, by his fame and great action, as well as by the consciousness of a good cause, he was justly entitled" (H,VI,22). Following his plea, Hume adds: "That as to himself, they [the covenanters] had in vain endeavoured to vilify and degrade him by all their studied indignities: The justice of his cause, he knew, would ennoble any fortune" (H,VI,23). Hume gives us a sense of Montrose's moral strength and depicts him as someone who, in Atkinson's words, is seen as *exercising* moral agency (205). In this instance, it is Montrose's sentence that conveys a sense of repugnance and horror, and Hume gives it to the reader verbatim as it was read in the trial to maximize its impact:

"That he, James Graham" (for this was the only name they vouchsafed to give him) "should next day be carried to Edinburgh cross, and there be hanged on a gibbet, thirty feet high, for the space of three hours: Then be taken down, his head be cut off upon a scaffold, and affixed to the prison: His legs and arms be stuck up on the four chief towns of the kingdom: His body be buried in the place appropriated for common malefactors; except the church, upon his repentance, should take off his excommunication." (H,VI,23)

Hume then gives Montrose's own written response which further illustrates the point about moral agency as seen through one living up to, or in this case dying for, his own principles:

"For my part," added he, "I am much prouder to have my head affixed to the place, where it is sentenced to stand, than to have my picture hang in the king's bed-chamber. So far from being sorry, that my quarters are to be sent to four cities of the kingdom; I wish I had limbs enow to be dispersed into all the cities of Christendom, there to remain as testimonies in favour of the cause, for which I suffer." This sentiment, that very evening, while in prison, he threw into verse. The poem remains; a signal monument of his heroic spirit, and no despicable proof of his poetical genius. (H,VI,24)

To recall the opening remark from the essay "Of the Study of History" (E,565), it is through examples like this one depicting Montrose's fate that history strengthens virtue. Such moral defiance is an important English trait and is captured in the Montrose Character.[12]

Hume also uses the Montrose Character as a way to exhibit tension between the clergy and the people. Concerning the clergy or the covenanters, Hume makes the following narrative statement that shows he thought that description needs the guidance of moral judgments: "The past scene displays in a full light the barbarity of this theological faction: The sequel will sufficiently display their absurdity" (H,VI,25). (The sentence on Montrose looks very similar to the severe sentence on William Wallace (H,II,135-136); Hume might well have connected the events, since in each case the popular cause was more unified by this "barbarity.") Regarding the people, Hume had this to say: "The populace, more generous and humane, when they saw so mighty a change of fortune in this great man, so lately their dread and terror, into whose hands the magistrates, a few years before, had delivered on their knees the keys of the city, were struck with compassion, and viewed him with silent tears and admiration. The preachers, next Sunday, exclaimed against this movement of rebel nature, as they termed it; and reproached the people with their profane tenderness towards the capital enemy of piety and religion" (H,VI,22). Here Hume uses contemporary information and opinions to make a point about Montrose and English life in 1650, thus exercising Oldfield's methodological elaboration of the historian's craft (271). And I would guess that most of Hume's readers in his day would have identified with the populace. Hume's account of the clergy fosters negative feelings in the reader, thereby allowing him or her to identify vice, and his account of the populace builds positive feelings in the reader, thereby enabling her or him to identify virtue. Hume also serves as Oldfield's "moral educator" here in painting the people as humane, more sympathetic and understanding than the clergy. His distrust of the clergy and the sort of evils he thinks they had committed throughout the history of England is perhaps only second to Shirer's distaste for totalitarian regimes like the Third Reich (see note 7). In most of Hume's accounts, a dialectical tension between virtue and vice is portrayed by the warring factions of his historical personages, and subtle judgments of morality guide the narrative descriptions.

An issue thus far unaddressed in our analysis is the relativity of morals. (Oldfield's analysis of the contemporary raises this question.) We have seen Hume describe historical agents, e.g., Montrose, in terms of their own standards or ideals. Moreover, he is explicit about this; in his discussion of Charles I, he reflects:

But as these [strict legal] limitations were not regularly fixed during the age of Charles, nor at any time before; so was this liberty totally unknown, and was generally deemed, as well as religious toleration, incompatible with all good government. No age or nation, among the moderns, had ever set an example of such an indulgence: and it seems unreasonable to judge of the measures embraced during one period, by the maxims which prevail in another. (H,V,240)

At first glance, it sounds as if Hume voices the doctrine of the relativity of morals. In the second *Inquiry*, he makes the following comment on unusual customs of the Romans that were recorded in Tacitus: "a sentiment of the historian which would sound a little oddly in other nations and other ages" (IM,78). In "Of National Characters," Hume observes: "The manners of a people change very considerably from one age to another, either by great alterations in their government, by the mixtures of new people, or by that inconstancy, to which all human affairs are subject" (E,205-206). And in the first *Inquiry*, Hume says that there are "many general observations concerning the gradual change of our sentiments and inclinations, and the different maxims which prevail in the different ages of human creatures" and "the manners of men [are] different in different ages and countries" (IU,95).

These statements help us cast doubt on the ploy of emphasizing the phrase "it seems" in Hume's last sentence in the first quotation above (H,V,240) in order to de-emphasize the view it contains. I make a point of this, because Hume as a historian has been accused of lacking a historic sense. What this amounts to is that he "judged the past as if it were the present; [he] ... took for granted that the same standards must be apt to past centuries as well. /The first duty of a historian is not, as Hume declared, to be true and impartial; but to understand. And none can begin to understand a past age unless they intermit their own scales of value. They must view the age from within itself."[13] No doubt Hume is guilty of partiality throughout the *History*, but such claims as Greig's are totally unsympathetic and in large part unsubstantiated. Hume understood in large measure the periods he was dealing with. He declares these intentions in the opening of chapter LII where he says of the reign of Charles (1629): "We shall endeavour to exhibit a just idea of the events which followed for some years; so far as they regard foreign affairs, the state of the court, and the government of the nation. The incidents are neither numerous nor illustrious, but the knowledge of them is necessary for *understanding* the subsequent transactions, which are so memorable" (V,217-218; emphasis added). I doubt whether any of Hume's writings offers evidence of moral relativism, as we speak of it. Rather, they, but especially the *History*, suggest that general moral rules, corrected sentiments, and virtuous qualities evolve throughout history: there are fewer moral strangers than we would expect, at least among our ancestors. The above passages which suggest relativism is of manners and not morals. As Hume writes:

No character can be so remote as to be, in this light, wholly indifferent to me. What is beneficial to society or to the person himself must still be preferred. And every quality or action, of every human being, must, by this means, be ranked under some class or denomination, expressive of general censure or applause. (IM,94)

To reinforce my point, in the chapter on Oliver Cromwell and his rejection of the crown, Hume insists that: "Most historians are inclined to blame his choice; but he *must* be allowed the best judge of his own situation" (H,VI,97; emphasis added). The reason he gives for this statement is most interesting, given the context above: "And in such complicated subjects, the alteration of a very minute circumstance, unknown to the spectator, will often be sufficient to cast the balance, and render a determination, which, in itself, may be ineligible, very prudent, or even absolutely necessary to the actor" (H,VI,97). The use of the actor/spectator distinction here in respect to historical knowledge qualifies Hume's principle of sympathy. This time, Hume agrees more closely with Butterfield than with Collingwood. At this point in his analysis, Hume, I think, would agree with Butterfield's assessment of the limits of historical knowledge:

It is true that an historian may feel that by imaginative sympathy he has almost completed the gaps in his picture of some historical personage, almost achieved what we might call an internal knowledge of the man. By great insight and by running all his molten experience into the mould that has been presented to him, he may feel that he has found the essential clue to a character—even to a man who has hitherto baffled the interpreters. Even this degree of knowledge fails, however, in that innermost region of all, which has to be reached before a personality can be assessed in a moral judgment. (117)

Hume seems to comply with such an account of historical knowledge. For example, when he levels a moral judgment on a historical figure, he usually qualifies it by a reference to the agent's own motives or abilities. In his report on Cromwell's protectorship, Hume adds that: "The scheme of foreign politics, adopted by the protector, was highly imprudent, but was suitable to that magnanimity and enterprize, with which he was so signally endowed" (H,VI,101). So Hume will label some scheme or event as "prudent" or "imprudent," but will immediately qualify that judgment by its "suitability" from the point of view of the agent. Butterfield does not explain his "mould" for interpreting a historical character, although, as we have seen, Hume does. His mould consists of pre-sensation and sympathy in which the historian builds the internal knowledge of an agent, like that of Montrose.

By focusing on sentiments, so Hume's theory goes, the historian possesses a capacity universally shared by all human beings, and hence something that transcends the actor/spectator distinction. The analogue between history and literature is so close here that Hume's recital of the theatrical experience gives us some clues as to how the principle of sympathy functions in history:

A man who enters the theater is immediately struck with the view of so great a multitude participating of one common amusement, and experiences, from their very aspect, *a superior sensibility* or disposition of being affected with every sentiment which he shares with his fellow creatures. /He observes the actors to be animated by the appearance of a full audience and raised to a degree of enthusiasm which they cannot command in any solitary or calm moment. /Every movement of the theater, by a skillful poet, is communicated, as it were, by magic to the spectators, who weep, tremble, resent, rejoice, and are inflamed with all the variety of passions which actuate the several personages of the drama. (IM,49; emphasis added)

By analogy, Hume thought that past actions were communicated by a skillful historian. The historian is to "animate" the historical personages in her or his narrative in ways by which the reader experiences this "superior sensibility." This is how history strengthens virtue. Hume continues: "In our serious occupations [like history], in our careless amusements [like theater], this principle [of sympathy] still exerts its active energy" (IM,48-49). He concludes that "the sentiments which arise from humanity [a universal principle along with sympathy, see IM,57] are not only the same in all human creatures and produce the same approbation or censure, but they also *comprehend* all human creatures; nor is there anyone whose conduct or character is not, by their means, an object, to everyone, of censure or approbation" (IM,94; emphasis added). So the sentiments are the same for mankind—past, present, or future. It is the influence of reason and custom that accounts for their difference (IM,33) and affords us with "the natural progress of human sentiments" (IM,23). This is the stuff of history—both lived and written.

In a penetrating study, J. C. Hilson argues that: "Within the total structural pattern, or non-pattern, of the *History*, one may discern localized movements which might be seen, as I have argued here, as the *aesthetic enactment* of the ethics of the *Enquiry* [IM]. For Hume, the narrative artist's major concern is with 'the *images* of vice and virtue' and their effect on the reader."[14] In this section my argument has been that the structural pattern of the *History* is not only the aesthetic enactment of the ethics of the second *Inquiry*, but also can be seen as the *epistemological enactment* of it. Moreover, the epistemological enactment is not only reflected in the structural pattern of the *History*, but is also an integral part of his theory of history.

III

Thus far we have examined *civil history* (Hume's term, E,97) in regard to how the past is evaluated. As we have seen, Hume generally thinks that the past is evaluated on its own terms and by comparisons with one's neighbors (again, a use of contemporaries by Hume). Regarding ancient history, he opens the *History* with this methodological comment: "The only certain means, by which nations can indulge their curiosity in researches concerning their remote origin, is to consider the language, manners, and customs of their ancestors, and to compare them with those of the neighbouring nations" (H,I,4). Comparisons form a large subclass of narrative sentences,[15] and we have witnessed their use with moral judgments in history by Hume; e.g., Charles's indulgence (H,V,240) and Cromwell's imprudence (H,VI,101). Nevertheless, Hume's comparisons are not all of this type. When it comes to the "history of learning and science" (E,97), Hume appears to have been an advocate of presentism—the view that the past is judged in terms of the present.[16] In his Character of Francis Bacon, Hume estimates that: "If we consider him merely as an author and philosopher, the light in which we view him at present, though very estimable, he was yet inferior to his cotemporary [*sic*] Galileo, perhaps even to Kepler" (H,V,153). Hume tempers the morality of the present with that of the historical agent's time and period, so moral presentism is not dominant in Hume's *History* as it is in Lord Acton's narratives.

To put the above section in perspective, I shall focus on various accounts of Cardinal Wolsey—including Acton's—and compare them to Hume's. In a review of J. S. Brewer's monumental work, Acton announces that Brewer "excuses him [Wolsey] by the examples of his age, and by the greater cruelty of [Sir Thomas] More" (SW,II,309). Conversely, Acton says: "Nor can we admit that the intolerance of Wolsey is excused by comparison with the greater intolerance of More" (SW,II,310-311). Acton's use of "excuse" here is made clearer by an earlier passage: "The argument which excuses Wolsey by the times he lived in, is a serious fallacy. Christians must be judged by a moral code which is not an invention of the eighteenth century, but is as old as the Apostles" (SW,II,309). The Christian moral code transcends history and remains unaffected by it. Relativism of morals, as espoused by Atkinson and Oldfield is fallacious for Acton because he believed there is a Universal History that is imminent in human history. He makes this clear in the *Lectures on Modern History*, where he asserts that: "Their story [the combined history of all countries or nations] will be told, not for their own sake, but in reference and subordination to a higher series [Universal History], according to the time and the degree in which they contribute to the common fortunes of mankind" (317). Hume obviously did not have a "higher series" or Universal History as Acton and von Ranke did, especially one that had moral and religious overtones. But Hume did think that standards, rules (e.g., moral ones), laws developed over a period of time, a "progress of human sentiments"

(IM,23). He gives them a historical interpretation rather than a religious one as Acton did.

These, no doubt, motivated Acton to argue against the relativity of morals,[17] and to call such appeals fallacious. This substantial disagreement between Hume and Acton is evident in their handling of Wolsey. Acton writes: "That which distinguishes the whole reign of Henry VIII, both in Wolsey's happier days and during the riotous tyranny of later years, the idea of treating ecclesiastical authority not as an obstruction, but as a convenient auxiliary to the Crown ..." (SW,II,260). And, "the intimate alliance with the Papacy through every vicissitude of political fortune which is characteristic of Wolsey's administration, actually prepared the way for separation after his disgrace" (SW,II,261). This is just a sample of what Acton has to say about Wolsey; he also labels him as a "Minister of tyranny," a "priest of immoral life," and a man of "an extreme indulgence" (SW,II,308).

Hume on the other hand attempts to give a balanced portrait of Wolsey, attempting to bring out his good qualities as well as his bad ones, but Hume makes it abundantly clear which ones predominate. He writes: "Whoever was distinguished by any art or science paid court to the cardinal; and none paid court in vain. Literature, which was then in its infancy, found in him a generous patron; and both by his public institutions and private bounty, he gave encouragement to every branch of erudition" (H,III,114). But Hume continues, "he strove to dazzle the eyes of the populace, by the splendor of his equipage and furniture, the costly embroidery of his liveries, the lustre of his apparel." After a description of the legatine court that Wolsey erected, Hume places moral judgments in the populace of the period: "the people were the more disgusted, when they saw a man, who indulged himself in pomp and pleasure, so severe in repressing the least appearance of licentiousness in others" (H,III,125). At the end of his account of Wolsey, Hume adds this footnote to one of his sources: "This whole narrative has been copied by all the historians from the author here cited [Polydore Virgil]: There are many circumstances, however, very suspicious, both because of the obvious partiality of the historian, and because the parliament, when they afterwards examined Wolsey's conduct, could find no proof of any material offence he had ever committed" (H,III,125n).

So Hume is careful here in assessing the moral character of the cardinal. But Wolsey's Character is perhaps the most revealing in this respect:

By the rapid advancement and uncontrolled authority, the character and genius of Wolsey had full opportunity to display itself. Insatiable in his acquisitions, but still more magnificent in his expanse: Of extensive capacity, but still more unbounded enterprize: Ambitious of power, but still more desirous of glory: Insinuating, engaging, persuasive;

and, by turns, lofty, elevated, commanding: Haughty to his equals, but affable to his dependents; oppressive to the people, but liberal to his friends; more generous than grateful; less moved by injuries than by contempt; he framed to take the ascendant in every intercourse with others, but exerted this superiority of *nature* with such ostentation as exposed him to envy, and made every one willing to recoil the original inferiority or rather meanness of his *fortune*. (H,III,100)

"Haughty" seems to be a frequently used word to describe Wolsey's moral character. Trevelyan employs a contemporary to make a moral judgment: "He was haughty and ostentatious to a degree that would hardly have been tolerated in a Prince of the Blood. He 'is the proudest prelate that ever breathed' reported a foreign observer, and such was the general opinion."[18] Charles M. Gray defends Wolsey on the grounds of moral relativism:

He [Wolsey] has been accused of turning England into a Papal satellite partly because he had hopes of becoming Pope himself. That charge is exaggerated and unfair if it implies betrayal of English interests. As the world goes and his age went, Wolsey's diplomacy was not ignoble. He was not insensitive to the humanists' critique of contemporary politics nor to their dream of a united Christendom. /Wolsey's life ... is emblematic of the good and bad in a passing era.[19]

Gray follows more closely in Hume's footsteps, but the latter does take delight in citing episodes of Wolsey's excessive pride: "Warham, the primate, having written him a letter, in which he subscribed himself, *your loving brother*, Wolsey complained of his presumption, in thus challenging an equality with him. When Warham was told what offence he had given, he made light of the matter. 'Know ye not,' said he, 'that this man is drunk with too much prosperity'" (H,III,124). Hume continues much in the same vein. The cardinal represents the vices that draw on an empire's ruin (E,566).

IV

In this last section, I wish to return to the positivistic doctrine (echoed by Butterfield at the beginning) that moral judgments are to be eliminated in order for history to be objective or scientific. As we have seen, Atkinson, Oldfield, and Hume have argued that moral judgments are an integral part of the historian's narrative. Their model for history, especially Hume's, is literature rather than science. At the close of section IV of "Historical Inevitability," Sir Isaiah Berlin spells out the mishaps of the positivistic doctrine:

The invocation to historians to suppress even that minimal degree of moral or psychological evaluation which is necessarily involved in viewing human beings as creatures with purposes and motives (and not merely as causal factors in the procession of events), seems to me to rest upon a confusion of the aims and methods of the humane studies with those of natural science. It is one of the greatest and most destructive fallacies of the last hundred years.[20]

Hume would have agreed with Berlin because the subject matter of history is human actions and they are understood in ways (sentiment, for instance) in which physical phenomena are not. For Hume, the aims and methods of the humane studies include presensation and sympathy. Indeed these ways are "lawlike," but their regularities are a symptom of human nature. Hume's view of history as a branch of literature was repudiated in the nineteenth century by people like Jacob Burckhardt (1818-1897), who argued against moral judgments in history.[21] This argument appeared persuasive then because of historicism and later because of positivism. Hume was not under siege by either of these movements; consequently, his position on this issue, especially since these doctrines have been generally repudiated, should contribute to the debate in ways that were not possible before.

Hume did not hold that history is identical to imaginative literature. One of the things that differentiates the two is that "truth ... is the basis of history" (E,564). Once the truth of some account is known, then the moral dimension of history emerges. One way this is accomplished is suggested in the *History*: "History, the great mistress of wisdom, furnishes examples of all kinds; and every prudential, as well as moral precept, may be authorized by those events, which her enlarged mirror is able to present to us" (H,V,545). A historical narrative becomes a mirror of some moral precept through eloquence. Hume mentions a generous action barely cited in an old history and then follows up with this remark:

Virtue, placed at such a distance, is like a fixed star which, though to the eye of reason it may appear as luminous as the sun in his meridian, is so infinitely removed as to affect the senses neither with light nor heat. *Bring this virtue nearer*, by our acquaintance or connection with the persons, or even *by an eloquent recital of the case, our hearts are immediately caught, our sympathy enlivened, and our cool approbation converted into the warmest sentiments of friendship and regard*. (IM,56-57; emphases added)

"An eloquent recital of the case" would presuppose the requirements of Premise 2: "In moral decisions, all the circumstances and relations must be previously known; and the mind, from the contemplation of the whole, feels some new impression of affection or disgust, esteem or contempt, approbation or blame" (IM,108-109). What is it that eloquence adds to a recital of a case that enables it to enliven our sympathy and convert our sentiments?

Eloquence inflames an audience, "so as to make them accompany the speaker in such violent passions, and such elevated conceptions," Hume says in "Of Eloquence" (E,101).[22] Then in a passage that clearly anticipates the expressionist theory of art, Hume contends that: "The orator, by the force of his own genius and eloquence, first inflamed himself with anger, indignation, pity, sorrow; and then communicated those impetuous movements to his audience" (E,104). The paradigm of such practice is Cicero. The orators in Hume's own day lacked eloquence. "Yet, whenever the true genius arises, *he* draws to him the attention of everyone, and immediately appears superior to his rival" (E,107). This occurs because "even a person, unacquainted with the noble remains of ancient orators, may judge, from a few strokes, that the stile or species of their eloquence was infinitely more sublime than that which modern orators aspire to" (E,100). Hume thinks that men of science and history are those who should be great orators (E,107). He speaks out against indifference (and this could be directed against Burckhardt's argument): "And though an indifferent speaker may triumph for a long time, and be esteemed altogether perfect by the vulgar, who are satisfied with his accomplishments, and know not in what he is defective ..." (E,107).

From the above line of argument, we can see that Hume indeed anticipates the expressionist theory of art, i.e., the theory that the function of art is to express or communicate the artist's emotions. The audience or observer feels certain emotions because the artist embedded those emotions in his or her creation. A good example of this theory is given by Sigmund Freud, who in "The Moses of Michelangelo" claims that: "In my opinion, what grips us so powerfully can only be the artist's *intention*, in so far as he has succeeded in expressing it in his work and in getting us to understand it. I realize that this cannot be merely a matter of *intellectual* comprehension; what he aims at is to awaken in us the same emotional attitude, the same mental constellation as that which in him produced the impetus to create."[23] Hume apparently thought this psychic process was true of history; he wants to connect the motivating force of moral sentiment with the enlightened understanding of reasoned interpretations of events, which Bacon had argued as the way to do history—to do justice to both the truthful and the good.

The theory has its problems. It is obviously possible for a historian to write effectively and even eloquently about a given emotional episode (like the trial of Montrose) without undergoing those same emotions, and in fact he or she may be feeling other emotions at the time—some emotion perhaps even contrary to the ones written about. History, for Hume, is to convey ultimately the feelings of the historical personage. This sounds more like a theory of history of the nineteenth-century than one of the eighteenth. Though one might find Hume similar to later expressionists because of the part played by the moral sentiment felt within the historian in order to write, that on closer inspection he looks more like a proto-Dilthey. Here is how Wilhelm Dilthey (1833-1911) describes the nature of historical knowing:

The comprehension of the system of interactions of history grows first of all from individual points at which remnants of the past belonging together are linked in understanding by their relation to experience; what is near and around us becomes a means of understanding what is distant and past. The condition for this interpretation of historical remnants is that what we put into them must be constant and universally valid. On the basis of the connections which the historian has experienced within himself he transfers his knowledge of customs, habits, political circumstances and religious processes to these remnants.[24]

Dilthey's account of historical knowing is similar to Hume's, especially the latter's notion of presensation—the telling what others will probably feel on the basis of what we feel. Dilthey puts it this way: "On the basis of experience and self-understanding and the constant interaction between them, understanding of other people and their expressions of life is developed" (116). This is remarkably close to Hume's position. And Dilthey writes: "Now they [people's deeds or actions and the institutions they forge, like the law] stand as signs of a mental content which once existed, as the remnant which survives" (76). Whereas Hume fashions it this way: "When any affection is infus'd by sympathy, it is at first known only by its effects, and by those external signs in the countenance and conversation, which convey an idea of it. This idea is presently converted into an impression, and acquires such a degree of force and vivacity, as to become the very passion itself, and produce an equal emotion, as any original affection" (T,II,I,XI). It is descriptions of sympathy like this that lead me to take issue with Farr's account. This passage and others suggest that Hume's understanding of sympathy was in line with those of his eighteenth-century contemporaries, notably Adam Smith and Edmund Burke whom Farr cites (306), which were ones of empathetic projection.[25] I think Hume's notion of sympathy is *both* one of empathetic projection, as the above passage and his employment of Shaftesbury's presensation testify to, *and* a principle of communication of signs (and/or effects).[26] So it is a much stronger view of sympathy than the others. I would like to believe Farr's anachronistic account of Hume, but I do not think Hume conceived sympathy along the lines of contemporary *Verstehen* theory—maybe Dilthey's version of it, but none of the later versions. The new problem of *Verstehen* focuses on questions of linguistic communication (308f). Dilthey, like Hume, claims more than communication. He states that: "It is only possible to grasp it [the past] through the reconstruction of the course of events in a memory which *reproduces* not the particular event but the system of connections and the stages of its development" (73; emphasis added). However, Hume was interested in larger units of communication (LUCs), and Farr is right about this.

Hume wanted to account for how government "*spreads* a national character" and "communicates ... a similarity of manners" (E,204: emphasis added). In "the annals of history," Hume continues reference to LUCs or what Dilthey called "systems," by which the latter meant things like government, economic life, education, etc.: "These systems have sprung from the same human nature as I experience in myself and understand in others" (66); compare Hume's "we shall discover everywhere signs of a sympathy or contagion of manners, none of the influence of air or climate" (E,204). The focus of history is LUCs or the phenomenon of contagion, or what Hume elsewhere called "a superior sensibility" (IM,49). The historian must inflame himself or herself, then communicate those "impetuous movements" (E,104) to his or her audience: Hume probably did this with his Montrose Character.[27] Consequently, this process is very similar to Collingwood's enactment idea or Dilthey's notion of empathy (74). Since Hume downplayed reason in so many human activities, like moral decisions and situations, he needed something to function in a similar fashion, and what he arrived at was sympathy. It had to play the roles of projection and communication in Hume's theories of history and social life. Good written history, like his *History of England*, was literally to transform the reader—to distill or spread the British national character, in addition to strengthening the moral character of its audience. Hume's use and account of sympathy in history has a distinctively *a priori* flair about it, as Farr points out (289ff.). This is perhaps a reason why Hume has been labeled as a rationalist historian. Donald Livingston was one of the first philosophers of history to appreciate this dimension of his thought and to see that "moral accounts are the main form of explanation used in Hume's *History of England*."[28] Livingston illustrates this with Hume's explanation of why Henry VII did not assume the title of conqueror after violently seizing the throne (H,III,6): "These views of Henry are not exposed to much blame, because founded on good policy, and even on a species of necessity." Livingston explains: "What Hume tried to show is that given Henry VII's intention, his conception of his situation, and the policy he was determined to follow, the act performed was the rational thing to have done. The 'species of necessity' under which Henry VII found himself is the sort framed in moral accounts, the rational necessity of not doing what, given the reasons he had, would have been patently foolish or absurd" (59). Historical explanations, like Hume's explanation of Henry VII's decision about the kind of title he would assume to the crown or any of the other accounts above, are rational explanations rather than causal ones. "Rational explanations," Farr reminds us, "rely for their force, not on general laws [as in causal explanations], but on actors' reasons for acting, whether in situations which are regular and uniform, or irregular and extraordinary" (57). Farr goes on to demonstrate that these two models of explanation are indeed operative in Hume's writings—models primarily developed in the *Essays* and put into practice in the *History*. I have tried to show here that Hume's rational explanations of human actions and decisions usually involve moral "judgments" or sentiments that are activated by sympathy and "tested" (and sometimes presented) by presensation. Hume uses this psychological apparatus, Farr rightly concludes, "not so much as an empirical theory, but as a rough-and-ready test or criterion for acceptable evidence in history and the moral sciences. In this way we can distinguish fact from fantasy, moral reality from miracles, and still appreciate the diversity of history amidst the uniformity of human nature" (76).[29]

Farr claims that Hume's use of the expression "we enter so deep into" is a misleading metaphor (308). Given my account of sympathy, I think the metaphor is appropriate, and that it does raise serious questions about its status in Hume's overall philosophy.[30] To answer these claims, I think we need to follow Nicholas Capaldi's lead in "Hume as Social Scientist" and argue for an "interpretationism" being present in Hume's thought; "That is, all explanations must make reference to the conscious interpretation which social participants give of their behavior" (113). This is evident from the Montrose and Wolsey Characters in addition to the other passages from the *History* which I have amassed here. My claim is that we learn more from Hume on this issue by comparing him to Dilthey and Collingwood than to positivistic thinkers or those under the sway of positivism like Butterfield. We now turn to Hume and the historiography of science, and here again we find Butterfield immensely helpful.

EIGHT

THE HISTORIOGRAPHY OF SCIENCE

The period in which the people of Christendom were the lowest sunk in ignorance, and consequently in disorders of every kind, may justly be fixed at the eleventh century, about the age of William the Conqueror; and from that era, the sun of science beginning to reascend, threw out many gleams of light, which preceded the full morning when letters were revived in the fifteenth century. (Hume, H, II,508)

In this final chapter I shall examine David Hume's historiographical category of Character (whenever I refer to this concept with the word, it shall be capitalized) and its application to important figures and institutions in the history of science that appear in his *History of England*. This aspect of Hume's thought has not been given much attention, at least not in reference to his *History*. Its six volumes were published between 1754 and 1762, a time when we first see the emergence of the history of science, and Hume played a part in narrating that beginning even though it has gone largely unnoticed. From the over forty Characters in the *History* we find ones such as Francis Bacon, the Royal Society, the French Academy of Science, Robert Boyle, William Harvey, and Isaac Newton. Hume evidently intended his Characters to be adopted by future historians.[1] By "Character" Hume means an account of an eminent person or group which he reduces to types associated with their profession or contribution (in this case science), their station in life, and their relation to the government or reign. Characters form an integral part of his historical narrative by supplying the needed periodization besides the usual annual chronology. Conjoined to these brief intellectual biographies and narrative descriptions of the European scientific groups are numerous other historical references to science that nicely illustrate Hume "adorning the facts."[2] Consequently, when these episodes are viewed together, we may legitimately claim that Hume was one of the first cultural historians of science and specifically that he had an interest in accounting for the growth or development of what we now call "science" in Great Britain.

Hume used the term "science" in two common senses: (1) a broad use as in the phrase "arts and sciences" when we speak of colleges housing those disciplines, or as in the title of Hume's essay "Of the Rise and Progress of the Arts and Sciences." Any body of knowledge organized by principles is called a science; for instance, the law would qualify under sense (1). This is the Aristotelian conception of science. There is also (2) a narrow use that is synonymous with natural philosophy or experimental science. These senses of "science" are usually distinguishable from the context. It is interesting to note that Hume, like Voltaire, did use "science" occasionally to mean natural or experimental philosophy—a practice that did not become common until the early nineteenth century.

At the outset let me declare that there are four fundamental issues in the historiography of science that Hume addresses in one way or another. The nature of scientific change is the first. Hume views notable change in science as comprising both gradual and sudden (radical) shifts in perspective and theory. As evidence, the prefatory passage indicates that he did not conceive of the progress of science in one steady upward movement of refinement in our understanding of nature. Rather, his idea of progress involves setbacks and reascents. Progress is sometimes met with decline, and then decline is often followed by rise in achievement. Such a view is atypical for the Enlightenment, for most Enlightenment thinkers, e.g., Voltaire, held to a gradual theory of scientific progress, ending, at their present time or where they wished to end their narrative, with Newton. Hume did not think of Newton as the crowning achievement of natural (experimental) philosophy. Contrary to the scholarship on this subject, I argue that William Harvey (1578-1657) is Hume's paradigm of *achievement* in natural or experimental philosophy, and the emphasis in my argument below is on experimental.

The second issue involves the portraiture of outstanding figures or events in the history of science. What is the point of such portraits? Such questions lead to a third issue that pertains to the placement of science with a viewpoint or historical context. Hume is opposed to the view (known as internalism) that science is an isolatable, autonomous system and that the great scientific geniuses are the bearers of this system.[3] From such a perspective science is abstracted from its historical setting and handled "objectively" or in an isolated fashion as if nothing from the outside affected it. In the *History of England* especially, Hume positioned science within a cultural-social process or history and appreciated their mutual interaction.

The last issue is Hume's ambivalence on the origin of science. Is it early or relatively late? He thought it was the latter until he narrated Britain's early history—then he changed his mind. The two views were never reconciled in the *History*. Part of the explanation is that he changed his discussion from unrestricted to restricted (national) considerations.

Auguste Comte (1798-1857) is usually considered by historians to be the first thinker to call for a synthetic history of science in which the emphasis is placed on the unity of science and its interplay with other parts of social, political, and cultural life.[4] My general contention is that Hume made the call before Comte. A set of new questions is asked about Hume's writings from a context previously not associated with him. What place, for Hume, does science occupy in history in general? What is Hume's overall picture of the history of science in England? What is Hume's general theory about this history of science, and how does it correspond to his theory of history? How do Hume's views arise from, and depart from, the views of earlier thinkers? And how does he view historical change in science? The evolution of the historiography of science begins here.[5]

It is well known among Hume scholars that Hume employed Character as a historiographical concept in his *History*,[6] but the variety of that use is still not fully appreciated. Most scholars examine his use of it with the British regal figures like Queen Elizabeth or famous religious and social individuals like Martin Luther and Joan of Arc. Below we shall encounter his use of Character with Bacon, Boyle, Harvey, Newton, and others. I shall also appraise them by placing them within their context and then within the broader view of the history of science.

Francis Bacon

Perhaps the most well known Character of a scientist in Hume's *History* is that of Francis Bacon, although there is some debate in the literature as to whether he is deserving of the title of scientist. Since Hume compares Bacon to Galileo and makes a reference to Kepler, I shall give Bacon's Character in full. It also gives us a good representation of that historiographical concept. As Hume narrates,

The great glory of literature in this island [sic] during the reign of James [I], was Lord Bacon. Most of his performances were composed in Latin; though he possessed neither the elegance of that, nor of his native tongue. If we consider the variety of talents displayed by this man, as a public speaker, a man of business, a wit, a courtier, a companion, an author, a philosopher, he is justly the object of great admiration. If we consider him merely as an author and philosopher, the light in which we view him at present, though very estimable, he was yet inferior to his cotemporary Galilaeo, perhaps even to Kepler. Bacon pointed out at a distance the road to true philosophy: Galilaeo both pointed it out to others, and made himself considerable advances in it. The Englishman was ignorant of geometry: the Florentine revived that science, excelled in it, and was the first that applied it, together with experiment, to natural philosophy. The former rejected, with the most positive disdain, the system of Copernicus: the latter fortified it with new proofs, derived both from reason and the senses. Bacon's style is stiff and rigid: his wit, thought often brilliant, is also often unnatural and farfetched; and he seems to be the original of those pointed similes and long-spun allegories which so much distinguish the English authors: Galilaeo is a lively and agreeable, though somewhat a prolix writer. But Italy, not united in any single government, and perhaps, satiated with that literary glory which it has possessed both in ancient and modern times, has too much neglected the renown which it has acquired by giving birth to so great a man. That national spirit which prevails among the English, and which forms their great happiness, is the cause why they bestow on all their eminent writers, and on Bacon among the rest, such praises and acclamations as may often appear partial and excessive. He died in 1626, in the 66th year of his age. (V,153-54)

There are three consequential points to be made concerning this Character. First, Hume holds that in order to assess historically a British scientist's place in the history of science, one must have an international context. National or regional considerations will not do for the history of science, although Hume falls victim to this latter view in the earlier periods of the history of England. Second, Hume's statement that Bacon "rejected, with the most positive disdain, the system of Copernicus" implies that his rejection of Copernicanism was the result of an imperious and unreasonable bias. Others who agreed with Hume's assessment are Karl Popper, who thought that Bacon "sneered at those who denied the self-evident truth that the sun and the stars rotated around the earth, which was obviously at rest,"[7] and Anthony Quinton.[8] In a more recent study, Peter Urbach corrects this distorted view of Bacon by showing that Bacon questioned empirically the earth's motion and concluded tentatively.[9] Urbach concludes that "Bacon never sneered at the heliocentric theory, nor did he come to, or advance, his opinion in the high-handed and intemperate manner which is insinuated" (131).

A third point concerning Hume's observation that Galileo "fortified it [the system of Copernicus] with *new* proofs, derived both from reason and the senses" (emphasis added) shows us that Hume thought that science does advance sometimes by sudden leaps. I point this out to correct an account given by Bernard Cohen in *Revolution in Science*, who unfortunately restricts

his discussion to a solitary passage from Hume's *Treatise*, so that his account
is inadequate in many respects.[10] The Bacon Character at least suggests that
Hume thought that what Copernicus and Galileo had done was more "than an
improvement" (Cohen's phrase) in the previous system of the world or astronomy. Whether or not Hume perceived this situation in the history of science
as a revolution is not altogether clear from the Bacon Character. "New" for
Hume could be "revolutionary," but the former was not ordinarily associated
with the latter term. The latter obviously was a political term for him (Cohen
points this out, 521), because he selected it among other things in discussing
the Glorious Revolution of 1688. Here Hume was just consciously following
the practice of previous historians in calling the 1688 event a revolution.
Besides the word "revolution," he sometimes used "reformation,"[11] although
he did use the word "revolution" once in connection with science in discussing "mighty innovations made in religion [1453]. Thus a general revolution was made in human affairs throughout this part of the world and men
gradually attained that situation, with regard to ... science" (III,81). However,
this passage suggests by its wording that Hume still means "improvement" or
simply "notable change."[12] Cohen claims that the term "revolution" was not
used in the sense of a radical departure or fundamental change until after 1789
with the French Revolution, and Hume's usage usually conforms to this observation.

But there are some interesting examples in Hume's writings that are decidedly ambiguous. One passage suggests a political sense in addition to the word's
old repetitious, cyclical meaning:

Philosophy can only account for a few of the greater and more sensible events of this
[mental] *war*, but must leave all the smaller and more delicate *revolutions*, as dependent
on principles too fine and minute for her comprehension. (T,438; emphases added)

In the sentence before this one Hume speaks of the "*struggle* of passion and
reason" that diversifies and intensifies human life. However, Hume seems to
have possessed the strong concept of revolution. In the essay "Of Eloquence"
he opens with these thought-provoking sentences:

Those, who consider the periods and revolutions of human kind, as represented in history, are entertained with a spectacle full of pleasure and variety, and see, with surprize,
the manners, customs, and opinions of the same species susceptible of such *prodigious
changes* in different periods of time. It may, however, be observed, that in *civil* history,
there is found a much greater uniformity than in the history of learning and science ....
(E,97; emphasis added)

"Revolutions" is probably used in the political sense, and Hume contrasts civil history with intellectual history—where the latter is subject to more abrupt changes. Hume's explanation for this is that learning and science are dependent upon education and example (98), whereas civil history is governed by the common passions (97). This characterization opens up interpretive possibilities with contemporary historiography of science.

In any case Hume has the main actors in the dramatic chronology of the history of science in place and has also briefly assessed their importance. As he remarked, "If we consider [Bacon] merely as an author and philosopher [scientist], *the light in which we view him at present,* though very estimable, he was yet inferior to his cotemporary Galilaeo, perhaps even to Kepler" (emphasis added). Who is possibly included in Hume's "we" shall be discussed below. So for science in the early seventeenth century, Hume's list so far includes: Copernicus, Galileo, Kepler, and Bacon. And presentism appears to be one of the views that Hume adheres to in the historical narration of science.

Robert Boyle

Concerning Boyle, Hume reports that

Boyle improved the pneumatic engine, invented by Otto von Guericke, and was thereby enabled to make several new and curious experiments on the air, as well as on other bodies: his chemistry is much admired by those who are acquainted with that art: his hydrostatics contain a greater mixture of reasoning and invention with experiment than any other of his works; but his reasoning is still remote from that boldness and temerity which had led astray so many philosophers. Boyle was a great partisan of the mechanical philosophy; a theory which by discovering some of the secrets of nature, and allowing us to imagine the rest, is so agreeable to the natural vanity and curiosity of men. He died in 1691, aged 65. (VI,541)

This Character appears at the end of Hume's discussion of the reign of James II. Hume's common practice is to close a given reign with the status of learning during that particular age, moving from uniformity to diversity of human nature. This is one reason why learning and science are usually delegated to appendices in the *History*. Earlier Hume had remarked, "Amidst the thick cloud of bigotry and ignorance, which overspread the nation, during the commonwealth and protectorship, there were a few sedate philosophers, who, in the retirement of Oxford, cultivated their reason, and established conferences for the mutual communication of their discoveries in physics and geometry" (VI,540). Hume mentions that after the Restoration these men procured patents and eventually formed the Royal Society of London in 1660. He condemns Charles II for supporting his courtiers and mistresses rather than the sciences but nevertheless calls him a "lover of the sciences, particularly chemistry and mechanics." Hume contrasts this situation with the one in France where:

the French academy of science was directed, encouraged and supported by the sovereign, [and] there arose in England some men of superior genius who were more than sufficient to cast the balance, and who drew on themselves and on their native country the regard and attention of Europe. Besides Wilkins, Wren, Wallis, eminent mathematicians, Hooke, an accurate observer by microscopes, and Sydenham, the restorer of true physic [medicine]; there flourished during this period a Boyle and a Newton; men who trod with cautious, and therefore the more secure steps, the only road which leads to true philosophy. (VI,541)

Again, international context is needed for a true or accurate contrast and comparison. Joseph Agassi is one of the few scholars who has placed Hume in the context of the historiography of science.[13] Agassi notes Hume on this account:

Hume had already criticized Bacon, but only to the extent of saying that Bacon was inferior to Galileo since the former only pointed the way, while the latter both pointed the way and travelled on it. Hume did not refer to Bacon's errors, and thus treated him more leniently than he treated Boyle, though he must have known that Boyle's errors were negligible by comparison. See Hume, *History of England*, Appendix to "Reign of King James I." (V,153-54)

I am not sure how Agassi arrived at his comparative judgment that Hume treated Bacon more leniently than Boyle. In comparing just the two Characters, it seems to me the converse—that he treated Boyle more leniently than Bacon—which is in keeping with what Hume does with Bacon elsewhere.[14]

It should be recalled in this connection that in the history of science there are two methods commonly employed in the post-Butterfield era (ca. 1950): the diachronic, which traces the history of one idea or a cluster of ideas, and the synchronic, which studies an individual scientist (e.g., Newton) and the affairs of his day.[15] Hume practices only the synchronic method, and that in an embryonic stage. His creation of a place for the sciences and scientists in his *History* may be seen as part of his secularization and broadening of the scope of British history. British histories prior to Hume's contained no historical accounts of science and scientists, or at least not to the extent that Hume's did. So much for the context; let us now turn to the Boyle passage itself.

In the opening sentence Hume cites, in conjunction with Boyle, the German experimentalist Otto von Guericke (1602-86), who is most famous for his experimental studies of air pressure—for Hume, significant enough to include in his discussion.[16] How Hume knew of von Guericke is not known, but his experiments were widely discussed during Hume's era, and it was perhaps through sources at the Advocates' Library (see note 41) that he knew of them. More specifically, he may have learned of these experiments from Voltaire.[17] But there are other possible sources, too.

Hume's Acquaintance with Science

At the age of sixteen young David had already distinguished himself in his course of study at the University of Edinburgh. Among those works he probably studied was Newton's *Principia*, or at least he knew of its content.[18] At this time (1727) Colin Maclaurin (1698-1746) was lecturing on mathematics and Newton's *Principia*. Maclaurin had taken up the chair in 1725, which is the year Hume left the University, "or perhaps not until 1726," Mossner conjectures.[19] Maclaurin's wife, Anne, published his book, *An Account of Sir Isaac Newton's Philosophical Discoveries* (London, 1748), posthumously; and it was undoubtedly a product of those lectures that Hume must have heard or with whose ideas he was at least acquainted. Anne Maclaurin writes in her "An Account of the Life and Writings of the Author" that "After this the mathematical classes soon became very numerous, there being generally upwards of an hundred young gentlemen attending his lectures every year."[20] Hume was probably not among those young gentlemen (since he was at the University from 1723 to 1725 or 1726), but he at least picked up the mathematics in a less formal setting. If he read Malezieu's *Elements*,[21] he could have easily read lecture notes from some acquaintance who was one of those fortunate young gentlemen who attended Maclaurin's lectures. The first book of Maclaurin's *Account*, entitled "Of the Method of Proceeding in Natural Philosophy, and the Various Systems of Philosophers," contains chapters from the ancient philosophers down through Descartes's followers (Spinoza and Leibinz) and ending with a detailed discussion of Newton's theory of motion that Maclaurin calls Rational Mechanics. Maclaurin's account follows a generally chronological order, so that in a rudimentary sense this work can be viewed as an analytical history of science or as expressing internalism. An earlier book that could have influenced Hume here also is Joseph Glanvill's *Plus Ultra, or The Progress and Advancement of Knowledge Since The Days of Aristotle* (1668).[22] This work was widely read and discussed during Hume's youth. Both of these works in one way or another probably influenced Hume to think about science in Great Britain as a historical phenomenon. Hume shows us that he is acquainted with the debate between the Cartesian and Newtonian theories of nature in the essay "Of the Rise and Progress of the Arts and Sciences":

What checked the progress of the CARTESIAN philosophy, to which the FRENCH nation shewed such a strong propensity towards the end of the last century, but the opposition made to it by the other nations of EUROPE, who soon discovered the weak sides of that philosophy? The severest scrutiny, which NEWTON'S theory has undergone, proceeded not from his own countrymen, but from foreigners; and *if* it can overcome the obstacles, which it meets at present [1742] in all parts of EUROPE, [then] it will *probably* go down triumphant to the latest posterity. (E,121-22; emphases added)

When Hume wrote this description of the controversy, he may have forgotten about or may not have known Berkeley's criticisms of Newton (see note 42). In addition to Copernicus, Galileo, Kepler, Bacon, von Guericke, Boyle, Descartes, and Newton, Hume was aware of Tycho Brahe (1546-1601) and his importance to the Copernican revolution in astronomy; and in "Of National Characters," he remarks, "An ENGLISHMAN will naturally be supposed to have more knowledge than a DANE; though TYCHO BRAHE was a native of DENMARK" (E,198). In "The Idea of a Perfect Commonwealth" Hume mentions Christiaan Huygens (1629-95) as the inventor who determined the "figure of a ship, which is the most commodious for sailing" (E,513).

There is also Hume's friend Adam Smith (1723-90), who wrote "histories" of science in the chronological sense. In the early 1740s Smith wrote *The History of Astronomy* and *The History of the Ancient Physics*. As D. D. Raphael and A. S. Skinner point out in their General Introduction to Smith's *Essays*,[23] Hume had an influence on these works that stemmed from the *Treatise*. But it is also quite possible that the influence ran in the other direction, too: Hume perhaps got the idea of writing a narrative history, not just a chronological history, from Smith. In any event the idea of the history of science was clearly in the air of Scotland and France at this time, and surely Smith, Maclaurin, Glanvill, and Voltaire all had contributed in one way or another to Hume's innovative idea. The prefaces of university courses such as that given by David Fordyce (1711-1751) in 1743-44 who saw all knowledge having the same "Origin, Progress and several Revolutions"—a point which he would probably say came from Shaftesbury. Fordyce's short piece prefaced lectures on philosophy and are not unlike the preface-like pieces done by Smith somewhat later. Hume could have very well come into contact with Fordyce's piece in addition to Smith's pieces.

Hume's inclusion of Boyle's Character helps us see that Hume championed the experimental sciences in the later periods of British history. Boyle was the major advocate of experimentalism; in the late 1600s he had to defend experimental practices from Hobbes's criticism of them and of the invention of the air pump.[24]

Isaac Newton

Newton's curious Character, which immediately follows that of Boyle, reads as follows.

In Newton this island may boast of having produced the greatest and rarest genius that ever arose for the ornament and instruction of the species. Cautious in admitting no principles but such as were founded on experiment [presumably referring to *"hypotheses non fingo"*], but resolute to adopt every such principle, however new or unusual: from modesty, ignorance of his superiority above the rest of mankind, and thence less careful to accommodate his reasoning to common apprehensions; more anxious to merit than to acquire fame; he was from these causes long unknown to the world; but his reputation at last broke out with a luster which scarcely any writer, during his own lifetime, had ever before attained. While Newton seemed to draw off the veil from some of the mysteries of nature, he showed at the same time the imperfections of the mechanical philosophy; and thereby restored the ultimate secrets to that obscurity, in which they ever did and ever will remain. He died in 1727, aged 85. (VI,542)

By "the imperfections of the mechanical philosophy" Hume probably had in mind (a) the hypothesizing of hidden or underlying mechanisms, e.g., gravity, in explaining motion by invoking "occult" forces, as Boyle, too, had done, and (b) the necessity for God to be present to periodically "wind up" the universe since it tends to run down (with an analogy to a clock).[25] Hume's reading of Newton as "cautious in admitting no principles but such as were founded on experiment" is a common one and probably owes something to Maclaurin's *Account* or his lectures. Hume's allusion to Newton being "long unknown to the world" probably refers to his poverty from which Edmund Halley frequently rescued him.

In "Of the Middle Station of Life" Hume makes a synoptic judgment about Galileo and Newton that should not go unnoticed in a discussion of this sort:

Were we to distinguish the Ranks of Men by their Genius and Capacity more, than by their Virtue and Usefulness to the Public, great Philosophers [scientists] wou'd certainly challenge the first Rank, and must be plac'd at the Top of human Kind. So rare is this Character, that, perhaps, there has not, as yet, been above two in the World, who can lay a just Claim to it. At least, *Galilaeo* and *Newton* seem to me so far to excel all the rest, that I cannot admit any other into the same Class with them. (550)

Here Hume adds Galileo to the first rank, whereas in Hume's opening remark on Newton's Character, Sir Isaac is the only one admitted to this superlative class, perhaps because Hume's *History* is a national history.

William Harvey

Outside of Boyle, William Harvey is perhaps the most interesting Character from our topical perspective:

Harvey is entitled to the glory of having made, by reasoning alone, without any mixture of accident, a capital discovery in one of the most important branches of science. He had also the happiness of establishing at once his theory on the most solid and convincing proofs; and posterity has added little to the arguments suggested by his industry and ingenuity. His treatise of the circulation of the blood is further embellished by that warmth and spirit which so naturally accompany the genius of invention. This great man was much favored by Charles I., who gave him the liberty of using all the deer in the royal forests for perfecting his discoveries on the generation of animals. It was remarked that no physician in Europe, who had reached forty years of age, ever, to the end of his life, adopted Harvey's doctrine of the circulation of the blood; and that his practice in London diminished extremely, from the reproach drawn upon him by that great and signal discovery. So slow is the progress of truth in every science, even when not opposed by factious or superstitious prejudices. He died in 1657, aged 79. (VI,153-54)

This passage exhibits two recurring themes in Hume's *History*: first, references to individuals with regal power and their role in the rise of science in Great Britain, in this case to Charles I; and second, Hume's anti-religious bias, which is indirectly exhibited in his statement about the progress of truth and about superstitious prejudices. The sociohistorical facts give Hume a chance to discuss bigotry and prejudice against important scientists. Hume used the Harvey Character to comment on the nature of the medical profession of the time (1650s). Hume's phrase "superstitious prejudices" also probably referred to the blind adherence to medical tradition. Similarly Thomas Kuhn says: "Nor do scientists normally aim to invent new theories, and they are often intolerant of those invented by others."[26] Physicians over forty in Europe were under the influence of Descartes's theory of the heart as a furnace more than Harvey's, which explained the function of the heart as a pump. One of the reasons why "posterity has added little to the arguments suggested by his industry and ingenuity" is that medicine *returned* to Harvey's explanation after giving up Descartes's.

Despite Cohen's assertion that Hume "gives no clue whether he believes science advances by sudden great leaps forward or by steady and gradual progress" (521), Hume actually claims the former, especially as seen in "Of Eloquence" (E,97). This is also appreciated in the Harvey Character, in which he calls Harvey's theory "a *capital* discovery" and adds that the theory is established on "proofs." By "proof" Hume means something is established by intuition, i.e., that it is self-evident and certain (Descartes's criteria), and by sensual demonstration (as opposed to instruction), i.e., that the circulation of the blood can be *self-administered*, i.e., that other scientists could easily replicate Harvey's demonstration.

Hume's position seems to imply that there are some "revolutions" in the sense of sudden great leaps, not only slow gradual change. For him the seventeenth century is probably revolutionary in this sense. But unlike other Enlightenment thinkers, Hume did not think of scientific change solely as slow steady progress or advancement, which was to culminate in Newton or the refinement of Newtonian physics, as did the French Encyclopedists. Moreover, as a historian he also believed in the *decline* of science. In his account of the Anglo-Saxon government and manners (I,160), Hume adds in an appendix that "*Military despotism ... had sunk the genius of men, and destroyed every noble principle of science* [sense 1] *and virtue ...*" (emphasis added). Such examples come from antiquity or the medieval period and not the modern era; whether Hume thought his own age might see a similar decline is an open question. However, a passage in the *Dialogues Concerning Natural Religion* suggests that he thought decline in the sciences during his age was not only possible but likely. In a reply to Philo, Cleanthes remarks:

Those who reason from the late origin of arts and sciences, though their inference wants not force, may perhaps be refuted by considerations derived from the nature of human society, which is in continual revolution, between ignorance and knowledge, liberty and slavery, riches and poverty; so that it is impossible for us, from our limited experience, to foretel with assurance what events may or may not be expected. (D,Part VI; other uses of the word in this sense follow.)

As we have seen, Hume does use the word "revolution" in an archaic sense meaning repetition. Obviously "*continual* revolution" is no "revolution" (in Cohen's sense) at all. Also this use still has a political context and has not been applied to science except for the opening reference to the "arts and sciences."

The Harvey Character is a good instance of Hume "adorning the facts"; for example, "This great man was much favored by Charles I" and "embellished by that warmth and spirit which so naturally accompany the genius of invention." Another interesting thing about the passage is the statement that follows it. Hume remarks that "This age affords great materials for history; but did not produce any accomplished historian." The statement would, it seems, include contextually the passage on Harvey; and it is equally plausible that science is an instance of the "great materials for history," even though the statement is a synoptic judgment. So in referring to the age as a whole, Hume demonstrates that this is so by the several passages on science in his volume on the Stuarts.

The *Dialogues* passage on "revolution" in Part VI (quoted above) implies the following query: Is Hume an advocate of the early or late origin of science? From the first few volumes of the *History* it appears that he was committed to the early origin of science, but later in the narrative, 1625, he seems to change to the late origin of science view. Let us look at the early view first.

Early British Science

Hume's treatment of the ancient and medieval periods usually lacks specific references to science, but he does make a few explicit references to the development of science in ancient Britain.[27] One good illustration of this is in his discussion of Alfred the Great:

But the most effectual expedient, employed by Alfred for the encouragement of learning, was his own example...that he might more exactly measure the hours, he made use of burning tapers of equal length, which he fixed in lanterns, an expedient suited to that rude age, when the geometry of dialling and the mechanism of clocks and watches were totally unknown. (I,80)[28]

References like the above to the status of scientific knowledge during given historical periods are fairly numerous. Related to the rise of mechanical measurements of time is Hume's mention of the different calendars used by the British and Roman priests and that these were computed with the aid of astronomical considerations (of the courses of the sun and moon).[29] In his discussion of King Alfred, Hume comments, "But we should give but an imperfect idea of Alfred's merit, were we to confine our narration to his military exploits, and were not more particular in our account of his institutions for the execution of justice, and of his zeal for the encouragement of arts and sciences" (I,75). He adds, "Those who cast their eye on the general revolutions of society will find, that, as almost all improvements of the human mind had reached nearly to their state of perfection about the age of Augustus, there was a sensible decline from that point or period; and man thenceforth relapsed gradually into ignorance and barbarism" (II,519). As in his reference to astronomical considerations, Hume provides the reader with an idea of the level of medical science at the time of Edward VI (mid-1500s). He narrates the incident of the King's physicians being dismissed because they were making him more ill and the admission of a medically ignorant woman to take over Edward's care! (III,398). Of Julius Agricola he remarks,

He [Agricola] introduced laws and civility among the Britons, taught them to desire and raise all the conveniences of life, reconciled them to the Roman language and manners, instructed them in letters and science, and employed every experience to render those chains which he had forged both easy and agreeable to them. (I,10)

Outside of royal patronages contributing to the development of science in ancient Britain, Hume considers two factors important in the stimulation and rise of modern science—the printing press and the discovery of the New World. Of the first, Hume says:

The art of printing, invented about that time [1453], extremely facilitated the progress of all these improvements [navigation, geography, astronomy, etc.]: the invention of gunpowder changed the whole art of war: Mighty innovations were soon after made in religion, such as not only affected those states that embraced them, but even those that adhered to the ancient faith and worship: And thus a general revolution was made in human affairs throughout this part of the world; men gradually attained that situation, with regard of commerce, arts, science, government, police [policy], and cultivation, in which they have ever since persevered. (III,81)

Not only science itself but also its historiography was stimulated by printing. The historian had much more material to select and work from after the emergence of the printing press. The last clause in this passage, "men gradually attained that situation, with regard of commerce, arts, science, government, police, and cultivation, in which they have ever since persevered," strongly implies the idea of progress that we find in other historians of the Enlightenment. Hume continues:

Here, therefore, commences the useful, as well as the more agreeable part of modern annals; certainty has place in all the considerable, and even most of the minute parts of historical narration; a great variety of events, preserved by printing, give the author the power of selecting, as well as adorning, the facts which he relates. (III,81-82)

This passage from the *History*—especially Hume's mention of "adorning the facts"—provides a better context for what he means by "moral reasoning" (reasoning with particulars) in history than in most of his other writings.

Hume also seems to suggest that the discovery of the New World served as a stimulus for invention and progress in art and industry and by implication in the sciences. For instance:

It was during this reign [Henry VII] ... that Christopher Columbus, a Genoese, set out from Spain on his memorable voyage for the discovery of the western world; and a few years after, Vasquez de Gama, a Portuguese, passed the Cape of Good Hope, and opened a new passage to the East Indies. The great events were attended with important consequences to all the nations of Europe, even to such as were not immediately concerned in those naval enterprises. The enlargement of commerce and navigation increased industry and the arts everywhere. (III,80)

The immense number of references throughout the *History* to geography indicate that Hume considered it an important factor in any kind of history. He regarded geographical factors as "physical causes," and he defines them as follows: "By *physical* causes, I mean those qualities of the air and climate which are supposed to work insensibly on the temper, by altering the tone and habit of the body, and giving a particular complexion, which, though reflection and reason may sometimes overcome it, will yet prevail among the generality of mankind, and have an influence on their manners" (E,198). When we survey the English histories before him we understand why he did this: he was apparently the first British historian to give geography any importance, either for its own sake or as a factor in history. For example, "Greenland is thought to have been discovered about this period" (IV,144 [1625]). Geography is still considered significant to the rise of scientific thought, but not as much as Hume thought and in a different way.

Science Narrated

Besides Hume's narration of the development of science in Great Britain and his historiographical principles that invoke science as subject matter for his *History*, there are many instances that show that he used science as well as politics and religion as a historical category. Hume inferred states of affairs from the absence of scientific inventions and activity. For example, in an appendix called "The Anglo-Saxon Government and Manners," Hume speculated that "It is easy to imagine that an independent people, so little restrained by law and cultivated by science, would not be very strict in maintaining a regular succession of their princes" (I,161). Later in the next appendix Hume indicates the difficulty under which early scientists in Britain had to work. "The barons and gentry ... gave no encouragement to the arts, and had no demand for any of the more elaborate manufactures: Every profession was held in contempt but that of arms" (I,463). However, Hume mentions some learning. In regard to the Kingdom of Mercia, he writes: "That emperor [Charlemagne] being a great lover of learning and learned men, in an age very barren of that ornament, Offa, at his desire, sent him over Alcuin, a clergyman much celebrated for his knowledge, who received great honours from Charlemagne, and even became his preceptor in the sciences" (I,42).

When discussing even earlier English history, Hume states that "the knowledge of natural causes was neglected [by the Saxons], from the universal belief of miraculous interpositions and judgments" (I,51).[30] This "negative inferential approach" is, from a contemporary point of view, a way of covering a historical situation where there is no positive evidence available, and it reveals something about the historian's knowledge of given periods, or the lack thereof. Hume speaks many times about "ignorance." "The perfidious prince [Offa]," Hume says, "desirous of reestablishing his character in the world, and perhaps of appeasing the remorses of his own conscience, paid great court to the clergy, and practised all the monkish devotion so much esteemed in that ignorant and superstitious age" (I,41-42). One may well ask, ignorant of what? Hume's answer would be the arts and sciences. Here Hume is typical of Enlightenment historians who are severe, nonsympathetic judges of ages deficient in arts and sciences.[31] This implicit frame of reference runs throughout the *History* and indicates, among other things, that Hume was attentive to the status and development of the sciences in different periods.

In accord with this bias or frame of reference, Hume usually notes rather harshly the absence of science in any given period. For example, in his discussion of the manners of the Anglo-Saxons, he comments: "The [Norman] conquest put the people in a situation of receiving slowly, from abroad, the rudiments of science and cultivation, and of correcting their rough and licentious manners" (I,85). This negative inferential approach is indicative of Hume's use of science as a category for the *History*. A statement that somewhat removes the condemning character of his judgments, though it makes a negative inferential point, is that:

Every science ... must be considered as being yet in its infancy [1625]. Scholastic learning and polemical divinity retarded the growth of all true knowledge. Sir Henry Saville, in the preamble of that deed by which he annexed a salary to the mathematical and astronomical professors in Oxford, says, that geometry was almost totally abandoned and unknown in England. The best learning of that age [James I] was the study of the ancients. (V,155)

There are three general points in the above passage that need to be emphasized in evaluating Hume's *History* from the standpoint of the historiography of science. First, we have to turn to the *Treatise* to find a description of the state of natural philosophy before Copernicus:

Here, therefore, moral philosophy is in the same condition as natural, with regard to astronomy before the time of *Copernicus*. The ancients, tho' sensible of that maxim, *that nature does nothing in vain*, contriv'd such intricate systems of the heavens, as seem'd inconsistent with true philosophy, and gave place at last to something more simple and natural. To invent without scruple a new principle to every new phaenomenon, instead of adapting it to the old; to overload our hypotheses with a variety of this kind; are certain proofs, that none of these principles is the just one, and that we only desire, by number of falsehoods, to cover our ignorance of the truth. (282; Hume's emphases)

And in "The Sceptic," Hume discusses the merits of the Ptolemaic and Copernican systems (E,164-65).

The second point is Hume's recognition that science was still in its "infancy" during the 1600s. One factor contributing to the development of science in Great Britain was individuals who promoted science but who themselves were not considered scientists or who did not contribute directly to the advancement of science by novel experiments or hypotheses. Hume's inclusion of Sir Henry Saville indicates such a class of individuals. Also, from Hume's historical generalization about the infancy of science the philosophical historian has to infer implicitly that he formulated his judgment on the basis of the dependence of science upon regal individuals. This is in part due to his use of Character as a historiographical concept in his history.

Third, Hume's estimation of scholastic theology is questionable and has been criticized by philosophical historians and by historians of history.[32] His antireligious bias is one of the cornerstones of his emphasis upon science. Moreover, his *History* pictures historical movement or change in terms of basic conflicts between organized religion and early modern science, as they are manifested in individuals or groups. Within this conflict, the interpretation he finds most suitable is that organized religion stifles man's genius and liberty, thus slowing down or stagnating the processes of history. Science, on the other hand, has advanced man historically toward enlightenment. The "sun of science" metaphor in the *History* (II,508) makes this point abundantly clear. Clarifying this movement is one of the chief values that Hume places on the writing of history as a way to make the past intelligible and instructive for the reader. He wrote about the English nation in terms of its struggle, which involved the development of science. His thoughts are vividly illustrated in the following passage:

All the efforts of the great Bacon could not procure an establishment for the cultivation of natural philosophy.... The only encouragement which the sovereign in England has ever given to any thing that has the appearance of science, was this short-lived establishment of James [a College at Chelsea]; an institution quite superfluous, considering the unhappy propension which at that time so universally possessed the nation for polemical theology. (V,132)

The illustrations of science within a historical perspective, as in the Bacon example above, have been mainly negative; that is, instances of science are coupled with instances of religion. But there are exceptions, such as his Character of Sir Henry Saville.[33] To judge from the variety of references cited, Hume was interested in writing more than just an outline of the history of science on the British Isles. In his *History* he includes not only individuals who may have made scientific contributions or practiced the activity but also those who supported the scientific enterprise by promoting it in one way or another, such as Alfred the Great. Hume's idea of history emerges from what he includes in the history of England; this shows that the history of science is an integral feature of his general conception of history and that he viewed science as a cultural-social process.[34]

Aside from such figures as Alfred the Great and Sir Henry Saville, Charles I and Charles II are also granted significance in the rise of science in Britain. For Hume both of these kings are more important than any other individuals in this respect in his *History*. For instance, Hume remarks that Charles II's "genius, happily turned towards mechanics had inclined him to study naval affairs, which, of all branches of business, he both loved the most and understood the best" (VI,446). As Hume points out, the kings did two significant things in promoting the rise of science in Britain: Charles I encouraged Harvey's anatomical research, and Charles II gave a patent for the formation of the Royal Society.

Some Objections Considered

One possible objection to my presentation of the above Characters of scientists is that I portray Hume as intending those to be an integral part of his narrative. I think that this is not just appearance but is reflected in his theory of history.

Toward the close of his discussion of the reign of Richard III (d. 1485) Hume concludes: "Thus have we pursued the history of England through a series of many barbarous ages; till we have at last reached the dawn of civility and science, and have the prospect, both of greater certainty in our historical narrations, and of being able to present to the reader a spectacle more worthy of his attention" (II,518). It is here that we find Hume advocating the late origin of science. Notice he says "the dawn of civility and science" and not that they have been reached—perhaps that attainment would be nearly a century later with the founding of the Royal Society of London and its illustrious members like Boyle and Newton. What would constitute the dawn of science, especially around 1485 in Great Britain? Inspecting the first three volumes of the *History* as I have done above gives us an idea of what Hume had in mind, but of course that "dawning" is also determined by what came in later periods. We have seen inventions such as the printing press and mechanized clocks, and discovery of the New World as well as those individuals and events that led to the dawning of science.

Again, one of the best expressions of Hume's philosophy of history comes from his narration of the reign of Richard III:

The rise, progress, perfection, and the decline of art and science, are curious objects of contemplation, and intimately connected with a narration of civil transactions. The events of no particular period can be fully accounted for, but by considering the degrees of advancement which men have reached in those particulars. (II,519)

Besides having historiographical implications, this statement concerning the objects of history is a justification of his inclusion of the state of learning and science in the *History*. It is not until the nineteenth century with Burkle, Marx, and Engels that historians begin to appreciate the interrelationship that Hume sees between scientific and political and economic developments. Hume also deals with this subject more topically or with a synchronic approach in his essay "Of the Rise and Progress of the Arts and Sciences."[35] The sciences, Hume speculates, arose in Greece because its geographical regions were naturally divided into several distinct governments; i.e., the regions give rise to their governments. Hume later gives up the geographic theory for a great man theory of the history of science, probably because he could see the weakness in the former. Harvey's Character clearly suggests the great man theory, along with the Character of the French academy of science. Men of superior genius in England offset the organized efforts of the French sovereign. Hume was not an inductivist historian of science who painted scientists as black or white with the criterion of whiteness being the up-to-date Newtonian science textbook.[36]

Besides the merits of inclusion there are the sins of omission. One particular glaring example is William Gilbert, best known for his work on magnetism (1600). Apparently Hume was unaware of Gilbert, from the remarks he made in his narration of the period in which Gilbert lived. In his discussion of Queen Elizabeth, Hume mentions the queen's physicians in passing (IV, 350) but does not note that Gilbert was among them.[37] (Hume's omission of Gilbert and his relationship to Elizabeth I colors his whole account of the queen and her reign.) Another omission—that of John Locke—comes from the history of medicine. In fact there is not a Character of Locke at all—even as a philosopher. William Turner, who is recognized as a pioneer or the father of English botany in the sixteenth century, is absent from Hume's *History*, and so is Dr. Henry Power (1623-68) and his microscopical experiments.[38] A fifth is Edmund Halley, whose feats in astronomy were well known and given more space in the *Annual Register* (1759) than Isaac Newton's anecdote (1772).[39] Halley's omission is doubly interesting because, as Westfall puts it, "History has agreed that without Halley, who not only encouraged Newton but financed the publication from his own slender resources, the *Principia* would not have been written" (151); and Newton himself acknowledges his indebtedness to Halley in his Preface. If Hume had read this, he could hardly have left Halley out. But he probably did not read it or at least failed to appreciate its importance. A more understandable omission is the British medieval pair Robert Grosseteste (ca. 1175-1253) and Roger Bacon (ca. 1214-95), both of whom devoted themselves to scientific investigations. Bacon wrote on experimental science in the *Opus Majus*, Grosseteste wrote a treatise on light and gave a rudimentary account of the rainbow, and no history of science in Great Britain would be complete without them.

Even though the recital of the history of science in Hume's *History* is primarily dependent upon secondary, historical sources,[40] this aspect of his historical work is one of his original contributions to the development of modern history as we know it today. In fact he expanded the Advocates' Library holdings which included scientific materials while he was the Keeper. W. K. Dickson relates:

It is in additions made to the Library ... that the personality of a Librarian best appears. The purchase lists during the greater part of Hume's Keepership are preserved. They cover a wide range of literature, chiefly foreign books, standard classics, and works in jurisprudence, history, and science.[41]

As Barfoot mentions, Hume was a member of the Physiological Library of Edinburgh (151f) and he had an ongoing interest in science, which manifests itself at the Advocates' Library and throughout his writings (and I have tried to show here that this includes his *History* in a significant way).

Conclusion

In "Of Civil Liberty" Hume writes that science is still in its infancy:

Men [e.g., Thomas Sprat, Locke, and Bacon are mentioned (E,91)], in this country, have been so much occupied in the great disputes of *Religion, Politics,* and *Philosophy,* that they had no relish for the seeming minute observations of grammar and criticism. And though this turn of thinking must have considerably improved our sense and reasoning; it must be confessed, that, even in those sciences above-mentioned, we have not any standard-book, which we can transmit to posterity: And the utmost we have to boast of, are a few essays towards a more just philosophy; which, indeed, promise well, but have not, as yet, reached any degree of perfection. (E,92)

Given what Hume has said about Newton, I think he would have included Newton in this group, especially in light of what Hume said of Newton in "Of the Rise and Progress of the Arts and Sciences" (E,121-22) which I quoted above.

From the Characters we have surveyed, it seems Harvey is the one whose work is for posterity. Recall that Hume speaks with unqualified superlatives:

Harvey is entitled to the glory of having made, by reasoning alone, without any mixture of accident, a capital discovery in one of the most important branches of science. He had also the happiness of establishing at once his theory on the most solid and convincing proofs; and posterity has added little to the arguments suggested by his industry and ingenuity. His treatise of the circulation of the blood is further embellished by that warmth and spirit which so naturally accompany the genius of investigation. (VI,153)

Harvey's treatise, *De Motu Cordis* (*The Motion of the Heart* [1628]), appears to be one of those few essays that have reached a degree of perfection and may rightfully be called a "standard-book" (E,92). So it is at least curious that Hume did not include Harvey in the first rank of men (along with Galileo and Newton). This is surprising, because one would suspect that Newton would have the most praiseworthy Character and that his *Principia* would be the "standard-book." But in "Of the Rise and Progress of the Arts and Sciences" Hume makes it clear that word is still out on Newton's theory: "*if* it can overcome the obstacles which it meets at present [1742] in all parts of Europe, it will *probably* go down triumphant to the latest posterity" (E,122; emphasis added).

Apparently Hume had his doubts here—maybe it was Berkeley's criticism[42] of Newton's concepts of absolute space and time—but not about Harvey's treatise.

This situation is also reflected in the *Treatise*, where in the conclusion of Book Three Hume describes himself as an "anatomist," and as having "proceed[ed] in the accurate anatomy of human nature, having fully explain'd the nature of our judgment and understanding" (I,IV,VII) at the end of Book One. In the section (XII) "Of the Pride and Humility of Animals" we can see the enormous influence of Harvey on Hume's methodology of the *Treatise*, and it is worth quoting in full here:

'Tis usual with anatomists to join their observations and experiments on human bodies to those on beasts, and from the agreement of these experiments to derive an additional argument for any particular hypothesis. 'Tis indeed certain, that where the structure of parts in brutes is the same as in men, and the operation of these parts also the same, the causes of that operation cannot be different, and that whatever we discover to be true of the one species, may be concluded without hesitation to be certain of the other. Thus tho' the mixture of humours and the composition of minute parts may justly be presum'd to be somewhat different in men from what it is in mere animals; and therefore any experiment we make upon the one concerning the effects of medicines will not always apply to the other; yet as the structure of the veins and muscles, the fabric and situation of the heart, of the lungs, the stomach, the liver and other parts, are the same or nearly the same in all animals, the very same hypothesis, which in one species explains muscular motion, the progress of the chyle, the circulation of the blood, must be applicable to everyone; and according as it agrees or disagrees with the experiments we may make in any species of creatures, we may draw a proof of its truth or falsehood on the whole. Let us, therefore, apply this method of enquiry, which is found so just and useful in reasonings concerning the body, to our present anatomy of the mind, and see what discoveries we can make by it. (325-26)

In the first *Inquiry* (section IX, "Of the Reason of Animals") Hume makes the same point: "The anatomical observations formed upon one animal are, by this species of reasoning [analogy], extended to all animals; and it is certain that, when the circulation of the blood, for instance, is clearly proved to have place in one creature, as a frog or fish, it forms a strong presumption that the same principle has place in all" (112). Such confident, laudatory descriptions of the anatomy and physiology of his day make it clear that Harvey rather than Newton was Hume's idol of scientific achievement. Why? Because Harvey's experiments are ones the readers can perform on themselves—they can convert the ideas into impressions.[43] One cannot do this with the motion of the planets, or very few natural philosophers were in the position to do so.

In light of twentieth-century philosophy and history of science, this Humean perspective is most unusual and intriguing. The "measurement" or periodization for the seventeenth century is no different *in movement* from the previous ones. Copernicus made one change, Kepler another, and so on. Pierre Duhem (1905) held a view similar to Hume's but for different reasons: "What are generally assumed to have been intellectual revolutions have almost always merely been slow, long prepared evolutions.... Respect for tradition is an important precondition for scientific progress."[44] The early history of England that Hume narrated strongly suggests that he would have agreed with Duhem. In "Of Commerce," Hume defines historical change: "A long course of time, with a variety of accidents and circumstances, are requisite to produce those great revolutions, which so much diversify the face of human affairs" (E,260).

In "Of National Characters," Hume laments:

All the sciences and liberal arts have been imported to us from the south [Greece and Italy]; and it is easy to imagine, that, in the first ardor of application, when excited by emulation and by glory, the few, who were addicted to them, would carry them to the greatest height, and stretch every nerve, and every faculty, to reach the pinnacle of perfection. Such illustrious examples spread knowledge everywhere, and begot an universal esteem for the sciences. (E,210)

These "illustrious examples" are the Characters of Bacon, Boyle, Harvey, Newton, and the rest. Hence the purpose of the history of science is to spread knowledge of the sciences and "beget an universal esteem for the sciences." But this is generally true of intellectual history. It is true of the English literature found in the *History*. Indeed, E. C. Mossner years ago made the observation that if Hume's "character-sketches" of British authors were collected together, they would constitute the first "History of English Literature."[45] Mossner's observation is even more true of science because even though Hume's historical remarks on science are limited to the "Miscellaneous Transactions," "Notes," and "Appendices," they play a prominent role in the *History*—in the narrative itself as part of the story of England. Science and philosophy foster "a manly, steady virtue, ... [the] calm sunshine of the mind" (NH, 73). And for the sun of science to shine it must be given a place where it may radiate. Historical change in Hume's narrative is not just political. Within a political framework, one finds social, economic, and intellectual forces at work.

Hume was not unique in what he had done historically with science. As I said earlier, Voltaire had popularized science in his philosophical and historical writings. In the *Revolution in Science* Cohen even goes so far as to declare that: "This is all the more remarkable in that Voltaire recognized how significant and fundamental were the creations in science of such major founding figures as Galileo and Newton" (204). The same may be said of Hume. He went beyond Voltaire in the way he wove the history of science into a national, political history and appreciated their interaction. Foreseeing that progress in the history of science was partially dependent upon regal figures was an insight not appreciated until the next century.

EPILOGUE

In the preceding chapters but especially the last two chapters we have seen major developments of the rise of modern history in the hands of David Hume. First, the shift in the audience or readers of Hume's *History* was something he sought to address: "an audience neither of politicians nor antiquarians [i.e., men], but of those who aspired to participate in polite conversation" [men and women] (284). David Wootton continues: "This gave history a new role: that of retelling a story already told. We take it for granted that there will be more than one history dealing with a particular subject [like we do with multiple interpretations of works of art], but to those living in the eighteenth century there was something novel about this idea" (*ibid.*). If one wanted to learn about English history, one would read the chronicles and histories, for example, those of Edward Hyde, Earl of Clarendon (1609-74). These historical pieces were regarded as self-sufficient narratives. Hume revised this notion by treating them as mere sources—histories to be re-written. (He also thought that few people were capable of making sense of all the source material; consequently, someone like himself was needed to interpret the mass of information.) "At the heart of Hume's undertaking," Wootton surmises, "was, therefore, a novel, and largely unstated, conception of progress in historical knowledge" (285). This had an impact on Hume's philosophy of history.

As Wootton draws the map:

When we speak nowadays of the philosophy of history we sometimes mean to refer to the detailed philosophical analysis of the nature of historical evidence, and sometimes to large-scale theories that claim to identify a pattern or a meaning in the course of history. Hume was familiar with both sorts of philosophy of history. He would not have thought it unreasonable to regard his history as a test of the large-scale theories of James Harrington (1611-77), Charles-Louis de Secondat, baron de Montesquieu (1689-1755), and Anne-Robert-Jacques Turgot, baron de l'Aulne (1727-81), who would have been in his eyes the most important exponents of the second sort of philosophy of history. (290)

Wootton then paints Hume as pro-Harringtonian, although Hume gave commerce more importance than Harrington (292). It is difficult for several reasons to trace Montesquieu's influence on Hume, but their thinking is so close that "reading Montesquieu can help in the interpretation of Hume's *History*" (293). One such place is in the historiography of science (chapter 8). It is useful to think about historical topics in Scotland, like the cultural history of science, with reference to two French writers whom Hume knew well—Charles Rollin (1661-1741) and Montesquieu. In his *Ancient History*,[1] Rollin adopted a pattern of historical analysis which originated with the Greeks, was refined by the Renaissance chorographers and was still in vogue among antiquarians and travel writers in 1750. He dealt with people's arms, trade, laws, government, customs and beliefs (both religious and other) and with their arts and sciences (=learning). Rollin had no good way of relating these historical sectors, but they got covered—however skimpily. What he thought they all reflected was the spirit of a people or their national character.

Montesquieu, I think, took these categories and showed how they impacted and changed one another.[2] He began this enterprise in the *Persian Letters* (1717-21) and continued it with greater clarity and explicitness in *The Spirit of Laws* (1748). This gives, then, a rationale for the history of science. But Montesquieu never wrote one, never even considered science in his great work, although in the 1720s he did speculate on the motives underlying work in the sciences.[3] By 1748 Henry Home or Lord Kames (1696-1782) had probably come to the conclusion that just as law changes with society and all its aspects, so too do learning and science. For him and for others that would be natural philosophy, so these thinkers should be included with Hume, Voltaire, and others as those beginning the cultural history of science before Comte that I discussed in chapter 8.

Additionally, Turgot, Wootton supplies, "had little influence on Hume, but his views provide a helpful contrast to Hume's own" (295). One such contrast is that "[h]istory itself, in Hume's view, provided no grounds for any faith in providence, even in the secularized form of a belief in the inevitability of progress" (295). As we saw in chapter 8, Hume believed that there were declines as well as progresses in human history. It may be true that "Hume never claimed to identify a single *esprit* running through all aspects of the life of an epoch" (295), but he does talk of National Character, like Rollin and Montesquieu did. Also I might add his history had shown that there is progress in civilization even though there may be temporary setbacks.

Now a brief word on the politics of the *History*. Wootton surveys various views in regard to this matter. These views tend to oversimplify its politics: "To make sense of Hume's *History*, we must take more seriously than commentators usually do the fact that his is a narrative history describing changing social and political circumstances. Hume's emphasis on change was, indeed, one of the most original aspects of his history" (298). Hume's politics in the *History* are close to the court Whig position (299), but his politics are Parliamentary and not Royalist, "in its account of the period from 1604 to 1641, and Parliamentary again in its account of the period from 1681 to 1688" (301). Towards the end Wootton concludes "Hume thus writes in favour of the mixed constitution to which both moderate Parliamentarians and Royalists aspired in 1641, and which was finally established in 1688. Towards the end of the *History*, he tells us that the English have established 'the most entire system of liberty, that ever was known amongst mankind' (H,VI,531), and, in one of the volumes written last, he claims that the main utility of history lies in instructing us to cherish the present constitution" (H,II,525) (306-07). Hume worried about how to balance stability with liberty, a concern which became a major issue for political philosophy to address after the late eighteenth-century.

Hume provides the philosopher of history with a unique opportunity in that he was both a philosopher and a historian. These were not separate pursuits for Hume. As Nicholas Phillipson argues: "For Hume's historical reasoning is so cogent and so carefully regulated by philosophical distinctions that it soon became clear that revising his revisionism would be a matter of attacking metaphysical premises [like the principles of human nature] rather than facts."[4] Much of Books Two and Three, "Of the Passions" and "Of Morals," of the *Treatise* finds its way into Hume's historical narrative, especially in his understanding of royal and military personages. Few historians have had the ambition and opportunity to think through the principles of human nature as Hume did. For most historians, an ordinary grasp of these principles is all they work with. Due to his circumstances, Hume earned the title of philosophical historian. But there was more to it than this. I have tried to show in the preceding pages that Hume had a philosophic concern for history throughout all of his writings. We see this is manifest from the *Treatise* and the *Essays* to the *Inquiries* and the *History*. Historiography is something Hume thought about both theoretically and practically.

Given what I have argued in the previous pages—that history is a central idea in Hume's overall philosophic program—what are we to make of the traditional appellation of "empiricism" to his philosophical outlook? Don Garrett lists five kinds of empiricism and each one can, in some measure, be attributed to Hume (29-40). Donald Livingston introduces a sixth—historical empiricism.[5] The claim of empiricism as a family of concepts is that all knowledge is derived from experience. Historical empiricism is a better identification of Hume's philosophy, Livingston explains, "because Hume's conception of experience has more affinity with the notion of historical experience as understood by the English Common Law tradition and the Latin rhetorical tradition in philosophy, as exemplified by Cicero, than with an empiricism which views sense experience as the historical foundation against which scientific theories are tested" (7) [which is what Garrett means by methodological empiricism]. Historical experience has a backward-looking character to it and it is used to understand the present. Again, Livingston says,

The present is understood to be what it is because of the past, because of traditions and customs built into it. And the greatest wisdom is not what an individual following a rational "method" can discern but the knowledge spontaneously collected by many generations, often working in ignorance of each other, and deposited in traditions, customs, and conventions. It is a philosophy whose favorite way of understanding something is to tell a story about its origins. (6)

Telling stories of the origins of things or events in philosophy, for Hume, employs the notion of historical narration. Hence the importance he gives it along with custom to the Humean enterprise (see chapter 5). Written history and lived history are essentially the same for Hume. The task of the historian is to recreate (represent) the past in such a way that the same emotions and feelings of historical figures can be relived (see chapter 7), but this is also true of any writer (see chapter 6). Knowledge begins with experience and experience, we have seen, is extended by history for Hume. He begins with a very narrow conception of experience (ideas derived from corresponding impressions) and expands this because of philosophical encounters (like the missing shade of blue thought experiment) and the study and practice of history. Hume was the first philosopher who took history seriously. In the first *Meditation* Descartes dismissed history as a source of confusion and error. With "the general demolition of my [Descartes's] opinions" (12) goes history. For Hume, history is one of the sources for understanding human nature. In Hume's own words, "history is not only a valuable part of knowledge, but opens the door to many other parts, and affords materials to most of the sciences" (E,566). The rest of the essay "Of the Study of History" provides an elaboration of this positive view of history.

I am reminded of Annette Baier's characterization of Hume's "Philosophy in This Careless Manner" (ch.1) when Hume ends the essay on history with these choice lines:

When a philosopher contemplates characters and manners in his closet, the general abstract view of the objects leaves the mind so cold and unmoved, that the sentiments of nature have no room to play, and he scarce feels the difference between vice and virtue.

History keeps in a just medium betwixt these extremes, and places the objects in their true point of view. The writers of history, as well as the readers, are sufficiently interested in the characters and events, to have a lively sentiment of blame or praise; and, at the same time, have no particular interest or concern to pervert their judgment. (E,568)

History warms the mind so that the sentiments have room to play, and hence, philosophy may be done in a "careless manner" and be a progress of thought and sentiment (T,120,455; Baier, viii). The upshot of this is to produce a humane, virtuous person. Towards the end of *The Natural History of Religion*, Hume writes:

Whatever weakens or disorders the internal frame promotes the interests of superstition: And nothing is more destructive to them than a manly, steady virtue, which either preserves us from disastrous, melancholy accidents, or teaches us to bear them. During such calm sunshine of the mind, these spectres of false divinity never make their appearance. (NH,73)

By "the calm sunshine of the mind" Hume means, in the words of Donald Siebert, that "the temper of the genuinely moral individual is an ideal of cheerful equanimity. It is to that moral ideal that Hume aspired in his own life."[6] This is close to the description Hume gives in the essay "My Own Life":

To conclude historically with my own character. I am, or rather was (for that is the style I must now use in speaking of myself, which emboldens me the more to speak my sentiments); I was, I say, a man of mild dispositions, of command of temper, of an open, social, and cheerful humour, capable of attachment, but little susceptible of enmity, and of great moderation in all my passions. (E,xl)

History warmed the mind whereby there could be the calm sunshine. As we saw in chapter 8, the metaphor is used by Hume to characterize the impact of science on civilization, "the sun of science" (H,II,508). But when speaking of individuals, it is "a manly, steady virtue" which produces the "calm sunshine of the mind." History strengthens virtue for Hume, so it contributes along with philosophy: "while we ourselves, during their, [opposing species of superstition] fury and contention, happily make our escape into the calm, though obscure, regions of philosophy" (NH,76). I hope our escape here in the region of philosophy of history has not been too obscure. Descartes thought there was not such a region; Hume thought it was the most important of them all. Hume personified history and philosophy as he conceived of them, but also the philosophy of history as I have portrayed them here.

NOTES

Introduction

[1]Although Hume exhibits a definite historical interest in the *Treatise* and in earlier juvenile writings, this claim about the *Treatise* is fairly noncontroversial; see S. K. Wertz, "When Did Hume Plan a History?" *Southwest Philosophical Studies* III (April 1982): 30-33. But Hume's historical interest is part of a larger philosophical project; see the rest of the Introduction and the following chapters.

[2]The phrase "the origin of ideas," or "the way of ideas" as I prefer to call it since Hume considerably broadened its meaning, comes from the opening section heading of the *Treatise* (I, I, I) and from section II, "Of the Origin of Ideas," in the *Inquiry Concerning Human Understanding*. In 1689 John Locke spoke of it as "Of Ideas in general, and their Original" [i.e., origin] in *An Essay Concerning Human Understanding*, edited by P. H. Nidditch (Oxford: Clarendon Press, 1975), Book II, chapter I. Hume clearly has a Lockean project in mind. "The Way of Ideas" is a phrase that comes from the correspondence of Thomas Reid (1710-1796), a friend and able critic of Hume and the founder of the Scottish school of common-sense philosophy that flourished well into the nineteenth century.

[3]R. G. Collingwood, *The Idea of History* (London: Oxford University Press, 1946), 75. For this work (hereafter IH) and the others, parenthetical page references are made in the body of the text after an initial citation in the notes. Bracketed phrases are added.

[4]Donald W. Livingston, "Hume on the Problem of Historical and Scientific Explanation," *The New Scholasticism* XLVII #1 (Winter, 1973): 38-67; and his *Hume's Philosophy of Common Life* (Chicago: University of Chicago Press, 1984).

[5]John W. Danford, *David Hume and the Problem of Reason: Recovering the Human Sciences* (New Haven: Yale University Press, 1990).

[6]Annette C. Baier, *A Progress of Sentiments: Reflections on Hume's "Treatise"* (Cambridge, Massachusetts: Harvard University Press, 1991), says "I take his *Treatise* to be one work. It appeared serially, first two of its books, then the third, and in my view we understand none of them properly unless we understand all of them, and the progression or thought within the work as a whole" (vii).

[7]Peter Jones reminds us that "we must recognize that for him" [Hume], literature "was

a very general category which included history and philosophy" in "Hume's Literary and Aesthetic Theory," in *The Cambridge Companion to Hume*, edited by David Fate Norton (Cambridge: Cambridge University Press, 1993), 258.

[8]See the author's "Descartes and the Argument by Complete Enumeration," *Southwest Philosophy Review* XV #1 (January 1999): 137-147.

[9]"The new approach," (which is to indulge his [Hume's] readers' sentiments) Baier says, "is to be careless in the older sense, carefree rather than negligent" (1). Hume's "most perfect character" (IU, 17-18) exemplifies this spirit of philosophy. History's contribution to this "new approach" is discussed in chapter 7.

1: The Status of the System

[1]Charles W. Hendel, *Studies in the Philosophy of David Hume* (New Edition; Indianapolis: Bobbs-Merrill, 1963), Appendix III: "On Space and Time: Correction of Former Errors," 498-504, which includes William T. Parry's criticisms from an unpublished paper. Their story is used to introduce the topic of systematicity.

[2]For example, there is no entry for "system" or its cognates in the Subject Index of Roland Hall's *50 Years of Hume Scholarship: A Bibliographical Guide* (Edinburgh: Edinburgh University Press, 1978), 148. Also there is no entry for "system" in the Selby-Bigge index to the *Treatise*, although there is an entry in the index for the *Enquiries*, for which three references given all refer to social groups. Perhaps the reason that there is no entry for "system" in the Selby-Bigge index to the *Treatise* is that Hume nowhere discusses what a system is or what he means by the word "system." Nevertheless, for that very reason an entry for "system" would have been especially helpful. The meaning or meanings that "system" has for Hume will have to be gleaned from the occasions in which he uses the term. This chapter is a beginning of this undertaking.

[3]Ernest Campbell Mossner, *The Life of David Hume* (Edinburgh: Nelson, 1954), 76. Elsewhere, Mossner describes Hume's *Treatise* as "the most sustained and systematic of his works"; see his introduction to his edition of the *Treatise* (London: Penguin Books, 1969), 7.

[4]Sir Isaac Newton, *Philosophiae Naturalis Principia Mathematica* (London, 1687), and translated by Andrew Motte, 1729, as *Sir Isaac Newton's Mathematical Principles of Natural Philosophy and His System of the World*, revised by Florian Cajori (Berkeley: University of California Press, 1946). It has been recently suggested that Hume was a more careful student of Newton and the calculus than has been claimed by people like James Noxon, *Hume's Philosophical Development: A Study of His Methods* (Oxford: Clarendon Press, 1973), Part II, and Peter Jones, *Hume's Sentiments: Their Ciceronian and French Context* (Edinburgh: Edinburgh University Press, 1982), ch. 1. I learned at the Hume Conference at the University of Lancaster, U.K., August 1989, that Professor M. A. Stewart had examined a handwritten manuscript of Hume's that was a recitation

of calculus problems. Unfortunately the manuscript was purchased by a private individual who has not made it available to scholars. Stewart testified to the manuscript's authenticity. And if we can take Stewart's word (and I think we can here), the manuscript shows that Hume knew enough mathematics that he could have read *Principia* and appreciated its line of thought. See Stewart's "Introduction," 8-9, and Michael Barfoot, "Hume and the Culture of Science in the early Eighteenth Century," in *Studies in the Philosophy of the Scottish Enlightenment*, edited by M. A. Stewart (Oxford: Clarendon Press, 1990), 151-190; specifically, "On the basis of my [Barfoot's] brief examination of the manuscript ["A Treatise of Fluxions" (1726)], it seems likely that Hume was an advanced student of mathematics" (190, note 76). Newtonianism manifests itself in numerous ways in Hume's system, but perhaps the most evident application is in Newton's "Rules of Reasoning in Philosophy," 398-400, which Hume judiciously follows in formulating the elements of his system. For instance, Hume refers to *Principia*, Book III, The System of the World, and "Newton's chief rule of philosophizing" at the end of Section III, Part II, of the second *Inquiry*, 34. See also James E. Force, "Hume's Interest in Newton and Science," *Hume Studies* XIII #2 (November 1987): 166-216, although Force is mainly interested in the *Dialogues*, the *Essays*, and the *History of England*; and see my chapter 8.

[5]Anthony Ashley Cooper, Third Earl of Shaftesbury, *An Inquiry concerning Virtue, or Merit*, edited by David Walford (Philosophical Classics; Manchester: Manchester University Press, 1977), 9.

[6]Robert Fendel Anderson, *Hume's First Principles* (Lincoln: University of Nebraska Press, 1965), xxiii: "This examination will employ all of Hume's philosophical writings. It will be assumed that in each he is presenting this system, or some aspect of that system."

[7]By "interpretive application," I mean a guess or hypothesis of what the whole means and that it guides us through difficult passages and issues.

[8]Humphrey Palmer, Review of *Humes verborgener Rationalismus (Hume's Hidden Rationalism)* by Lother Kreimendahl, *Hume Studies* X #2 (November 1984): 174-180, see 178.

[9]John Locke, *An Essay Concerning Human Understanding*, edited by P. H. Nidditch (Oxford: Clarendon Press, 1975), 654 (Bk. IV, ch. 15, para 1): "demonstration is the shewing the Agreement, or Disagreement of two *Ideas*, by the intervention of one or more Proofs, which have a constant, immutable, and visible connexion one with another. . . ." For Hume, see the *Treatise*, esp. 31-32, 161, for passages that echo Locke's definition.

[10]I am indebted to David Owen on this point—one of several he made in his paper "Hume and the Lockean Background: Induction and the Uniformity Principle," which he read at the Hume Conference held at the University of Lancaster in August 1989 and subsequently published in *Hume Studies* XVIII #2 (November 1992): 179-207.

[11]Later Hume anticipates objections: "I doubt not but these consequences ['the mind is *determin'd* by custom" and "Tis this impression, then, or *determination*, which affords me the idea of necessity"] will at first sight be receiv'd without difficulty, as being evident deductions from principles, which we have already establish'd, and which we have often employ'd in our reasonings. This evidence both in the first principles, and in the deductions, may seduce us unwarily into the conclusion [the denial of the above consequences], and make us imagine it contains nothing extraordinary, nor worthy of our curiosity" (156). Newton's fourth Rule of Reasoning in Philosophy is manifestly identifiable in these passages.

[12]Thomas Reid, *An Inquiry into the Human Mind on the Principles of Common Sense*, in *Thomas Reid's Inquiry and Essays*, edited by Ronald E. Beanblossom and Keith Lehrer (Indianapolis: Hackett Publishing Company, 1983), 108-109; Reid's emphasis.

[13]Hans Lenk of the University of Karlsruhe first drew my attention to Kreimendahl's work, *Humes verborgener Rationalismus* (Berlin and New York: Walter de Gruyter, 1982).

[14]David Pears, *Hume's System: An Examination of the First Book of His "Treatise"* (Oxford: Oxford University Press, 1990). For a review of this book which contains this criticism, see William Davie, *Bulletin of the Hume Society* XXI #1 (Spring 1992): 4; and Annette Baier's study *A Progress of Sentiments: Reflections on Hume's "Treatise"* (Cambridge, Massachusetts: Harvard University Press, 1991).

[15]See the extended discussion of identity in Section II of Part IV, Book One, of the *Treatise* for a particularly good example of the generation of one of these fictions.

[16]R. G. Collingwood, *The Principles of Art* (London: Oxford University Press, 1938/1958), 295-296; emphasis added.

[17]I wish to thank Houghton B. Dalrymple of the University of Texas at Arlington for his insightful comments on an earlier draft of this chapter. He assisted me in sharpening its focus. Among his numerous perceptive articles on Hume, I found his "Hume's Difficulties with Dispositions," *Southwest Philosophical Studies* (Fall 1987), particularly helpful.

[18]For a critical discussion of the argument in this chapter, see A. Mark Williamson, "Hume's Systematicity," *Southwest Philosophy Review* X #2 (July, 1994): 189-192.

2: The Missing Shade and Its Implications

[1]The same passage occurs in the first *Inquiry*, IU, 29.

[2]See, e.g., Don Garrett, *Cognition and Commitment in Hume's Philosophy* (New York: Oxford University Press, 1997), ch. 2 (esp. 50ff) and 3 (esp. 73ff); Karann Durland, "Hume's First Principle, His Missing Shade, and His Distinctions of Reason," *Hume Studies* XXII #1 (April 1996): 105-121; John Losee, "Hume's Demarcation Project," *Hume Studies* XVIII #1 (Apr. 1992): 51-62; Reginald O. Savage, "Hume's Missing

Shade of Blue," *History of Philosophy Quarterly* IX #2 (Apr. 1992): 199-206; John O.
Nelson, "Hume's Missing Shade of Blue Re-Viewed," *Hume Studies* XV #2 (Nov. 1989):
353-363; D. M. Johnson, "Hume's Missing Shade of Blue Interpreted as Involving
Habitual Spectra," *Hume Studies* X #2 (Nov. 1984): 109-124; John Morreall, "Hume's
Missing Shade of Blue," *Philosophy and Phenomgical Research* XLII #3 (Mar. 1982):
407-415; and Robert Cummins, "The Missing Shade of Blue," *The Philosophical Review*
LXXXVII #4 (Oct. 1978): 548-565.

[3]It might prove useful to have a contemporary summational account of color to serve
us in the evaluation of Hume's account. I draw upon Stephen Davies's *Definitions of Art*
(Ithaca: Cornell University Press, 1991): "If parts of the world are differentiated across
continua (that is, with each part grading imperceptibly into the next and, hence, not being
clearly demarcated from the next), then the way in which we categorize those parts of
the world reveals as much about us as it reveals about the world's structure. Rather than
discovering the world's natural boundaries, we, as observers, impose our own divisions
upon its continuities. The colors are not natural property kinds (and, of course, neither
are they natural substance kinds such as those just mentioned). Although yellow and vio-
let are quite different colors, the color spectrum contains within it no discontinuities to
work a natural boundary between the two. Because color classifications are made by us
and are not merely discovered in the world, they do not simply map its natural divisions.
The number of colors into which we divide the range reveals something of the percep-
tual discriminations of which we are capable and something of the importance that color
discrimination plays in the conduct of our lives. Our classification of the world's colors
is not indifferent, as it is supposed to be in the case of natural kinds, to the fact that we
are (have been/might be) present in the world as describers of it. Accordingly, the defining properties of colors will be relational, since what makes a color what it is is a function of the properties of observers as well as of the properties of light wavelengths and
the like. The relational character of the definition will be more or less emphasized in
accordance with the particularity or universality of the relation. On the one hand, if all
human beings discriminate the primary colors, for example, then the relation drops out
of account. If something is red to everyone (under standard conditions), then it is red and
not merely red-to-me. On the other hand, if the color distinctions being drawn are finer
than is usual and/or are tied to interests not universally shared (such as those of a person
producing a photographic catalog of the paintings in an exhibition), the relational element must be treated with more care. This would be the case if we were to try to define
the meaning of 'magenta' for example" (23-24; emphases added). For a more complete
account of color, which is beyond the scope of this chapter, see C. L. Hardin, *Color for
Philosophers: Unweaving the Rainbow* (Expanded Edition; Indianapolis: Hackett
Publishing Company, 1993), and for discussion of Hume, see esp. 42, 81, 96, 97, 108,
128, and 140.

[4]For a discussion of complete enumeration as explanation, see Daniel Garber, "Science

and Certainty in Descartes," in *Descartes: Critical and Interpretive Essays*, edited by Michael Hooker (Baltimore, Maryland: Johns Hopkins University Press, 1978), 114-151. Consult Descartes's *Discourse on Method, Rules for the Direction of the Mind, Meditations* III & V, and the *Geometry*. A simple example of complete enumeration is triangles: equilaterial (all three angles are equal), scalene (no two angles are alike), isosceles (two angles are equal, one is smaller), right (one angle is a strong 90 - degree corner), and obtuse (greater than one right angle and less than two). For further discussion, see my essay, "Descartes and the Argument by Complete Enumeration," *Southwest Philosophy Review* XV #1 (January 1999): 137-147.

[5]For a critical discussion of commonality and Wittgensteinian resemblance, see Robert J. Richman, "'Something Common,'" *Journal of Philosophy* LIX #26 (December 20, 1962): 821-830.

[6]David F. Pears, *Hume's System: An Examination of the First Book of His "Treatise"* (Oxford: Oxford University Press, 1990), 25.

[7]Alexander Rosenberg, "Hume and the Philosophy of Science," in *The Cambridge Companion to Hume*, edited by David Fate Norton (Cambridge: Cambridge University Press, 1993), 83.

[8]René Descartes, *Meditations on First Philosophy with Selections from the Objections and Replies*, translated by John Cottingham (Cambridge: Cambridge University Press, 1986), 79.

[9]George Berkeley, *Philosophical Works Including the Works on Vision*, Introduction and Notes by M. R. Ayers (London: Dent, 1975), 10.

[10]George Berkeley, *Three Dialogues between Hylas and Philonous*, edited by R. M. Adams (Indianapolis: Hackett Publishing Company, 1979), 17, 19.

[11]Michael Dummett, "Common Sense and Physics," in *Perception and Identity: Essays Presented to A. J. Ayer with His Replies to Them*, edited by G. F. Macdonald (Ithaca: Cornell University Press, 1979), 1-40, and Ayer's Reply, 277-298, esp. 282-285, and Ayer's "A Defence of Empiricism," in *A. J. Ayer: Memorial Essays*, edited by A. Phillips Griffiths (Cambridge: Cambridge University Press, 1991), 8ff.

3: History and Human Nature

[1]David H. Fischer, *Historians' Fallacies: Toward a Logic of Historical Thought* (New York: Harper & Row, 1970), 203-06.

[2]Kenneth Stampp, *The Peculiar Institution: Slavery in the Ante-Bellum South* (New York: Knopf, 1965), vii. My discussion of Stampp as an example of the fallacy of the universal man varies from Fischer's: mine is couched more in argumentative terms and in the context of inference, where Fischer's is concerned with assumptions. For a criticism of Fischer's general conception of fallacies, see Louis O. Mink's review essay in *History and Theory* X #1 (1971): 107-22, especially 109f.

[3]J. B. Black, *The Art of History: A Study of Four Great Historians of the Eighteenth Century* (New York: Russell & Russell, 1965), 86.

[4]Black, "Hume," *The Art of History*, 77-116. The following historians also adopt the standard interpretation: H. E. Barnes, *History of Historical Writing* (2nd ed., New York: Dover, 1963), 148, 155-59, 167; S. B. Barnes, "The Age of Enlightenment," *The Development of Historiography*, M. A. Fitzsimmons and A. G. Pundt, eds. (Harrisburg: The Stackpole Co., 1954), 155-57; Duncan Forbes, "Introduction," in his edition of Hume's *History of Great Britain* (Baltimore: Penguin Books, 1970), 16; T. P. Peardon, *The Transition in English Historical Writing, 1760-1830* (New York: AMS Press, 1966), 9-23; and J. W. Thompson, *History of Historical Writing*, 2 vols. (New York: Macmillan, 1942), II, 69-72.

[5]Alfred Stern, *Philosophy of History and the Problem of Values* (s'Gravenhage: Mouton, 1962), 147. Stern cites the same passage from the *Inquiry* that Fischer does.

[6]R. G. Collingwood, *The Idea of History* (London and New York: Oxford University Press, 1946), 76 and 82 respectively.

[7]Laurence L. Bongie, *David Hume: Prophet of the Counter-Revolution* (Oxford: Clarendon Press, 1965), 71.

[8]The basis for this can be seen, for example, in the *Treatise* (II,I,XI) where Hume says that our ability to sympathize with others and "to receive by communication their inclinations and sentiments" extends to those whose sentiments are "different from, or even contrary to our own." How this applies to the past I show below and in chapter 7.

[9]William Dray, "Explanatory Narrative in History," *Philosophical Quarterly* IV #1 (1954): 15-27, and his *Laws and Explanations in History* (London and New York: Oxford University Press, 1957).

[10]No doubt there is an unnoticed parallel between Collingwood and Hume on this point of historical epistemology. See note 12 below.

[11]For Hume's discussion of probability, see the *Treatise*, for instance, II,III,I.

[12]Karl Lambert and Gordon G. Brittan, Jr., *An Introduction to the Philosophy of Science* (Englewood Cliffs: Prentice-Hall,1970), 96. Let me digress a moment. These gentlemen would not completely agree with my interpretation, for they (like many others) see the "Humean" account of explanation solely in terms of Hume's famous and overworked analysis of causality. My argument is that Hume's own explanations in the *History*, and their foundations we have seen thus far from the *Treatise*, suggest an alternative view of history and explanation in Hume than the one traditionally painted by those who wish to put Hume in the positivists' camp. I am arguing here that one finds considerable evidence to see the definite beginnings of Bradley's, Collingwood's, and Dray's theories of history and historical explanation in Hume's thought. See 27ff. of Lambert and Brittan for their account of Hume's view.

[13]Black, *The Art of History*, 98.

[14]The idea of "relief by variety" reminds one of Aristotle's *Poetics* (1459a35), in

which he says of the historian that "some episodes ... relieve the uniformity of his narrative," *The Basic Works of Aristotle*, Richard McKeon, ed. (New York: Random House, 1941), 1480.

[15]H,II,464-65. Hume's procedure in documentation is perhaps best seen in H, Vol. I in a note [A] at the beginning in which he discusses the difficulty of writing a history of remote ages. He uses the similarities and dissimilarities of language as a means of historical dating and of inferring what happened among the ancient Britons. Guided by the inferences of earlier historians, Hume says: "We may infer from two passages in Claudian, and from one in Orosius and another in Isodore, that the chief seat of these Scots was in Ireland" (H,I,489-90). The common consensus criterion also explains why Hume's treatment of the ancient and medieval periods is weak; for there were then few known facts, source material, and techniques for handling data relating to those periods, in addition to there being a certain lack of interest on Hume's part. But even this is not wholly true, for he does give an excellent, unprecedented account of the plight of the Jews in medieval England. However, for later historical periods Hume relies less and less on the common consensus criterion.

[16]H,IV,141. An example of a proper inference for a historian to make would be in determining the origin of an event that had significant consequences; for instance, H,III,463: "Then [ca. 1558] seems to have been the first intercourse which that empire [Russia] had with any of the western potentates of Europe." However, Hume probably had more in mind than this. He would also have included political and moral judgments, or at least judgments that are not capable of being true or false by the facts alone, for example, "the best form of government is ...." So on the issue of moral judgments in history, Hume would have sided with those who argue for their inclusion: with Herbert Butterfield, not with Lord Acton; see the former's "Moral Judgments in History," in *History and Human Relations* (New York: Macmillan, 1952), 101-30, esp. 103, 127, and 124 for an illustration. This issue in philosophy of history is discussed in some detail in chapter 7.

[17]For further discussions of human nature in Hume's thought compatible with the lines sketched here, see David Miller, *Philosophy and Ideology in Hume's Political Thought* (Oxford: Clarendon Press, 1981), ch. 5; Frederick G. Whelan, *Order and Artifice in Hume's Political Philosophy* (Princeton: Princeton University Press, 1985), ch. III; and Jennifer A. Herdt, *Religion and Faction in Hume's Moral Philosophy* (Cambridge: Cambridge University Press, 1997), ch. 4. For someone who ignores these lines, see Leon Pompa, *Human Nature and Historical Knowledge: Hume, Hegel and Vico* (Cambridge: Cambridge University Press, 1990), Introduction, chs. 1 and 4.

[18]David Fate Norton, "Hume, Human Nature, and the Foundations of Morality," in *The Cambridge Companion to Hume*, ch. 6.

[19]Terence Penelhum, "Hume's Moral Psychology," in *The Cambridge Companion to Hume*, ch. 5.

4: Experience and Evidence

[1]D. F. Norton, "History and Philosophy in Hume's Thought," in PH, xxxii-1. Norton to this day asks his readers to consult this essay (see *The Cambridge Companion to Hume*, 5,29,374). Consequently, Norton's argument is still very much with us today and needs careful analysis because I think he misreads Hume.

[2]James Noxon, *Hume's Philosophical Development: A Study of His Methods* (Oxford: Clarendon Press, 1973), 176-77, and esp. 185-86.

[3]Donald Livingston goes so far to say that: "The essay by Norton is the first and still the best discussion on the conceptual connections that exist between Hume's philosophical and historical work." In "The Hume Literature of the 1970s: III. Philosophy of History and Philosophy of Religion," *Philosophical Topics* XII #3 (1982): 182-192, 191, note 31.

[4]David Wootton, "David Hume, 'the historian,'" in *The Cambridge Companion to Hume*, where he says of Norton's essay: it "is particularly helpful on the links between Hume's scepticism and historical study" (309).

[5]Antony Flew, "Impressions and Experiences: Public or Private?" *Hume Studies* XI #2 (November 1985): 183-91.

[6]Noxon, 176n, tempers his acceptance of Norton's theses by citing a case from the *History* that casts doubt on Norton's argument. In detail: "Hume considers whether the conspiratorial letters by which Mary, Queen of Scots was convicted of high treason were genuine or forgeries. Although Hume (naturally) was much more sympathetic toward Mary ('the most amiable of women') than toward Elizabeth ('an excellent hypocrite'), his scrupulous sifting of circumstantial evidence and sensitive probing of the behavior of the chief personages involved led him to conclude 'that all the suppositions of ... forger ... fall to the ground.'" See the Blair letter quoted earlier on the historian's relying on his own experience in cases or instances of conflicting evidence or testimony (more on this reliance later).

[7]Ludwig Wittgenstein, *Remarks on the Foundations of Mathematics* (Oxford: Blackwell, 1964), part 2, secs. 65-69, esp. 69, and *inter alia*.

[8]R. G. Collingwood, *The Idea of History* (London: Oxford University Press, 1946), 244-45. I wonder whether Norton would emphasize the personal pronouns in Collingwood's method and suggest that Collingwood, too, is a "naive subjectivist"? If not, why not? What is the difference between Hume and Collingwood on this point? None that I see. The rudiments of a reconstructionist's theory of history are in Hume's thought. His historical thinking is more highly developed than a common sense view of history that emphasizes facts, givens, and authorities. Hume had definitely moved away from the latter toward the former. Chapters 5, 6, and 7 assist substantiating this interpretive claim.

Between Hume's Philosophy and History

5: The Nature of Historical Narration

[1]H. Stuart Hughes, *History as Art and as Science: Twin Vistas on the Past* (New York: Harper & Row, 1964), 70.

[2]Morton White, *Foundations of Historical Knowledge* (New York: Harper & Row, 1965), 224. I have utilized White's categories (encyclopedism, essentialism, abnormalism, and so on) in interpreting Hume's account. White's *Foundations* is a classic study in analytical philosophy of history.

[3]For more detail (and criticism) of this view, see White's *Foundations*, ch. IV, sec. 2; and for a view of narration, see 247-48.

[4]An Abstract of *A Treatise of Human Nature*, in IU, 192. This characterization would hold equally for the nature of our past judgments for Hume.

[5]Rudolph H. Weingartner, "Review Essay" (of White's *Foundations*), *History and Theory* VII #3 (1968): 346n. I shall return to the idea of the causal relation as the paradigm for the model of historical narration later.

[6]John Passmore, "The Objectivity of History," *Philosophy* XXXIII #1 (1968): 104-05; reprinted in *Philosophical Analysis and History*, William H. Dray, ed. (New York: Harper & Row, 1966), 84-85.

[7]This analytical bias toward general topics and histories has been allowed to dominate far too long over theoretical models of historical studies. There are many good modern general histories that fulfil an important educational need. Furthermore if historical narration is to be adequately understood by those who have theoretical or philosophical interests in history, these general narratives need to be sympathetically studied. *The Columbia History of the World*, John A. Garraty and Peter Gay, eds. (New York: Columbia University Press, 1972), written by members of the faculty of Columbia University, is a case in point. Historical works, like this one, should be judged by what purpose they are written for. Much of what Passmore, Hughes, and company say about general histories is correct. But not all such histories, like the one above, are written with a metaphysic of Mankind lurking behind them. (I wish to thank Professor J. H. Plumb for pointing out and discussing the above-mentioned book with me.)

[8]R. F. Atkinson, "Explanation in History," *Proceedings of the Aristotelian Society* LXXII (1971/72): 256.

[9]White, *Foundations*, 248-57. According to this view, "The historian, it might be said, wishes to approximate the whole truth about his central subjects, and therefore one basis for a chronicle will be adjudged superior to another if it characterizes the central subject in a fuller way than the other does" (248-49).

[10]An essentialist, according to White, is one who holds the view of historical narration that some truths are more important or *deeper* than others, and that a historical narrative of any given entity is to express the essence of that entity. See White's *Foundations*, 240-47.

[11]See LC,I,367-417,II,1-85,120-48; LS, e.g., 212-216,233-34.

[12]This review is included in PH,379f.

[13]Trygve R. Tholfsen, *Historical Thinking* (New York: Columbia University Press, 1967), 98-99.

[14]For an excellent lengthy discussion of this concern of Hume's, see Jennifer A. Herdt, *Religion and Faction in Hume's Moral Philosophy* (Cambridge: Cambridge University Press, 1997).

[15]The movement was given this name by Dugald Stewart. Hume labeled it as *philosophical history*. According to this school of "historical sociology or anthropology," one "was to concentrate on the reconstruction of unknown stages in the development of society from known stages, by means of certain hypotheses about social, cultural, physiological, or economic phenomena." From George H. Nadel, "Philosophy of History before Historicism," *History and Theory* III #3 (1964), 312. Reprinted in *Studies in the Philosophy of History*, George H. Nadel, ed. (New York: Harper & Row, 1965), 71. For further detail, see Nadel's essay and the material he has cited.

[16]G. E. Aylmer, *A Short History of Seventeenth-Century England: 1603-1689* (New York: New American Library, 1963), 123-24; the italics are mine. (This book was published in England under the title *The Struggle for the Constitution, 1603-1689* [London: Blandford Press, 1963].)

[17]A good example of this view is seen in Cecil B. Currey's narrative, *Road to Revolution: Benjamin Franklin in England, 1765-1775* (Anchor Books; Garden City, New York: Doubleday & Company, 1968).

[18]The best way to make clear what R. G. Collingwood meant by "the *a priori* historical imagination" is by an example he gives in *The Idea of History* (London: Oxford University Press, 1946): "A commander's dispatches may claim a victory; the historian, reading them in a critical spirit, will ask: 'If it was a victory, why was it not followed up in this way or that way?'" (237). Embedded in this question is an appeal to the meaning of words—to our understanding of what a victory consists of—which leads us to think along certain lines of thought, viz., "in this or that way."

[19]Conceptual evidence, as opposed to documentary evidence, is the relationship between concept and instance, and is what the historian can plausibly infer from "our general concepts"; see A. C. Danto, *Narration and Knowledge* including the integral text of *Analytical Philosophy of History* (New York: Columbia University Press, 1985), 122-23, where he gives the following example: "There are many sources from which support for a story, as well as suggestions for a story, might be drawn. In addition to actual records and documents, we almost certainly rely upon what we might call *conceptual* evidence. Simply to identify someone as an artist, for instance, already locates that individual under a concept, and permits us, with some measure of plausibility, to apply a whole set of different and, ... *acceptable* or *possible*, sentences to that individual." For instance, "knowing the title of the painting and *understanding* it allows us to entertain

some idea of the sorts of things it had to contain, and we can suppose, as well, that if an artist of note painted a picture of note, and the latter had a religious motif, there was some more or less intimate connection between art and religion: at all events, we can get some general idea of who the patron was. These connections having been established, we can go on seeking for further ones, and for evidence to support the ones we had made." So bit by bit we piece together a plausible narrative of the artist's life, and the narrative will be plausible to the extent that it tells us what might typically happen to an artist in his lifetime. Danto's discussion here sounds very similar to Hume's idea of conjectures (see ch. 2, sec. 2), and the role they play in providing a well-rounded picture of the past.

[20]A. R. Louch, "History as Narrative," *History and Theory* VIII #1 (1969), 57.

[21]The distinction between monistic and pluralistic views is one I have borrowed from White; see his *Foundations*, 257ff.

6: The Paradox of Taste

[1]Mary Mothersill, "Hume and the Paradox of Taste," in *Aesthetics: A Critical Anthology*, edited by George Dickie, Richard Scalfani, and Ronald Roblin (Second Edition; New York: St. Martin's Press, 1989), 269-286. For Mothersill's more conventional reading of Hume's essay "Of the Standard of Taste," see her *Beauty Restored* (Oxford: Clarendon Press, 1984), ch. VII.

[2]Francis Hutcheson, *An Inquiry into the Original of Our Ideas of Beauty and Virtue* (Third Edition; London, 1729), reprinted in *Aesthetics: A Critical Anthology*, 223-241, esp. 235 and 238 on the Association of Ideas.

[3]IU,33-39. This addition triples the length of the section "Of the Association of Ideas" (III), and hence much was sacrificed by its final omission, one part of which is the change in the tenor of the whole section from a humanistic one to a universalistic, scientific one. Hume's deletion has misled scholars in the interpretation of this section for decades.

[4]For details, see Jones in note 8 below.

[5]Adrian Oldfield, "Moral Judgements in History," *History and Theory* XX #3 (1981): 260-76, see 261. This topic is discussed in greater detail in the next chapter (7).

[6]See John P. Wright, *The Sceptical Realism of David Hume* (Minneapolis: University of Minnesota Press, 1983), and Galen Strawson, *The Secret Connexion: Causation, Realism, and David Hume* (Oxford: Clarendon Press, 1989).

[7]Dr. Linda K. Hughes, Professor in the Department of English, Texas Christian University, Fort Worth.

[8]For recent readings of Hume's theory of taste, see Christopher MacLachlan, "Hume and the Standard of Taste," *Hume Studies* XII #1 (April 1986): 18-38; Peter Jones, *Hume's Sentiments: Their Ciceronian and French Context* (Edinburgh: Edinburgh University Press, 1982), ch. 3, his "Hume's Literary and Aesthetic Theory," in *The*

Cambridge Companion to Hume, ch. 9; Theordore A. Gracyk, "Rethinking Hume's Standard of Taste," *Journal of Aesthetics and Art Criticism* LII #2 (Spring 1994): 169-182, who also provides a critical discussion of Mothersill's interpretive argument; and for a new, different spin on Hume's argument, see Roger A. Shiner, "Hume and the Causal Theory of Taste," *JAAC* LIV #3 (Summer 1996): 237-249; Mary Mothersill, "In Defense of Hume and the Causal Theory of Taste," *JAAC* LV #3 (Summer 1997): 312-317; John W. Bender and Richard N. Manning, "On Shiner's 'Hume and the Causal Theory of Taste,'" *JAAC* LV #3 (Summer 1997): 317-320; and Roger A. Shiner, "Causes and Tastes: A Response," *JAAC* LV #3 (Summer 1997): 320-324.

7: Moral Judgments in History

[1]R. F. Atkinson, *Knowledge and Explanation in History* (Ithaca, New York: Cornell University Press, 1978), ch. VI, sec. 3.

[2]Herbert Butterfield, "Moral Judgments in History," in his *History and Human Relations* (New York: Macmillan, 1951/52), 101-130; reprinted in *The Philosophy of History in Our Time: An Anthology,* edited by Hans Meyerhoff (Garden City, New York: Doubleday and Company, 1959), 228-249.

[3]Adrian Oldfield, "Moral Judgments in History," *History and Theory* XX #3 (1981): 260-277.

[4]Lord Acton, *Lectures on Modern History* (London: Macmillan, 1906, 1960), and *Historical Essays and Studies* (Freeport, New York: Books for Libraries Press, 1907, 1967), *inter alia.* My references, wherever possible, will be to the *Selected Writings of Lord Acton,* edited by J. Rufus Fears (Indianapolis: Liberty Press, 1985), which shall be abbreviated as "SW," followed by the volume and page numbers parenthetically.

[5]R. G. Collingwood, *The Idea of History* (London: Oxford University Press, 1946), Part V, esp. 244: "The web of imaginative construction [of the historian] is something far more solid and powerful than we have hitherto realized. So far from relying for its validity upon the support of given facts, it actually serves as the touchstone by which we decide whether alleged facts are genuine."

[6]In "Explanatory Narrative in History," *Philosophical Quarterly* IV #4 (January 1954): 15-27, William Dray comments that the Hanoverian settlement (1714) actually emerged during the last fifteen years of Elizabeth (1588-1603). This raises a temporal problem in English history—"a problem which can only be solved by a description of the transition in all its detail" (26). And, "an historical explanation may thus amount to *telling the story of what actually happened,* and telling it in such a way ... [that] answers to likely objections are *built into* the narrative" (27; Dray's emphases). Historical explanation is a certain kind of narrative description, for Dray, as it is for Butterfield and Hume.

[7]I am reminded of William L. Shirer, who says in the Foreword of *The Rise and Fall of the Third Reich: A History of Nazi Germany* (New York: Fawcett Crest, 1959/1960):

"No doubt my own prejudices, which inevitably spring from my experience and make-up, creep through the pages of this book from time to time. I detest totalitarian dictatorships in principle and came to loathe this one the more I lived through it and watched its ugly assualt upon the human spirit. Nevertheless, in this book I have tried to be severely objective, *letting the facts speak for themselves* and noting the source for each" (xii; emphasis added).

[8]For Hume's Italian historiographical connections (Francesco Guiccardini and Paolo Sarpi), see David Wootten, "David Hume, 'the historian,'" in *The Cambridge Companion to Hume*, edited by David Fate Norton (Cambridge: Cambridge University Press, 1993), 281-312, esp. 283ff.

[9]James Farr, "Hume, Hermeneutics, and History: A 'Sympathetic' Account," *History and Theory* XVII #3 (1978): 285-310; and his companion piece, "Humean Explanations in the Moral Sciences," *Inquiry* XXV #1 (March 1982): 57-80.

[10]Hume adopted this term from Shaftesbury's *Characteristics* (London, 1711), II, 307, 412, in *The Moralists, A Philosophical Rhapsody, Being a Recital of certain Conversations on Natural and Moral Subjects* (1709), II, 4, and III, 2. But the term goes back as far as Henry More's *Conjectura Cabbalistica* (1653). John Laird, in *Hume's Philosophy of Human Nature* (Hamden, Connecticut: Archon Books, 1932/1967), 197, is one of the few commentators to mention *presensation* in Hume's account of sympathy (in ch. VII).

[11]*Thought* is founded on feeling in Collingwood's theory of imagination, see *The Principles of Art* (New York: Oxford University Press, 1938/1958), Book Two.

[12]Whenever I refer to Hume's historiographical category of Character, the word is capitalized. By "Character," Hume means an account of eminent persons or groups wherein he reduces them to types associated with their profession, their station in life, and their relation to the government or reign. Characters form an integral part of his historical narrative by supplying the needed periodization besides the usual, temporal chronology. The historiographical category of Character was probably suggested to Hume from his reading of *Ancient History* (4 Vols.) by French historian Charles Rollin (1661-1741) who divided narrative order into Religion, People, War, Arts and Sciences, and the Character, Manners, and Qualities of Nations, like the Carthaginians. Hume's narrative structure is essentially Rollin's. See Donald C. Ainslie's important study, especially his discussion of National Character, in "The Problems of the National Self in Hume's Theory of Justice," *Hume Studies* XXI #2 (November 1995): 289-313, esp. 295ff, in the context of recent political philosophy. Also see chapter 8 in this regard.

[13]J. Y. T. Greig, *David Hume* (London: Jonathan Cape, 1931), 268-269. Backslash ("/") indicates that indention for a new paragraph is ignored for purposes of quotation.

[14]J. C. Hilson, "Hume: The Historian as Man of Feeling," in *Augustan Worlds: New Essays in Eighteenth-Century Literature*, edited by J. C. Hilson, M. M. B. Jones, and J. R. Watson (New York: Barnes and Noble, 1978), 205-222; 218-19.

[15]The term "narrative sentences" is Arthur Danto's, who in *Narration and Knowledge* (New York: Columbia University Press, 1985), ch. VIII, gives this characterization: "Commonly they take the past tense, and ... they refer to at least two time-separated events though they only *describe* (are only *about*) the earliest event to which they refer" (143).

[16]For a spirited discussion of this view, see David L. Hull, "In Defense of Presentism," *History and Theory* XVII #1 (1979): 1-15. John Dewey, too, argued that history must be written from the standpoint of the present; see his "Historical Judgments," from *Logic: The Theory of Inquiry* (New York: Henry Holt and Co., 1938), 230-239; reprinted in *The Philosophy of History in Our Time*, 163-172.

[17]For an excellent account of Lord Acton's position on moral judgments in history, see Terrence Murphy's study, "Lord Acton and the Question of Moral Judgments in History: The Development of His Position," *The Catholic Historical Review* LXX #2 (April 1984): 225-250.

[18]G. M. Trevelyan, *A Shortened History of England* (Baltimore, Maryland: Penguin Books, 1942/1959), 213.

[19]Charles M. Gray, *Renaissance and Reformation England: 1509-1714* (New York: Harcourt Brace Jovanovich, 1973), 30.

[20]Sir Isaiah Berlin, "Historical Inevitability" (1954), reprinted in *The Philosophy of History in Our Time*, 271.

[21]For a brief selection of Jacob Burckhardt's argument against moral judgments in history, see "On Fortune and Misfortune in History," reprinted in *The Philosophy of History in Our Time*, 273-290.

[22]Recently Hume's "Of Eloquence" has been of interest among eighteenth-century scholars; see Adam Potkay, *The Fate of Eloquence in the Age of Hume* (Ithaca: Cornell University Press, 1994); M.A. Box's review in *Hume Studies* XXI #2 (November 1995): 333-339; and Potkay's reply, *Ibid.*, 340-343.

[23]Sigmund Freud, "The Moses of Michelangelo" (1914), in the *Standard Edition of the Complete Psychological Works of Sigmund Freud* (London: The Hogarth Press and the Institute of Psycho-Analysis, 1955), XIII, 212. For a discussion of Hume in the midst of Descartes and Tolstoy on the topic of the expression theory of art, see my "Human Nature and Art: From Descartes and Hume to Tolstoy," *Journal of Aesthetic Education* XXXII #3 (Fall 1998): 75-81.

[24]Wilhelm Dilthey, *Pattern and Meaning in History: Thoughts on History and Society*, edited by H. P. Rickman (New York: Harper and Row, 1961), 139-140.

[25]In *The Theory of Moral Sentiments*, edited by D. D. Raphael and A. L. Macfie (Indianapolis: Liberty Press, 1979), Adam Smith gives a more conservative description of sympathy than Hume: "As we have no immediate experience of what other men feel, we can form no idea of the manner in which they are affected, but by conceiving what we ourselves should feel in the like situation. Though our brother is upon the rack, as

long as we ourselves are at our ease, our senses will never inform us of what he suffers. They never did, and never can, carry us beyond our own person, and it is by imagination only that we can form any conception of what are his sensations. Neither can that faculty help us to this any other way, than by representing to us what would be our own, if we were in his case. It is the impressions of our own senses only, not those of his, which our imaginations copy. By the imagination we place ourselves in his situation, we conceive ourselves enduring all the same torments, we enter as it were into his body, and become in some measure the same person with him, and thence form some idea of his sensations, and even feel something which, though weaker in degree, is not altogether unlike them" (9). This description sounds more like Butterfield's than Hume's. Edmund Burke's description is much closer to Hume's. In *A Philosophical Enquiry into the Origin of Our Ideas of the Sublime and Beautiful*, edited by Adam Phillips (New York: Oxford University Press, 1990), Burke writes: "It is by the first of these passions [sympathy, imitation, and ambition] that we enter into the concerns of others; that we are moved as they are moved, and are never suffered to be indifferent spectators of almost any thing which men can do or suffer. For sympathy must be considered as a sort of substitution, by which we are put into the place of another man, and affected in many respects as he is affected; so that this passion may either partake of the nature of those which regard self-preservation, and turning upon pain may be a source of the sublime; or it may turn upon the ideas of pleasure; and then, whatever has been said of the social affections, whether they regard society in general, or only some particular modes of it, may be applicable here. It is by this principle chiefly that poetry, painting, and other affecting arts, transfuse their passions from one breast to another ..." (41). Evidently Hume thought that it is by this principle that history transfuses agents' passions from one breast to another twice: from the agent to the historian, and then from the historian to the reader.

[26]I am not alone in reading this passage and the others this way: Nicholas Capaldi, in "Hume as Social Scientist," *Review of Metaphysics* XXXII (1978): 99-123, says that: "Sympathy is defined by Hume as the process in which our idea of someone else's inner mental state is enlivened to become the very same mental state in ourselves" (117), and Capaldi refers specifically to T,II,I,XI.

[27]David Wootton gives us an interesting example of this "communication:" "Hume deliberately sought to move his audience to tears by his account of the execution of Charles I (L, I, 210, 222, also 344; "My Own Life"). He was certainly successful: indeed, we have letters from female admirers testifying to how his history had moved their passions. One of them told him that she had never had such a good opinion of herself as when reading his history: evidently Hume had inspired virtuous sentiments in her, and thereby made her feel virtuous and admirable (L, II, 347, 366-67)." (282)

[28]Donald W. Livingston, "Hume on the Problem of Historical and Scientific Explanation," *The New Scholasticism* XLVII #1 (Winter 1973): 38-67, see 59; his

account is updated and greatly enhanced in *Hume's Philosophy of Common Life* (Chicago: University of Chicago Press, 1984), chs. 4, 7, 8, and 9.

[29]For a recent discussion of this topic, see Simon Evnine's study, "Hume, Conjectural History, and the Uniformity of Human Nature," *Journal of the History of Philosophy* XXXI #4 (1993): 589-606.

[30]For a critical discussion of some of these problems, see John J. Jenkins, "Hume's Account of Sympathy—Some Difficulties," in *Philosophers of the Scottish Enlightenment*, edited by Vincent Hope (Edinburgh: Edinburgh University Press, 1984), 91-104.

8: The Historiography of Science

[1]David Hume, "A Character of Sir Robert Walpole" (1742), in E, 575, where Hume imagines that "I shall flatter myself with the pleasing imagination, that the following character will be adopted by future historians."

[2]H, III, 82. This is not a negative phrase; Hume thought this a legitimate and primary function of historiography.

[3]See Helge Kragh, *An Introduction to the Historiography of Science*, tr. Jean Lundskjaer-Nielsen (Cambridge: Cambridge University Press, 1987), 18ff, and ch. 9 on anachronical history of science—the view that the past should be studied in the light of the knowledge we have today, also known as presentism.

[4]Kragh, *Introduction*, 11ff.

[5]See, for example, scholars who have made considerable advances in answering these questions: Michael Barfoot, "Hume and the Culture of Science in the Early Eighteenth Century," in *Studies in the Philosophy of the Scottish Enlightenment*, ed. M. A. Stewart (Oxford: Clarendon Press, 1990), 151-90; Roger L. Emerson, "Sciences and the Origins and Concerns of the Scottish Enlightenment," *History of Science* XXVI (1988): 333-66, also in Stewart's *Studies*, 11-36; James E. Force's "Hume's Interest in Newton and Science," *Hume Studies* XII (1987): 166-216.

[6]For example, J. Y. T. Greig, *David Hume* (London: Jonathan Cape, 1931), ch. XX, esp. 270ff.

[7]Karl Popper, *The Open Society and Its Enemies* (4th ed.; London: Routledge and Kegan Paul, 1962), II, 16.

[8]Anthony Quinton, *Francis Bacon* (Oxford: Oxford University Press, 1980), 79: "he [Bacon] disdained Copernicus and ignored Kepler and Galileo."

[9]Peter Urbach, *Francis Bacon's Philosophy of Science* (LaSalle, Ill.: Open Court Publishing Co., 1987), 131-32.

[10]I. Bernard Cohen, *Revolution in Science* (Cambridge, Mass.: Harvard University Press, 1985), 519-21. Cohen's discussion first appeared in "The Eighteenth Century

Origins of the Concept of Scientific Revolution," *Journal of the History of Ideas* XXXVII #2 (April-June 1976): 257-88.

[11]Hume, T, xvii, 412. See the *History*, III, 409, for use of both "reformation" and "revolution", also *History*, IV, 8: "These declarations of her intention [Queen Elizabeth's], concuring with preceding suspicions, made the bishops foresee with certainty a revolution in religion"; Appendix III, "But the change of manners was the chief cause of the secret revolution of government, and subverted the power of the barons" (IV, 385), and (IV, 384), "Whatever may be commonly imagined, from the authority of Lord Bacon, and that of Harrington, and later authors, the laws of Henry VII. contributed very little towards the great revolution, which happened about this period in the English constitution."

[12]Cf. (V, 545), "From the memorable revolutions, which passed in England during this period [1649], we may naturally deduce the same useful lesson, which Charles himself, in his later years, inferred; that it is dangerous for princes, even from the appearance of necessity, to assume more authority, than the laws have allowed them." In the opening paragraph of the *History* Hume talks about "the sudden, violent, and unprepared revolutions, incident to Barbarians" (I,3); also I, 24, 26, 39; and "Of National Characters" (examples of *moral* causes as opposed to *physical* ones), "Of this kind are, the nature of government, the *revolutions* of public affairs, the plenty or penury in which the people live, the situation of the nation with regard to its neighbours, and such like circumstances" (198; emphasis added).

[13]Joseph Agassi, *Towards an Historiography of Science, History and Theory*, Beiheft 2 (Middletown, Connecticut: Wesleyan University Press, 1963), 88n.

[14]For instance in "Of Miracles," Part II, Hume criticizes Bacon's method of reasoning concerning the novel or extraordinary in nature, i.e., to record everything, or as Westfall put it, "unguided observation" (*The Construction of Modern Science: Mechanisms and Mechanics* [Cambridge: Cambridge University Press, 1977], 114); see Hume's IU, section X on miracles, 139. But in fairness to Professor Agassi there are other references to Bacon in the *History* that have a more laudatory tone: "Bacon, so much distinguished afterwards by his high offices, and still more by his profound genius for the sciences ..." and "All the efforts of the great Bacon could not procure an establishment for the cultivation of natural philosophy" (V,132). In the Abstract to the *Treatise* Hume remarks that "my Lord Bacon ... [is] the father of experimental physicks" (T,646). There is another place in the *Treatise* (469) where Hume used the word "physics" instead of "natural philosophy" or "experimental philosophy." All this points to the fact that Hume is at best ambivalent toward Bacon. On the latter portion of Bacon's Character, where Hume views the contemporary adulation of Bacon as a reflection of the English "national spirit" and some of the praise bestowed upon him as "partial and excessive," see Richard Yeo, "An Idol of the Market-Place: Baconianism in Nineteenth Century Britain," *History of Science* XXIII (1985): 251-98, esp. 259.

[15]Edward Harrison, "Whigs, Prigs and Historians of Science" (commentary), *Nature* CCCXXIX (1987): 213-14; "Whig History" in *Macmillan Dictionary of the History of Science*, ed. W. F. Bynum, E. J. Browne, and Roy Porter (London: The Macmillan Press, Ltd., 1981), 445-46; Herbert Butterfield, "The Historian and the History of Science," *Bulletin of the British Society for the History of Science* I (1950): 49-57, and Butterfield's other works. For an example of the diachronic method, see Horace Freeland Judson, *The Eighth Day of Creation: The Makers of the Revolution in Biology* (New York: Simon and Schuster, 1979). For an example of the synchronic method see R. S. Westfall, *Never at Rest: A Biography of Isaac Newton* (Cambridge: Cambridge University Press, 1980).

[16]On this experiment see A. P. Usher, *A History of Mechanical Inventions* (Boston: Beacon Press, 1959 [1929]), 340-41.

[17]L, I,226. Hume admired Voltaire's *The Age of Louis XIV* (1751), and he may even have gotten the idea to include science in his historical narrative from Voltaire since the latter devoted two short chapters (31 and 34) to the subject and wrote extensively about it in numerous, other writings, e.g., *Elements of the Philosophy of Newton* (1738/41), although Hume explicitly denies such a connection: "In this Country, they [e.g., Horace Walpole] call me his Pupil, and that my History is an Imitation of his Siecle de Louis XIV. This Opinion flatters very much my Vanity; but the Truth is, that my History was plan'd, & in a great measure compos'd, before the Appearance of that agreeable Work" (*ibid.*).

[18]In *Hume's Philosophical Development* (Oxford: Clarendon Press, 1973) James Noxon argues that Hume probably never read Newton's *Principia* and that he got its ideas secondhand (68ff), and so does Peter Jones, *Hume's Sentiments: Their Ciceronian and French Context* (Edinburgh: Edinburgh University Press, 1982), ch. 1. There is evidence to the contrary (see Barfoot's investigation in note 5); furthermore, Hume did read Nicolas de Malezieu's *Eléments de Géometrie* (1722) while he was in France composing the *Treatise*, so it is probable that he could understand the mathematical parts of *Principia* (see note 21). Hume also studied mathematics with George Campbell and Hume served as secretary for the Edinburgh Philosophical Society for a few years (c.1749-c.1762). He succeeded Maclaurin. And as secretary, Hume would presumably have read all that *Essays and Observations, Physical and Literary* contained. The programmatic statements about science in volume I may be his although they are usually credited to Alexander Mouro on no good evidence, at least no conclusive evidence.

[19]E. C. Mossner, *The Life of David Hume* (Edinburgh: Nelson, 1954), 49.

[20]Colin Maclaurin, *An Account of Sir Isaac Newton's Philosophical Discoveries*, a facsimile of the first edition with a new introduction and index of names by L. L. Laudan (The Sources of Science, No. 74; New York: Johnson Reprint Corporation, 1968), v. (*An Account* was written by Patrick Murdoch and Mrs. Maclaurin wrote the dedication.)

[21]See Marina Frasca Spada, "Some Features of Hume's Conception of Space," *Studies in History and Philosophy of Science* XXI (1990): esp. 382ff.

22Joseph Glanvill, *Plus Ultra, or The Progress and Advancement of Knowledge Since the Days of Aristotle* (1668), a facsimile reproduction with an introduction by Jackson I. Cope (Gainesville, Fla.: Scholar's Facsimiles and Reprints, 1958).

23Adam Smith, *Essays on Philosophical Subjects*, ed. W. P. D. Wightman and J. C. Bryce (Indianapolis: Liberty Press, 1982), 1-21, esp. 11ff.

24.See Steven Shapin and Simon Schaffer, *Leviathan and the Air-Pump: Hobbes, Boyle, and the Experimental Life* (Princeton: Princeton University Press, 1986).

25See the *Leibniz-Clarke Correspondence*, ed. H. G. Alexander (Manchester: Manchester University Press, 1956), esp. 11ff, for the classic debate on this latter requirement; Hume, *Dialogues Concerning Natural Religion*, esp. Parts IX and X, shows his familiarity with this debate.

26Thomas S. Kuhn, *The Structure of Scientific Revolutions* (2nd ed.; Chicago: The University of Chicago Press, 1970), 24.

27Hume's general historiography is one of the recent past (which R. G. Collingwood calls "Illuminism"), on which see S. K. Wertz, "Collingwood's Understanding of Hume" (paper read at the 19th Hume conference, University of Nantes, France, July 1992), in *Hume Studies* XX #2 (November 1994): 261-287.

28Hume mentions mistakenly (I, 79) that Alfred founded, repaired, and endowed Oxford University. Also Hume provides us with some idea about the rise of mechanical measurement of time by making another reference much later in the *History*: "The author of the Present State of England, says, that about 1577, pocket watches were first brought into England from Germany. They are thought to have been invented at Nuremberg" (IV, 370). Cf. Steven F. Mason, in his *A History of the Sciences* (rev. ed.; New York: Collier, 1962), 109, who cites the same information: "craftsmanship rapidly improved, and by the sixteenth century pocket watches were being constructed at Nuremberg."

29*History*, I,49. For his time Hume knew a great deal about astronomy, contrary to what Cohen claims; and in the *Treatise* he mentioned Copernicus more than just once, the Cartesians, esp. Malebranche (152-53), Isaac Barrow's *Mathematical Lectures* (46), Malezieu (30), "the satellites of Jupiter" (342), and in the Introduction he obviously alludes to Newton's *Principia* when he promises to "render all our principles as universal as possible" (xvii). In the *Dialogues* Hume discusses Copernicus and Galileo in some detail (Parts II and V). Incidentally he also mentions Galen in Part XII.

30Cf. *History*, I,50-51, for the context of this remark.

31Cf. Voltaire, *Essay on the Manner and Spirit of Nations*, in *The Portable Voltaire*, ed. B. R. Redman (New York: The Viking Press, 1949), 549-50: "In those times of darkness and ignorance, which we distinguish by the name of the Middle Ages...." Recently there has been a greater appreciation of the role of religion in the rise of modern science; see Jacob's book (note 34). Maclaurin says: "The cloud was, at length, gradually dispell'd in *Europe*: the active genius of man could not be enslaved for ever. The love of knowledge revived, the remains of ancient learning, that had escaped the wreck of the dark ages, were diligently sought after; the liberal arts and sciences were restored, and none of them has gained more by this happy revolution than natural philosophy" (44).

[32]Some of the historians following Hume who were critical were William Robertson, Edward Gibbon, William Godwin, and Henry Hallam. See Francis Palgrave, "Hume and His Influence upon History," *Quarterly Review* LXXXIII (1844): 536-92.

[33]According to Robert S. Westman, "The Astronomer's Role in the Sixteenth Century: A Preliminary Study," *History of Science* XVIII (1980): 146, a full study of Saville's life and works is very much needed.

[34]See especially Margaret C. Jacob, *The Cultural Meaning of The Scientific Revolution* (New York: Alfred A. Knopf, 1988).

[35]E,111-17. Hume observes (124) that "a republic is most favourable to the growth of the sciences," while in "Of Civil Liberty" (90) he says of Florence that it "made its chief progress in the arts and sciences, after it began to lose its liberty by the usurpation of the family of MEDICI. ARISTO, TASSO, GALILEO, more than RAPHAEL, and MICHELANGELO, were not born in republics." (These individuals were born in Italian principalities.)

[36]See Agassi's seminal work, *Towards an Historiography of Science*; also Maurice A. Finocchiaro, *History of Science as Explanation* (Detroit: Wayne State University Press, 1973), Part 2; James W. McAllister, "Theory-Assessment in the Historiography of Science," *British Journal of the Philosophy of Science* XXXVII (1986): 315-33; and Helge Kragh, *Introduction*.

[37]Hume cites John Strype's (1643-1737) *Annals of the Reformation and Establishment of Religion, and Other Occurrences in the Church of England, during Queen Elizabeth's Happy Reign: Together with an Appendix of Original Papers of State, Records, and Letters* (Oxford: The Clarendon Press, 1824), IV,521-22 (doc. #276).

[38]Henry Power, *Experimental Philosophy, In Three Books: Containing New Experiments Microscopical, Mercurial, Magnetical...* (The Sources of Science, No. 21; New York: Johnson Reprint Corp., 1966).

[39]On Halley's character, see "Some Particulars of the Life of Dr. Halley," *Annual Register* (1759), 283-90; Newton's anecdote, *Annual Register* (1772), 34-37.

[40]Francis Palgrave, *op. cit.*, suggests that Hume paraphrased many passages from the works of earlier British historians, but it is also true that many later historians had to follow his lead because they had to use the archives he had discovered; see Hugh Trevor-Roper, "Hume as a Historian," in *David Hume, A Symposium*, ed. D. F. Pears (London: Macmillan, 1963), 99.

[41]William K. Dickson, "David Hume and the Advocates' Library," *Juridical Review*, XLIV (1932): 9.

[42]George Berkeley, *De Motu* (1721/52), in *Philosophical Works*, ed. M. R. Ayers (London: Dent, 1975), 209-27.

[43]See Alec Fisher, *The Logic of Real Arguments* (Cambridge: Cambridge University

Press, 1988), 184/186, discussing Harvey, *The Motion of the Heart*, and how the values function in the veins of the arm.

[44]Pierre Duhem, *Les origines de la statique* (Paris, 1905-7), I, 111, quoted from Kragh, *Introduction*, 18.

[45]E. C. Mossner, "An Apology for David Hume, Historian," *Proceedings of the Modern Languages Association* LVI (1941): 657-690; 679 and 687.

Epilogue

[1]Charles Rollin, *Histoire Romaine* (1738-41) "was the first attempt to retell the history of ancient Rome for a modern audience," [an English translation began to appear in 1739] Wootton reports (284). *Oeuvres complétes de Rollin* (Nouvelle Édition in 30 vols.; Paris: chez Firmin Didot Fréres, Libraires, 1825-30) and *Ancient History* (4 vols.; New York: Belford, Clarke and Co., n.d.), in which Rollin has two discussions on "Arts and Sciences," vol. I, book II, part I, sec. VII; book IV, chapter I, article III.

[2]In his lengthy Introduction David Wallace Carrithers does not mention the influence of Rollin on Montesquieu; however, it is undoubtably there; Montesquieu, *The Spirit of Laws* edited by Carrithers (Berkeley: University of California Press, 1977), Carrithers's Introduction, 3-88.

[3]Montesquieu, *Discours sur les motifs qui doivent nous encourager aux sciences* (1725) and it is mentioned in Carrithers's Introduction, 9.

[4]Nicholas Phillipson, *Hume* (London: Weidenfeld and Nicolson, 1989), 138.

[5]Donald W. Livingston, *Philosophical Melancholy and Delirium: Hume's Pathology of Philosophy* (Chicago: The University of Chicago Press, 1998), 7. After having introduced this useful term, he dismisses it as either misleading or paradoxical. This I do not agree with for mainly the reasons Garrett outlines in his chapter (1) on cognition and imagination—"empiricism" is a useful term to characterize not only the British tradition of which Hume was a part, but the legacy he left the next two centuries mainly in Britain and America. Nevertheless, I find the term—historical empiricism—helpful, especially in light of what I argued in chapter 4 on experience and evidence.

[6]Donald T. Siebert, *The Moral Animus of David Hume* (Newark: University of Delaware Press, 1990), 195.

BIBLIOGRAPHY

The books and articles referred to in the notes of each chapter are listed below. The editions of Hume's writings that have been used are listed under the List of Abbreviations on pages vii-viii.

Acton, Lord, *Lectures on Modern History*. London: Macmillan, 1906/1960.
_____. *Historical Essays and Studies*. Freeport, New York: Books for Libraries Press, 1907/1967.
Agassi, Joseph. *Towards an Historiography of Science, History and Theory* II #3, Beiheft 2 (1963). Middletown, Connecticut: Wesleyan University Press.
Ainslie, Donald C. "The Problems of the National Self in Hume's Theory of Justice," *Hume Studies* XXI #2 (November 1995): 289-313.
Alexander, H. G. (ed.). *Leibniz-Clarke Correspondence*. Manchester: Manchester University Press, 1956.
Anderson, Robert Fendel. *Hume's First Principles*. Lincoln: University of Nebraska Press, 1965.
Anonymous. "Some Particulars of the Life of Dr. Halley," *Annual Register, 1750*. London, 283-290.
_____. Newton's Anecdote, *Annual Register, 1772*. London, 34-37.
Aristotle. *Poetics*. In Richard McKeon's (ed.) *The Basic Works of Aristotle*, 1455-1487.
Atkinson, R. F. "Explanation in History," *Proceedings of the Aristotelian Society* LXXII (1971/72).
_____. *Knowledge and Explanation in History*. Ithaca, New York: Cornell University Press, 1978.
Ayer, A. J. "A Defence of Empiricism," in *A. J. Ayer: Memorial Essays*, ch. 1.
Ayers, M. R. (ed.). *George Berkeley, Philosophical Works including the Works on Vision*. London: Dent, 1975.
Aylmer, G. E. *A Short History of Seventeenth-Century England: 1603-1689*. New York: New American Library, 1963.
Baier, Annette C. *A Progress of Sentiments: Reflections on Hume's "Treatise."* Cambridge, Massachusetts: Harvard University Press, 1991.

Barfoot, Michael. "Hume and the Culture of Science in the Early Eighteenth Century," in M. A. Stewart's *Studies in the Philosophy of the Scottish Enlightenment*, 151-90.

Barnes, H. E. *History of Historical Writing*. Second Edition; New York: Dover, 1963.

Barnes, S. B. "The Age of Enlightenment," in *The Development of Historiography*, edited by M. A. Fitzsimmons and A. G. Pundt. Harrisburg: The Stackpole Co., 1954.

Barrow, Isaac. *The Geometrical (Mathematical) Lectures*, 1670, translated by J. M. Child. Chicago: The Open Court Publishing Company, 1916.

Bender, John W., and Richard N. Manning. "On Shiner's 'Hume and the Causal Theory of Taste," *Journal of Aesthetics and Art Criticism* LV#3 (Summer 1997): 317-320.

Berkeley, George. *Three Dialogues between Hylas and Philonous* (1713), edited by R. M. Adams. Indianapolis: Hackett Publishing Company, 1979.

_____. *De Motu*, 1721/1752, reprinted in M. R. Ayers's *Philosophical Works*, 209-227.

Berlin, Isaiah (Sir). "Historical Inevitability" (1954), reprinted in *The Philosophy of History in Our Time*, 249-271.

Black, J. B. *The Art of History: A Study of Four Great Historians of the Eighteenth Century*. New York: Russell & Russell, 1965.

Bongie, Laurence L. *David Hume: Prophet of the Counter-Revolution*. Oxford: Clarendon Press, 1965.

Burckhardt, Jacob. "On Fortune and Misfortune in History," reprinted in *The Philosophy of History in Our Time*, 273-290.

Burke, Edmund. *A Philosophical Enquiry into the Origin of Our Ideas of the Sublime and Beautiful*, edited by Adam Phillips. New York: Oxford University Press, 1990.

Butterfield, Herbert. "The Historian and the History of Science," *Bulletin of the British Society for the History of Science* I (1950): 49-57.

_____. *History and Human Relations*. New York: Macmillan, 1951/52.

Bynum, W. F., E. J. Browne, and Roy Porter. (eds.). *Macmillan Dictionary of the History of Science*. London: The Macmillan Press Ltd., 1981.

Capaldi, Nicholas. "Hume as Social Scientist," *Review of Metaphysics* XXXII (1978): 99-123.

Chappell, V. C. (ed.). *Hume: A Collection of Critical Essays*, Garden City, New York: Doubleday, 1966.

Cohen, I. Bernard. "The Eighteenth Century Origins of the Concept of Scientific Revolution," *Journal of the History of Ideas* XXXVII #2 (April-June 1976): 257-288.

_____. *Revolution in Science*. Cambridge, Massachusetts: Harvard University Press, 1985.

Collingwood, R. G. *The Principles of Art*. London: Oxford University Press, 1938/1958.

_____. *The Idea of History*, edited by T. M. Knox. London: Oxford University Press, 1946.

Cooper, Anthony Ashley, Third Earl of Shaftesbury. *An Inquiry Concerning Virtue, or Merit* (1699), edited by David Walford. Philosophical Classics; Manchester: Manchester University Press, 1977.

_____. *The Moralists, A Philosophical Rhapsody, Being a Recital of certain Conversations on Natural and Moral Subjects* (1709).

_____. *Characteristics* (London, 1711).

Cummins, Robert. "The Missing Shade of Blue," *The Philosophical Review* LXXXVII #4 (Oct. 1978): 548-565.

Currey, Cecil B. *Road to Revolution: Benjamin Franklin in England, 1765-1775.* Anchor Books; Garden City, New York: Doubleday & Company, 1968.

Dalrymple, Houghton B. "Hume's Difficulties with Dispositions," *Southwest Philosophical Studies* (Fall 1987).

Danto, Arthur C. *Narration and Knowledge.* New York: Columbia University Press, 1985.

Davie, William. Review of *Hume's System: An Examination of the First Book of His Treatise* by David Pears, *Bulletin of the Hume Society* XXI #1 (Spring 1992): 4.

Davies, Stephen. *Definitions of Art.* Ithaca: Cornell University Press, 1991.

Descartes, René. *Discourse on Method.* (1637).

_____. *Geometry.* (1637).

_____. *Meditations on the First Philosophy.* (1641), *with Selections from the Objections and Replies,* translated by John Cottingham. Cambridge: Cambridge University Press, 1986.

_____. *Rules for the Direction of the Mind* (ca. 1628/1651).

Dewey, John. *Logic: The Theory of Inquiry.* New York: Henry Holt and Company, 1938.

Dickie, George, Richard Scalfani, and Ronald Roblin (eds.). *Aesthetics: A Critical Anthology.* Second Edition; New York: St. Martin's Press, 1989.

Dickson, William K. "David Hume and the Advocates' Library," *Juridical Review* XLIV (1932): 1-14.

Dilthey, Wilhelm. *Pattern and Meaning in History: Thoughts on History and Society,* edited by H. P. Rickman. New York: Harper and Row, 1961.

Dray, William. "Explanatory Narrative in History," *Philosophical Quarterly* IV #14 (January 1954): 15-27.

_____. *Laws and Explanations in History.* London: Oxford University Press, 1957.

_____. (ed.). *Philosophical Analysis and History.* New York: Harper and Row, 1966.

Duhem, Pierre. *Les Origins de la Statique,* Paris, 1905-1907.

Dummett, Michael. "Common Sense and Physics," in *Perception and Identity,* 1-40.

Durland, Karánn. "Hume's First Principle, His Missing Shade, and His Distinctions of Reason," *Hume Studies* XXII #1 (April 1996): 105-121.

Edwards, Paul (ed.). *Voltaire Selections.* New York: Macmillan, 1989.

Emerson, Roger L. "Sciences and the Origins and Concerns of the Scottish

Enlightenment," *History of Science* XXVI (1988): 333-366.

_____. "Science and Moral Philosophy in the Scottish Enlightenment," in M. A. Stewart's *Studies in the Philosophy of the Scottish Enlightenment*, 11-36.

Evnine, Simon. "Hume, Conjectural History, and the Uniformity of Human Nature," *Journal of the History of Philosophy* XXXI #4 (1993): 589-606.

Farr, James. "Hume, Hermeneutics, and History: A 'Sympathetic Account," *History and Theory* XVII #3 (1978): 285-310.

_____. "Humean Explanations in the Moral Sciences," *Inquiry* XXV #1 (March 1982): 57-80.

Fears, J. Rufus (ed.). *Selected Writings of Lord Acton*. 3 volumes; Indianapolis: Liberty Press, 1985.

Finocchiaro, Maurice A. *History of Science as Explanation*. Detroit: Wayne State University Press, 1973.

Fischer, David H. *Historians' Fallacies: Toward a Logic of Historical Thought*. New York: Harper & Row, 1970.

Fisher, Alec. *The Logic of Real Arguments*. Cambridge: Cambridge University Press, 1988.

Fitzsimmons, M. A., and A. G. Pundt. (eds.). *The Development of Historiography*. Harrisburg: The Stackpole Co., 1954.

Flew, A. G. N. "Impressions and Experiences: Public or Private?" *Hume Studies* XI #2 (November 1985): 183-191.

Forbes, Duncan. "Introduction," in his edition of Hume's *History of Great Britain*. Baltimore: Penguin Books, 1970.

Force, James E. "Hume's Interest in Newton and Science," *Hume Studies* XIII #2 (November 1987): 166-216.

Freud, Sigmund. "The Moses of Michelangelo" (1914), in the *Standard Edition of the Complete Psychological works of Sigmund Freud*. London: The Hogarth Press and the Institute of Psycho-Analysis, 1955, XIII.

Garber, Daniel. "Science and Certainty in Descartes," in *Descartes: Critical and Interpretive Essays*, 114-151.

Garraty, John A., and Peter Gay. (eds.). *The Columbia History of the World*. New York: Columbia University Press, 1972.

Garrett, Don. *Cognition and Commitment in Hume's Philosophy*. New York: Oxford University Press, 1997.

Gillispie, C. C. (ed.). *Dictionary of Scientific Biography*. New York: Charles Scribner's Sons, 1972.

Glanvill, Joseph. *Plus Utra, or The Progress and Advancement of Knowledge Since the Days of Aristotle* (1668), a facsimile reproduction with an introduction by Jackson I. Cope. Gainesville, Florida: Scholars' Facsimiles and Reprints, 1958.

Gracyk, Theodore A. "Rethinking Hume's Standard of Taste," *Journal of Aesthetics and*

Art Criticism LII #2 (Spring 1994): 169-182.

Gray, Charles M. *Renaissance and Reformation England: 1509-1714*. New York: Harcourt Brace Jovanovich, 1973.

Greig, J. Y. T. *David Hume*. London: Jonathan Cape, 1931.

Hacking, Ian (ed.). *Scientific Revolutions*. Oxford: Oxford University Press, 1981.

Hall, A. R., and M. B. Hall. *The Revolution of Science, 1500-1750*. London: Longmans, Green and Company, 1983.

Hall, Roland. *50 Years of Hume Scholarship: A Bibliographical Guide*. Edinburgh: Edinburgh University Press, 1978.

Hardin, C. L. *Color for Philosophers: Unweaving the Rainbow*. Expanded Edition. Forward by Arthur Danto. Indianapolis: Hackett Publishing Company, 1988/1993.

Harrison, Edward. "Whigs, Prigs and Historians of Science" (commentary), *Nature* CCCXXIX (17 September 1987): 213-214.

Hendel, Charles W. *Studies in the Philosophy of David Hume*. New Edition; Indianapolis: Bobbs-Merrill, 1963.

Herdt, Jennifer A. *Religion and Faction in Hume's Moral Philosophy*. Cambridge: Cambridge University Press, 1997.

Hilson, J. C. "Hume: the Historian as Man of Feeling," in *Augustan Worlds: New Essays in Eighteenth-Century Literature*, edited by J. C. Hilson, M. M. B. Jones, and J. R. Watson. New York: Barnes and Noble, 1978.

Hooker, Michael. (ed.). *Descartes: Critical and Interpretive Essays*. Baltimore, Maryland: John Hopkins University Press, 1978.

Hope, Vincent (ed.). *Philosophers of the Scottish Enlightenment*. Edinburgh: Edinburgh University Press, 1984.

Hughes, H. Stuart. *History as Art and as Science: Twin Vistas on the Past*. New York: Harper and Row, 1964.

Hull, David L. "In Defense of Presentism," *History and Theory* XVII #1 (1979): 1-15.

Hutcheson, Francis. *An Inquiry into the Original of Our Ideas of Beauty and Virtue*. Third Edition: London, 1729, reprinted in *Aesthetics: A Critical Anthology*, edited by Dickie, Scalfani, and Roblin, 223-41.

Jacob, Margaret C. *The Cultural Meaning of the Scientific Revolution*. New York: Alfred A. Knopf, 1988.

Jenkins, John J. "Hume's Account of Sympathy—Some Difficulties," in *Philosophers of the Scottish Enlightenment*, edited by Vincent Hope. Edinburgh: Edinburgh University Press, 1984, 91-104.

Jones, Peter. *Hume's Sentiments: Their Ciceronian and French Context*. Edinburgh: Edinburgh University Press, 1982.

_____. "Hume's Literary and Aesthetic Theory," in *The Cambridge Companion to Hume*, ch. 9.

Johnson, D. M. "Hume's Missing Shade of Blue Interpreted as Involving Habitual

Spectra," *Hume Studies* X #2 (Nov. 1984): 109-124.

Judson, Horace Freeland. *The Eighth Day of Creation: The Makers of the Revolution in Biology.* New York: Simon and Schuster, 1979.

Kragh, Helge. *An Introduction to the Historiography of Science,* translated by Jean Lundskjaer-Nielsen. Cambridge: Cambridge University Press, 1987.

Kreimendahl, Lother. *Humes verborgener Rationalismus (Hume's Hidden Rationalism).* Berlin and New York: Walter de Gruyter, 1982.

Kuhn, Thomas S. *The Structure of Scientific Revolutions.* Second Edition, Enlarged; Chicago: University of Chicago Press, 1970.

_____. "Second Thoughts on Paradigms," in Frederick Suppe's *The Structure of Scientific Theories,* 459-482.

_____. *The Essential Tension,* Chicago: University of chicago Press, 1977.

Lambert, Karl, and Gordon G. Brittan, Jr. *An Introduction to the Philosophy of Science.* Englewood Cliffs: Prentice-Hall, 1970.

Lard, John. *Hume's Philosophy of Human Nature.* Hamden, Connecticut: Archon Books, 1932/1967.

Livingston, Donald W. "Hume on the Problem of Historical and Scientific Explanation," *The New Scholasticism* XLVII #1 (Winter 1973): 38-67.

_____. "The Hume Literature of the 1970s: III. Philosophy of History and Philosophy of Religion," *Philosophical Topics* XII #3 (1982): 182-192.

_____. *Hume's Philosophy of Common Life.* Chicago: The University of Chicago Press, 1984.

_____. *Philosophical Melancholy and Delirium: Hume's Pathology of Philosophy.* Chicago: University of Chicago Press, 1998.

Locke, John. *An Essay Concerning Human Understanding,* edited by P. H. Nidditch. Oxford: Clarendon Press, 1975.

Losee, John. "Hume's Demarcation Project," *Hume Studies* XVIII #1 (Apr. 1992): 51-62.

Louch, A. R. "History as Narrative," *History and Theory* VIII #1 (1969).

Macdonald, G. F. (ed.). *Perception and Identity: Essays Presented to A. J. Ayer with His Replies to Them.* Ithaca: Cornell University Press, 1979.

MacLachlan, Christopher. "Hume and the Standard of Taste," *Hume Studies* XII #1 (April 1986): 18-38.

Maclaurin, Colin. *An Account of Sir Isaac Newton's Philosophical Discoveries,* a facsimile of the first edition with a new introduction and index of names by L. L. Laudan. The Sources of Science, No. 74; New York: Johnson Reprint Corporation, 1968.

McAllister, James W. "Theory-Assessment in the Historiography of Science," *British Journal of the Philosophy of Science* XXXVII (1986): 315-333.

McKeon, Richard. (ed.). *The Basic Works of Aristotle.* New York: Random House,

1941.

Malezieu, Nicolas de. *Elements de Geometrie* (1722).

Mason, Steven F. *A History of the Sciences.* New Revised Edition; New York: Collier, 1962.

Meyerhoff, Hans (ed.). *The Philosophy of History in Our Time: An Anthology.* Garden City, New York: Doubleday and Company, 1959.

Mink, Louis O. Review of Fischer's *Historians' Fallacies* in *History and Theory* X #1 (1971): 107-122.

Miller, David. *Philosophy and Ideology in Hume's Political Thought.* Oxford: Clarendon Press, 1981.

Montesquieu, baron de. (See Charles-Louis de Secondat).

More, Henry. *Conjectura Cabbalistica* (1653).

Morreall, John. "Hume's Missing Shade of Blue," *Philosophy and Phenomenological Research* XLII #3 (Mar. 1982): 407-415.

Mossner, Ernest Campbell. "An Apology for David Hume, Historian," *Proceedings of the Modern Language Association* LVI (1941): 657-690.

_____. *The Life of David Hume.* Edinburgh: Nelson, 1954.

_____. "Introduction" to Hume's *Treatise.* London: Penguin Books, 1969.

Mothersill, Mary. *Beauty Restored.* Oxford: Clarendon Press, 1984.

_____. "Hume and the Paradox of Taste," in Dickie, Scalfani, and Roblin's *Aesthetics: A Critical Anthology,* 269-86.

_____. "In Defense of Hume and the Causal Theory of Taste," *Journal of Aesthetics and Art Criticism* LV #3 (Summer 1997): 312-317.

Murphy, Terrence. "Lord Acton and the Question of Moral Judgments in History: The Development of His Position," *The Catholic Historical Review* LXX #2 (April 1984): 225-250.

Nadel, George H. "Philosophy of History before Historicism," *History and Theory* III #3 (1964).

— (ed.). *Studies in the Philosophy of History.* New York: Harper and Row, 1965.

Nelson, John O. "Hume's Missing Shade of Blue Re-Viewed," *Hume Studies* XV #2 (Nov. 1989): 353-363.

Newton, Isaac. *Philosophiae Naturalis Principia Mathematica,* London, 1687, translated by Andrew Motte, 1729, as *Sir Isaac Newton's Mathematical Principles of Natural Philosophy and His System of the World,* revised by Florian Cajori. Berkeley: University of California Press, 1946.

Norton, David Fate. "History and Philosophy in Hume's Thought," in *David Hume: Philosophical Historian,* xxxii-1.

_____ and Richard H. Popkin (eds.). *David Hume: Philosophical Historian.* Indianapolis: Bobbs-Merrill, 1965.

_____ (ed.). *The Cambridge Companion to Hume.* Cambridge: Cambridge University

Press, 1993.

_____. "An Introduction to Hume's Thought," in *The Cambridge Companion to Hume*, ch. 1.

_____. "Hume, Human Nature, and the Foundations of Morality," in *The Cambridge Companion to Hume*, ch. 6.

Noxon, James. *Hume's Philosophical Development: A Study of His Methods*. Oxford: Clarendon Press, 1973.

Oldfield, Adrian. "Moral Judgments in History," *History and Theory* XX #3 (1981): 260-277.

Owen, David. "Hume and the Lockean Background: Induction and the Uniformity Principle," *Hume Studies* XVII #2 (November 1992): 179-207.

Palgrave, Francis. "Hume and his Influence upon History," *Quarterly Review* LXXXIII (1844): 536-592.

Palmer, Humphrey, Review of *Humes verborgener Rationalismus* by Lother Kreimendahl, *Hume's Studies* X #2 (November 1984): 174-80.

Passmore, John. "The Objectivity of History," *Philosophy* XXXIII #1 (1968); reprinted in Dray's *Philosophical Analysis and History*.

Peardon, T. P. *The Transition in English Historical Writing, 1760-1830*. New York: AMS Press, 1966.

Pears, D. F. (ed.). *David Hume: A. Symposium*. London: Macmillan, 1963.

_____. *Hume's System: An Examination of the First Book of His "Treatise"*. Oxford: Oxford University Press, 1990.

Penelhum, Terence. "Hume's Moral Psychology," in *The Cambridge Companion to Hume*, ch. 5.

Phillipson, Nicholas. *Hume*. London: Weidenfeld and Nicolson, 1989.

Pompa, Leon. *Human Nature and Historical Knowledge: Hume, Hegel and Vico*. Cambridge: Cambridge University Press, 1990.

Popper, Karl. *The Open Society and Its Enemies*. Fourth Edition; London: Routledge and Kegan Paul, 1962.

Potkay, Adam. *The Fate of Eloquence in the Age of Hume*. Ithaca: Cornell University Press, 1994.

Power, Henry *Experimental Philosophy, In Three Books: Containing New Experiments Microscopical, Mercurial, Magnetical....* The Sources of Science, No. 21; New York: Johnson Reprint Company, 1966.

Quinton, Anthony. *Francis Bacon*. Oxford: Oxford University Press, 1980.

Redman, B. R. (ed.). *The Portable Voltaire*. New York: The Viking Press, 1949.

Reid, Thomas. *An Inquiry into the Human Mind on the Principles of Common Sense*, in *Thomas Reid's Inquiry and Essays*, edited by Ronald E. Beanblossom and Keith Lehrer. Indianapolis: Hackett Publishing Company, 1983.

Richman, Robert J. "'Something Common,'" *Journal of Philosophy* LIX #26 (Dec. 20,

1962): 821-830.

Rollin, Charles. *Oeuvres complétes de Rollin*. Nouvelle Édition in 30 vols.; Paris: chez Firmin Didot Fréres, Libraires, 1825-30.

_____. *Historie Romaine* (1738-41).

_____. *Ancient History*. 4 vols.; New York: Belford, Clarke and Co., n.d.

Rosenberg, Alexander. "Hume and the Philosophy of Science," in *The Cambridge Companion to Hume*, ch. 3.

Savage, Reginald O. "Hume's Missing Shade of Blue," *History of Philosophy Quarterly* IX #2 (Apr. 1992): 199-206.

Secondat, Charles-Louis de, baron de Montesquieu. *Persian Letters*. (1717-21).

_____. *Discours sur les motifs qui doivent nous encourager aux sciences*. (1725).

_____. *The Spirit of Laws*. (1748). Edited by David Wallace Carrithers. Berkeley: University of Caliifornia Press, 1977.

Shaftesbury, see A. A. Cooper.

Shapin, Steven, and Simon Schaffer. *Leviathan and the Air-Pump: Hobbes, Boyle, and the Experimental Life*. Princeton, New Jersey: Princeton University Press, 1986.

Shiner, Roger A. "Hume and the Causal Theory of Taste," *Journal of Aesthetics and Art Criticism* LIV #3 (Summer 1996): 237-249.

_____. "Causes and Tastes: Á Response," *JAAC* LV #3 (Summer 1997): 320-324.

Shirer, William L. *The Rise and Fall of the Third Reich: A History of Nazi Germany*. New York: Fawcett Crest, 1959/1960.

Siebert, Donald T. *The Moral Animus of David Hume*. Newark: University of Delaware Press, 1990.

Smith, Adam. *The Theory of Moral Sentiments*, edited by D. D. Raphael and A. L. Macfie. Indianapolis: Liberty Press, 1979.

_____. *Essays on Philosophical Subjects*, edited by W. P. D. Wightman and J. C. Bryce. Indianapolis: Liberty Press, 1982.

Spada, Marina Frasca. "Some Features of Hume's Conception of Space," *Studies in History and Philosophy of Science* XXI (1990): 371-411.

Spinoza, Baruch (Benedict). *Ethics (Ethica Ordine Geometrico Demonstrata)*, 1677.

Stampp, Kenneth. *The Peculiar Institution: Slavery in the Ante-Bellum South*. New York: Knopf, 1965.

Stern, Alfred. *Philosophy of History and the Problem of Values*. s'Gravenhage: Mouton, 1962.

Stewart, M. A. (ed.). *Studies in the Philosophy of the Scottish Enlightenment*. Oxford: Clarendon Press, 1990.

Strawson, Galen. *The Secret Connexion: Causation, Realism, and David Hume*. Oxford: Clarendon Press, 1989.

Strype, John. *Annals of the Reformation and Establishment of Religion, and Other Occurrences in the Church of England, during Queen Elizabeth's Happy Reign:*

150 Between Hume's Philosophy and History

Together with an Appendix of Original Papers of State, Records, and Letters. Oxford: The Clarendon Press, 1824, in four volumes.

Suppe, Frederick (ed.). *The Structure of Scientific Theories.* Urbana: The University of Illinois Press, 1974.

Tholfsen, Trygve R. *Historical Thinking.* New York: Columbia University Press, 1967.

Thompson, J. W. *History of Historical Writing.* 2 vols., New York: Macmillan, 1942.

Trevelyan, G. M. *A Shortened History of England.* Baltimore, Maryland: Penguin Books, 1942/1959.

Trevor-Roper, Hugh. "Hume as a Historian," in David Pears's *David Hume: A. Symposium,* 89-100.

Urbach, Peter. *Francis Bacon's Philosophy of Science.* LaSalle, Illinois: Open Court Publishing Co., 1987.

Usher, A. P. *A History of Mechanical Inventions.* Boston: Beacon Press, 1929/1959.

Voltaire, Jean Francois Marie Arouet de. *Elements of the Philosophy of Newton,* 1738/1741, with brief selections in Paul Edwards's *Voltaire Selections,* 98-103.

_____. *The Age of Louis XIV,* translated by Martyn P. Pollack and preface by F. C. Green. Everyman's Library; New York: Dutton, 1926, 1969. Originally published in 1751.

_____. *Essay on the Manners and Spirit of Nations,* 1754, translated by W. F. Fleming, in Redman's *The Portable Voltaire,* 547-555.

Weingartner, Rudolph H. Review of White's *Foundations, History and Theory* VII #3 (1968).

Wertz, S. K. *Humean Models of Historical Discourse.* Ph.D. dissertation; Norman: University of Oklahoma, 1970.

_____. "When Did Hume Plan a History?" *Southwest Philosophical Studies* III (April 1978): 30-33.

_____. "Collingwood's Understanding of Hume," *Hume Studies* XX #2 (November 1994): 261-287.

_____. "Human Nature and Art: From Descartes and Hume to Tolstoy," *Journal of Aesthetic Education* XXXII #3 (Fall 1998): 75-81.

_____. "Descartes and the Argument by Complete Enumeration," *Southwest Philosophy Review* XV #1 (January 1999): 137-147.

Westfall, R. S. *The Construction of Modern Science: Mechanisms and Mechanics.* Cambridge: Cambridge University Press, 1977.

_____. *Never at Rest: A Biography of Isaac Newton.* Cambridge: Cambridge University Press, 1980.

Westman, Robert S. "The Astronomer's Role in the Sixteenth Century: A Preliminary Study," *History of Science* XVIII (1980): 105-147.

Whelan, Frederick G. *Order and Artifice in Hume's Political Philosophy.* Princeton: Princeton University Press, 1985.

White, Morton. *Foundations of Historical Knowledge*. New York: Harper and Row, 1965.

Williamson, A. Mark. "Hume's Systematicty," *Southwest Philosophy Review* X #2 (July 1994): 189-192.

Wittgenstein, Ludwig. *Remarks on the Foundations of Mathematics*, translated by Anscombe. Oxford: Blackwell, 1964.

Wootton, David. "David Hume, 'the historian,'" in *The Cambridge Companion to Hume*, ch. 10.

Wright, John P. *The Sceptical Realism of David Hume*. Minneapolis: University of Minnesota Press, 1983.

Yeo, Richard. "An Idol of the Market-Place: Baconianism in Nineteenth Century Britain," *History of Science* XXIII (1985): 251-298.

INDEX

Cooper, A. A.. See Shaftsbury
copy, theory of ideas, xii, 12–13, 62. See
   Pears for alternative use of "copy"
cultural relativism, xiii. See also customs
   or human nature, diversity
custom, 50, 51, 77, 80, 93, 116; contrasted
   with reason, 46, 50

Danford, John, xi
Danto, A. C., 129 n. 19 (54), 133 n. 15 (80)
Davies, Stephen, 123 n. 3 (10). See also
   color
decimal, repeating, 29
deduction. See reasoning, deductive
demonstration, in narratives, 6, 100,
   32–33, 54, 126 n. 15 (33)
Descartes, René, xi, 13, 99–100, 116
Dilthey, Wilhelm, 85
diversity, 24, 51, 53, 58. See also human
   nature
Dray, William, 23, 131 n. 6 (68)
Dummett, Michael, 14
Durland, Karann, 11

eloquence, 83–84
empathy, also called enactment, 86. See
   also passions
empiricism, 115. See also science
encyclopedism, 49–51, 58; use of periodization in, 50
essentialism, 51, 53
ethics, 4. See also system, vulgar
evidence, conceptual, 53–54; 129 n. 19
   (54); documentary, 54. See also
   demonstration
experience, and credibility, 37; and evidence, xii; acquired through history,
   37–38, 70, 116; individual (sensory),
   xiii, xv, 10, 34, 35–36, 41; interpretational, xiii; moral, 70. See also virtue;
   orderly, 15–16; social (or common), xv,
   15–16, 31–33, 85
experiment, missing shade of blue:
   described, 9; implications of, 15–16;
   interpolation in, 11, related to copy theory of ideas, ii
experimentalism, 97–98

Farr, James, 72, 85–87
facts. See history, critical reconstruction
   of. See also truth
Fischer, David, 19–20, 22
Flew, Antony, 35

Gassendi, Pierre, 13; in contrast to
   Berkeley, 13–14
general rules. See probabilities, species of
Gray, Charles M., 82
Greig, J. Y. T., 77

Hardin, C. L., 11
Harvey, William. See Characters
Hendel, Charles, 1, 4, 62; on system(s), 1,
   2, 3
Henry, Robert, 50
Hilson, J. C., 79
historical knowing, 85
historical narrative, xii, 16, 17, 27.
   106–107; enumeration in, xiv, 10–13;
   purpose of, 47; structure of (See also
   periodization), 17, 43–44, 51–52; sub-
   jectivity in, 49, 69, 75–83; types of:
   analytical, 49, 51, general, 48, 128 n. 7
   (49), explanatory, 45, 131 n. 6 (68),
   topical, 49, 97, 107; unity in, 21, 29,
   48, 125 n. 14 (29)
historiography, of science, xiii, 19, 23, 43,
   56, 89, 132 n. 12 (75); diachronic versus synchronic approach to, 95, 101,
   107; internalism, 90; international
   viewpoint in, 91; post-Butterfield
   (1950), 95; portraiture in, 90
history, aided by conjecture, 16, 31;
   alliance with philosophy, xii, 31–33,
   41–42; and human nature, xii, 19–21;
   civil, 41, 79, 93; contrasted with chronicle, 45; diversity in, 57, 87, dynamic
   nature of, 90, 93, 111, 114–115;
   explanatory function, 30–31; Hume's
   concept of, 70; intellectual, 94; key to
   ideas, xiii–xiv; monistic versus pluralistic viewpoints in, 58, 130 n. 21 (58);
   philosophical, 129 n. 15 (51); reconstructions of, 41, 42, 72–73, 127 n. 8

(42), 131 n. 5 (68); universal, 80. See also experience, social

human nature, 7, 19–21, 37, 58, 110, 115, 126 n. 17–18 (33), diversity in, 24–25, 94; component of historical analyses, 31–33; contingency in, 26, 31, 66; dynamic, xiii, 31–32, 33, 77; power of sympathy, 72–73; subject to error, 29, 64; uniformity of, 20–21, 22, 33, 87, 94; See also, customs, morals

Hutcheson, Francis, 2, 62

ideas, 4, 8, 44; as revolutionary, 93; copy theory of, xii, xvi, 11–12, complex, 10–12; Descartes' use of the term, 6; deductive, 4, interpretive, 121 n. 7 (4); nature of 61; not derived from impressions, 9–10; simple 10–12. See also association of ideas

imagination, 2, role of perception, 2; importance in history, 30–31

impressions, 8, 10; as equivalent to ideas, xii, 9, 12, 110; origin of, xiii–xiv. See also resemblance

induction, 6. See also uniformity

interpolation. See color

Johnson, D. M., 15

judgment, and taste, 61; moral: appropriateness in written histories, xii, 67, 78, 82, 103–104; distinguished from aesthetic judgments, 71; implicit 68, 87; loss of objectivity, 68, 82; role of rhetoric in, 126 n. 16 (#), 103;

knowledge, xii, 37, 104; as science, 89, 97; extended by conjecture, 45, 48; limits of historical, 78; probability in, xiv. See also experience

Kriemendahl, Lother, 6

Lambert, Karl, 25

larger units of communication (LUCs), 86

liberty, 23

literature, 63, 64, 108; analogous to history, 78; Hume as critic of, 64; defined, xiii, 83. See also composition or historical narrative

Locke, John, xiv, 6, 108, 121 n. 10 (6)

Lord Acton. See Acton

Louch, A. R., 57

Maclaurin, Colin, 96, 98, 138 n. 31 (104)

mankind, 19, 20, 26, 49, 51, 128 n. 7 (49); sympathy, 23–24; unchanging, 20–21, 22. See also human nature

manners. See customs

metaphors, chain/link, 2–3, 45, 49, 52, 54, 57, 62, 63; channel, 4; fabric 25, 68, 110; sun, 117; train, 2–3, 27, 58, 62

miracles, 35, 37, 63, 87, 104

missing shade of blue. See experiment

moral, agency, 75, 115; judgments (See judgments, moral); necessity, 27–28; relativity of, 76–77, 80–81; sensitivity, 69–70, 73

mortality, 33; and miracles, 35–37

Mossner, E. C., 2, 11

Mothersill, Mary, 59–61, 64, 131 n. 8 (62). See also paradox of taste

narrative order, 4–5, 6, 32, 43, 45, 57, 69; reversal of, 44; sentences, 80. See also historical narrative

necessity, 25; danger in literal use, 26; physical versus moral, 27–28

Newton, Sir Isaac. See Characters

Nietzsche, 5

Norton, David Fate, 33, 39, 41; criticism of Hume's methodology, 35–37, 127 n. 1 (35); supporters of. See Noxon, Livingston, Wooten

novelty, in history. See history, diversity

Noxon, James, 35, 39, 127 n. 2, 6 (#), 137 n. 18 (96); on reasoning, 40

objectivity, increased by selectivity, 49

Oldfield, Adrian, 65, 67, 69, 76

opinions, 74, 93; Hume's system as more than, 5; instantaneous formation of, 59

order, 5; chronological. See periodization; in color spectrum, 13, 14–15; natural, 54;. See also metaphors or narrative order

thought experiment, see experiment, missing shade of blue
time, 1, 57; mechanical measurement of,
  101, 107, 138 n. 28 (101); overcome
  through presensation, 73. See also periodization
train. See metaphors
truth, 99, 105, 110; basis of history, 83;
  compared to taste, 60–61; relative
  importance of 49–50, 128 n. 7, 10 (49).
  See also history, reconstructions of

uniformity, contrasted with abnormalism,
  46; defined, 24; diversity, 24, 87, 125
  n. 14 (29); in history, 93; methodological, 29; similarity, 22–23; substiantial,
  29; uniting cause and effect, 25, 46.
  See also mankind.
unity, principle of, 58, 62–63. See also
  association of ideas

universal man. See mankind
Urbach, Peter, 92

vice, 70, 82, 116; dialectical tension with
  virtue, 76
Vico, Giambattista, xiii
virtue, 70, 111, 116, 117; change through
  time, 77; strengthened by history,
  71–72, 79. See also vice

way of ideas. See ideas
White, Morton, 45, 49, 50, 58. See also
  positivism
Wolsey, Cardinal, 80–81
Wootten, David, 35, 50, 51, 113–114;
  acceptance of Norton, 127 n. 4 (35)
writing. See composition

ABOUT THE AUTHOR

Born in Amarillo, Texas, in 1941, Spencer K. Wertz earned his bachelors and masters degrees in philosophy at Texas Christian University in Fort Worth and his Ph.D. at the University of Oklahoma in Norman where he studied under Kenneth R. Merrill and Jitendra N. Mohanty. S. K. Wertz did postgraduate work with Patrick H. Nowell-Smith in the philosophy of history at Eliot College, the University of Kent at Canterbury (U.K.) and is an alumni member of Phi Beta Kappa (TCU chapter). He is the past president of the Southwestern Philosophical Society, the New Mexico-West Texas Philosophical Society, the North Texas Philosophical Association, and the Philosophic Society for the Study of Sport. His books include *Sport Inside Out: Readings in Literature and Philosophy* (1985/88) and *Talking a Good Game: Inquiries into the Principles of Sport* (1991). He is an active member of The Hume Society and has published over a hundred articles, discussion notes and reviews in various areas of philosophy. Currently he is professor of philosophy at Texas Christian University and lives on the North Texas prairie, west of Fort Worth with his wife Linda and their miniature donkeys, Abby, Peekaboo, and a yellow Lab, Cammie.

DATE DUE

Demco, Inc. 38-293